Revisiting Insider–Outsider Research in Comparative and International Education

To Anne, Allan and Adrian

Bristol Papers in Education
comparative and international studies

Revisiting Insider–Outsider Research in Comparative and International Education

Edited by
MICHAEL CROSSLEY, LORE ARTHUR & ELIZABETH McNESS

Bristol Papers in Education: comparative and international studies
Series Editor: Michael Crossley

Symposium Books Ltd
PO Box 204, Didcot, Oxford OX11 9ZQ, United Kingdom
www.symposium-books.co.uk

Published in the United Kingdom, 2016

ISBN 978-1-873927-67-0

Series: *Bristol Papers in Education* Number 6
(Seven earlier volumes in the the series were published
from 1992 by the University of Bristol; see
www.bris.ac.uk/education/research/centres/ics)

Printed and bound in the United Kingdom by Hobbs the Printers, Southampton
www.hobbs.uk.com

Contents

BRISTOL PAPERS IN EDUCATION

comparative and international studies

Previous volumes in this series

Languages and Education in Africa
a comparative and transdisciplinary analysis
Edited by BIRGIT BROCK-UTNE & INGSE SKATTUM
2009 356 pages US$64.00 ISBN 978-1-873927-17-5

Higher Education and International Capacity Building
twenty-five years of higher education links
Edited by DAVID STEPHENS
2009 240 pages US$56.00 ISBN 978-1-873927-22-9

Culture in Education and Development
principles, practice and policy
DAVID STEPHENS
2007 246 pages US$48.00 ISBN 978-1-873927-70-0

Narrative Research on Learning
comparative and international perspectives
Edited by SHEILA TRAHAR
2006 280 pages US$48.00 ISBN 978-1-873927-60-1

Research and Evaluation for Educational Development
learning from the PRISM experience in Kenya
MICHAEL CROSSLEY, ANDREW HERRIOT, JUDITH WAUDO, MIRIAM MWIOTSI, KEITH HOLMES & MAGDALLEN JUMA
2005 144 pages US$48.00 ISBN 978-1-873927-20-5

Acknowledgements

We would like to thank the British Association for International and Comparative Education (BAICE) for funding and supporting the inaugural BAICE Thematic Forum (BTF), 'Revisiting Insider–Outsider Perspectives in International and Comparative Education', from which this book has developed. Thanks are also extended to all BTF participants and reviewers of the chapters, and to Maria Viviani, Lizzi Milligan and Terra Sprague who provided administrative assistance throughout the lifetime of the project (2012-2015). The Centre for Comparative and International Research in Education (CIRE) at the University of Bristol hosted the initial events that inspired and launched the initiative.

Foreword

For several years now, the British Association of International and Comparative Education (BAICE) has been supporting a range of Thematic Fora. Each Thematic Forum enables a group of interested scholars to come together to investigate, interrogate and debate the particular topic they have chosen. This volume is a reflection of the first such Forum: *Revisiting Insider/Outsider Perspectives in International and Comparative Education.* Led by Lore Arthur, Michael Crossley and Elizabeth McNess, it comprised two well-attended workshops and inspired a popular symposium, *Revisiting Insider/Outsider Perspectives: methodological considerations in the context of researcher mobilities and international partnership,* at the 2012 BAICE Conference on 'Education Mobility and Migration: people, ideas, and resources' held at the University of Cambridge.

Notions of 'insider' and 'outsider' have, as the Editors remind us in their Introduction, been with us for a long time. So why, they ask, focus on revisiting these notions now? Their key point of departure is the need to focus closely on the relative positioning of researchers and how this might be changing at a time of increasing actual, and virtual, mobility – of people, ideas and resources. A powerful and controversial example of this, cited in their text, is the global comparison of schooling system performance indicators. These are both constructed and critiqued by people whose value positions as researchers are powerful, for they both shape and can champion particular policy positions. Other examples abound in other chapters. If the internationalisation of educational ideas has brought new opportunities, so too has it brought new challenges; and here we are concerned with the challenges of thinking very carefully about who and how we are as researchers and learners concerned with 'education'.

This volume is an exciting exploration of researcher positioning and how globally shifting identities frame constructions of self and the 'other' within and across particular cultural, historical and political contexts. Its chapters offer a wide-ranging, serious investigation of the contemporary relevance of the terms 'insider' and 'outsider' in comparative and international education research, and to attendant theoretical and methodological issues that are pertinent across the social sciences. Despite the juxtaposition in the title of terms that might imply simplistic duality, there is no binary divide of inside and outside here.

Rather, there is fluidity, reflection and recognition that researchers constantly move in and out of spaces along a dynamic continuum, and that their identities may thus be better characterised in other ways – such as 'alongsider', or 'inbetweener'. This is a stimulating collection that offers a remarkable richness and diversity of experience. I congratulate the Editors and all contributors on a project that offers their readers so much to enjoy and learn from.

Caroline Dyer
Professor of Education and International Development, University of Leeds, UK
Chair, British Association of Comparative and International Education

INTRODUCTION

Positioning Insider–Outsider Research in the Contemporary Context

LORE ARTHUR, ELIZABETH McNESS & MICHAEL CROSSLEY

Why this book? Why revisit the concepts of the insider and outsider in the research arena? There are many ways of answering these questions, albeit from very different perspectives and time frames, and cloaked in the mantles of different academic disciplines. In the main, insider–outsider research is concerned with individuals, or groups of individuals, having experience of, or moving into and out of, different cultural communities and the challenges they face when accommodating cultural perspectives and ways of thinking other than their own. The underlying concepts of 'insideredness' and 'outsideredness' focus on thought processes which enhance critical awareness and the creation of new knowledge and understanding. All compel researchers to examine their own subjectivity and shifting positions within their chosen research paradigm. The authors of the chapters in this book examine the obstacles, complexities and blurred boundaries of educational research, at the same time as they explore liminal or 'third spaces', and related intellectual positions. They seek to defy simple juxtapositions of the 'either–or' as the basis for critical reflection which, though common to all research processes, are multiplied when dealing with two or more cultural and/or linguistic communities within the broad field of comparative and international education. We, as editors, welcome this rich diversity.

Since initiating this discussion on the contemporary relevance of the terms 'insider' and 'outsider', we have become acutely aware of how this connects directly with the work of so many researchers and colleagues worldwide. Surprisingly often we also hear, read and refer to 'insiders' and 'outsiders' on an almost daily basis. These words are part and parcel of our everyday language and consciousness. We speak of outsiders who are, or are not, welcome; outsider art, insider traders, the inner circle, the outer walls. Other terms, such as newcomers, strangers, migrants and refugees highlight similar sentiments. All have their own connotations and place in history. In the contemporary context they point to the global and local, time and space, power and boundaries, embeddedness and distanciation. An example of such contradictions occurred during the Venice Biennale in 2015 when a contemporary artist who is Swiss was sponsored by the Icelandic government to produce a showpiece in relation to the exhibition theme of 'Power' (*ArtNews*, 2015). He set out to convert an old Venetian Catholic church, which had been empty for many years, into a 'mosque', a first in such a historic city. In this instance, tensions arose between the global and the local, the old and the new, the newcomers and the established communities, and the powerful and powerless. But who were the outsiders and insiders here? Where were the boundaries and where were the shared spaces? It is increasingly apparent that in a complex world of shifting identities and competing economies there are clear tensions between those on the inside and those looking in from the outside; between those who want to, above all, hold on to their cultural identity and those who welcome the richness that other cultural communities can offer; those who seek to facilitate the shift from being an outsider to becoming an insider (Guo, 2010).

Why Revisit the Concepts of the Insider/Outsider?

All societies produce strangers by drawing and charting cognitive, aesthetic and moral maps, argues Bauman (1995). For thousands of years human beings have erected boundaries to protect their own against intruders from elsewhere. Today the accommodation of large numbers of strangers or migrants remains complex and a highly sensitive political issue affecting often the survival and human rights of those on the margins – the outsiders – as well as those in the host communities, the insiders. It is not surprising that Simmel's (1908 [1958]) and Schuetz's (1944) concepts of the 'stranger' have endured the course of time; they have shaped scholarly debates and theoretical perspectives of 'insider- and outsiderness' ever since (see e.g. Merton, 1972; Bauman, 1995, among many others referred to in the various chapters of this book). We, too, as 'insiders' or 'outsiders' try to make sense of our own life experiences and place them into a meaningful conceptual framework appropriate to the academic area we explore. All contributors to this book have travelled in various places and modalities and collected, sometimes indiscriminately, bits of baggage, possibly without a full appreciation of the context from which they were wrenched. The more we travel, experience and research, the more we are aware of the various strands and layers that mesh in and out of what is commonly understood as 'culture' in the context of the 'other' (Arthur, 2001). Furthermore, modern times have made us members of network nations, exchanging vast amounts of both information and socio-emotional communication with researchers, colleagues and family/friends across numerous national and cultural boundaries. As Castells (1996) predicted, computer networks have created an abundance of forms and channels of communication, shaping life and being shaped at the same time, making it increasingly difficult to differentiate between the various ways of perceiving the world around us. Not surprisingly, the theoretical constructs and practical issues they raise defy the duality or juxtapostioning of the concepts revisited here.

As educationalists and researchers, we may lament the fact that education has become a global commodity, often embedded within a range of power-related economic agendas. Policy-makers increasingly rely on large-scale *international* surveys such as PISA (Programme for International Student Assessment) or TIMMS (Trends in International Mathematics and Science Study) for comparison between one state and another; they seek 'evidence' to support *national* changes in education – often without regard to different cultural/historical/linguistic contexts. Writers such as Crossley (2000, 2014) and Alexander (2000, 2010) challenge current funding and policy preoccupations with large-scale surveys that compare pupil attainment across countries in an aggregated, de-contextualised way. They also draw attention to the value of context specific studies which can do more to reveal the culturally determined links between discourse, pedagogy and practice.

The increasing internationalisation of higher education has also facilitated the mobility and collaboration of both researchers and students working across national boundaries, often in cross-disciplinary groups, actual and virtual. This is something that is now widely encouraged by research sponsors and funders. Such circumstances, we argue, contribute further to the need for an updating and re-envisioning of the ways in which we conceptualise being an insider or an outsider in the research process. Not only should this include a better understanding of the ways in which more traditional boundaries, such as nationality, language, ethnicity, culture, gender and age, interact, it should also include a recognition and understanding of various ontological, epistemological and disciplinary boundaries that might be encountered, and the ways in which these might impact on the generation of new knowledge. Attention to such theoretical and methodological issues has informed our collective thinking over recent years, and this has inspired our interest in revisiting notions of 'insiderness' and 'outsiderness' in relation to cross-cultural comparative studies in education. We see this as especially pertinent in rapidly changing times where traditional conceptualisations of 'national identity' (Hans, 1949; Bereday, 1964,

Mallinson, 1975) and essentialist constructions of the 'other' are increasingly being questioned. As Bhabha maintains:

> The very concepts of homogeneous national cultures, the consensual or contiguous transmission of historical traditions, or 'organic' ethnic communities – *as the grounds of cultural comparativism* – are in a profound process of redefinition. (Bhabha, 1994, p. 7; italics in original)

In this book, as editors, we are not offering our own theoretical constructs or other model answers that researchers might be looking for; nor do we intend to promote the duality of the 'insider–outsider'; indeed, we aim to problematise such terms . We do, however, acknowledge that they are often used as a kind of shortcut to highlight positions adopted within many helpful methodological and theoretical frameworks. Other concepts, images or metaphors may better express the range, diversity and fluidity of perspectives relating to the 'other' and related boundaries. We hope the reader will find these emerge in many of the chapters of this book. All of these contributions encourage increased reflexivity and critical awareness in contemporary research within and beyond the field of comparative and international education. The chapters themselves draw upon research carried out in a wide range of countries worldwide, generating insights from British, European, Latin American, Indian Ocean, South Asian, African and Chinese contexts and cultures.

The Structure of the Book

This book draws on the work of an international group of colleagues involved in the inaugural BAICE-sponsored Thematic Forum (BTF) *Revisiting Insider/Outsider Perspectives in International and Comparative Education.* Some of the authors are academics and researchers, others are teachers, administrators or professional leaders and practitioners: importantly, they are also insiders and outsiders, with origins and different levels of experience worldwide. Our analysis challenges the existing methodological literature by developing a number of critical arguments that were first explored in two BAICE, BTF workshops held at the Research Centre for International and Comparative Studies, University of Bristol, in February 2012 and 2014. We also presented our emergent thinking in a symposium at the Annual BAICE Conference held at the University of Cambridge in September 2012. Since then we have given further talks and led related doctoral research seminars in a number of universities in the UK and in Hong Kong and mainland China. Most of the chapters in the book have thus been written by participants in these well-attended and successful project events. In doing so, the many participants have helped us to advance our understanding of the complexities, ambiguities and ways of thinking that we believe have much to offer the comparative and international research community and the wider social sciences.

The initial chapters revisit and debate a variety of theoretical perspectives relating to conceptualisations of the insider and the outsider. Then follow chapters which progressively bridge the gap between theory and practice by drawing on personal research experience to examine and demonstrate the implications of such challenges, both as relative 'insiders' and then as more obvious 'outsiders' to the cultural contexts concerned. This is followed by work that engages with the experience of marginalised outsiders within a majority culture, together with attention to the phenomenon of researchers and research participants moving between positions as outsiders and insiders. The final two chapters consider new approaches to working collaboratively within professional and practitioner contexts.

The Nature and Scope of the Chapters

Chapter 1 by McNess, Arthur and Crossley is a shortened and amended version of the first BTF output published in the BAICE peer-reviewed journal *Compare* (McNess et al, 2015). The chapter traces the historical origins of insider–outsider debates and seeks to illustrate how this duality has influenced philosophical, sociological and methodological thinking over many years. At the same time the authors challenge this construct and seek to explore cultural meaning in what Bhabha (1994) calls the 'Third Space'. The chapter refers to linguistic complexities when researching in an international context, and examines Hellawell's (2006) plea for empathy with reference to his understanding of the insider–outsider continuum. All researchers, the authors argue, need to come to terms with their own position in the research process and engage with a diversity of expectations and perspectives which may be fragmented, imaginary or even contradictory and divisive. Chapter 2 is an article that, as keynote speaker, Anna Robinson-Pant presented at the second BTF workshop held in Bristol during 2014. In this chapter the author takes a critical stance and argues that the application of the 'insider–outsider' continuum is problematic as an analytical tool for research. Inside and outside of what?, she asks. Like other dualisms, such concepts can be seen to close down rather than open up understanding, pushing us into categories with a tendency to polarise people's identities. In contrast, Robinson-Pant draws on Pike's (1990) concept of the 'emic' and 'etic' and offers three vignettes, based on her own research experience, to illustrate a range of different perspectives in support of her personal positioning. In doing this Robinson-Pant argues that, within ethnography, formal and informal learning between the researcher and the researched can lead to a dialectical construction of knowledge and related processes for getting to know 'each other's' cognitive maps. In chapter 3 Kelly challenges traditional, colonial and international approaches to comparative research and argues for a more relational stance which enables researchers to explore the power relations within their own research groups, the contexts in which they work, and the wider research community which legitimates their work. He identifies three idealised social collectives – emergent, established and exclusive – and discusses the mechanisms by which each of these types of collectives constructs insiders and outsiders. Kelly goes on to call for more democratic approaches to research which can guide ways of working relationally and offer improved opportunities for wider participation and influence in decision-making. The themes of politicisation and power are taken up by Hawthorne in chapter 4 when she contends that the discourse of insiders and outsiders in social research is not only descriptive of perceived social realities but also constructs and so partially constitutes those same realities. This chapter is developed in three parts: first, some of the theoretical issues underpinning critical discourse analysis and discursive subject positioning are discussed; second, it looks at the broader landscapes in which researcher roles, identities and subjectivities are positioned; and finally, this is applied to the prevailing discourse of the 'global knowledge economy' and the potential threat to the presence of an independent academic voice on educational matters within the public sphere.

The bridges between theory and practice are examined in chapters 5, 6, 7 and 8. In chapter 5 Planel considers five research projects that explored the embedded cultural values of several European countries. She uses her research experience within these projects, together with her bilingual and bicultural background, to tease out the ways in which she moved between being inside and outside the research context. In doing so, Planel concludes that the concept of the 'third space' is important because it can help researchers to cross national boundaries of meaning and allow underlying cultural understandings to rise to the surface. Planel also considers the debate around 'cultural borrowing' and argues that the positioning of the researcher will depend upon the positioning of the research, and that this should be seen as an additional methodological dimension in international and comparative research that impacts on the value and relevance of findings in different educational contexts. The authors of chapter 6, Savvides, Al-Youssef, Colin and Garrido, argue that the polarised debates of insiderism and outsiderism are fundamentally flawed because they do not take into account the multiple identities of individuals involved in the research process, nor do they consider the agencies with which all have to interact. They also argue that an exploration of the 'space-in-between' within the qualitative research paradigm calls for methodological rigour and critical reflexivity. Critical reflexivity, it is emphasised, should not be regarded merely as a technique but should question the positions, identities and ethicality between the researcher and the researched. These authors offer four vignettes, based on their separate research experiences, that explore different aspects of the insider–outsider debate. Milligan, writing in chapter 7, turns her attention to the methodological and ethical dilemmas that she experienced when conducting cross-cultural research into secondary education in western Kenya. Her status and role as a white researcher from the UK was defined not by herself as the outsider but by the local insiders, the participants in the project. With the help of their own photographs and diaries her students allowed her to enter spaces both within and outside the school environment. In this way, she argues, the hitherto uneven power relationship between the researcher and the researched was evened out. Milligan proposes a new positioning and term, that of the 'inbetweener', to address agency and power relationships by sharing part of the research activity with those investigated. Khan, in chapter 8, also explores the implications of being both an insider and an outsider during a period of her own research on teachers' perceptions of 'feeling valued' in northern Pakistan. She draws upon the varying dimensions of her professional and personal characteristics to discuss the ways in which they had influence in the field. Episodes from her data are used to demonstrate how being a previous senior manager for the educational charity that employed the teachers, a former teacher and teacher trainer, and a western-educated female with bicultural origins and bilingual facility, created tensions as well as insights. Ultimately, Khan considered herself to be an external researcher affiliated to a UK university, British-born of Pakistani origin, and 'middle class' through education. The multiple and fluid aspects of being a bicultural 'insider' and 'outsider' are seen to have enabled a more nuanced understanding of the teachers' perspectives. Attention to both ethical and power issues allowed for further challenging, reflective and rich perspectives, generating more effective communication and understanding.

Chapters 9, 10 and 11 turn attention to the experience of marginalised outsiders within a majority culture, albeit from very different perspectives. Insider–outsider tensions arise when social, cultural and political barriers are obstacles in the way of effective research, not only in the international context but also close by in home communities. McCaffery, in chapter 9, recounts how problematic her research was, when she, as a 'Gaujo', a non-gypsy, tried to access gypsy and traveller communities within the UK. She had not anticipated the distrust that she encountered by people who she maintains are disadvantaged, misunderstood and rejected by established home communities. Her research and interactions, based on the theoretical frameworks of ethnography, cultural identity and constructivism, eventually allowed her to become at least partially accepted. 'Inside-out and outside-in' was the phrase she used to describe her attempts to bridge the gap in understanding and knowledge for the potential benefit of both communities. International students studying in the UK are at the core of the chapters by Gu (chapter 10) and Salter-Dvorak (chapter 11). Gu's research draws on empirical evidence from three collaborative studies, carried out over ten years, that investigated the pedagogical, sociocultural and emotional challenges that international students encounter when studying at British universities. By creating their own social spaces, many lead dual lives. They feel 'outsiders' not only in the country where they are studying but also when returning back home. The migration of international students, according to Gu, highlights the interaction, dynamics and tensions between local, regional and global politics, cultures, economics and social processes. She cites the theory of transnationalism which is, in essence, concerned with linkages between people, places and institutions across nation-state borders, along with globally intensified cross-border relationships and affiliations. The interconnectedness of student experience calls for new approaches to teaching and research, particularly when associated with societies such as China that are currently undergoing their own far-reaching transformation in a fast-changing but unequal world. Salter-Dvorak, by contrast, examines a small-scale longitudinal study in the interpretive epistemological tradition of participant research with two international students, one from China and the other from Iran. The central purpose of this study was to provide a contrastive analysis of the dynamic between dominant discourse and language, power relations, agency and identities on two very different master's degree courses. In her analysis Salter-Dvorak employed a 'frontstage' and 'backstage' metaphor with which she challenges the insider–outsider duality. The former, she explains, is the physical space where formal interactions (lectures, tutorials, etc.) act as the literacy events concerned with knowledge transfer, while the latter is the space, physical or virtual (corridor, email, telephone, etc.), where informal interactions may provide support, clarification and reflection, which, in turn, can enhance overall 'frontstage' learning experiences. Her findings report that these two notions are distinct and complementary, and she maintains that it is possible to be an insider and an outsider in different ways, either frontstage or backstage.

The final chapters, 12 and 13, address professional knowledge within the insider–outsider continuum. In chapter 12, Wickins and Crossley reflect on the position of the researcher, which shifted during the course of a study of headteacher leadership challenges in the international school sector in Hong Kong. They examine how the researcher initially adopted a neutral observer stance when conducting fieldwork interviews. This positioning changed in the course of time when, during a second stage of research, the headteacher participants began to get more closely involved in the discussion and construction of findings. A reflexive process evident in the course of the third stage, the data analysis, led to insider positions being adopted by all when the participants and the researcher recognised that they were members of the same educational culture ... and constrained by the same set of rules. Using the metaphor of a research vessel observing data through a shaky telescope across a choppy sea, the authors developed the concept of the 'Alongsider' researcher. In their view, this term opens up new methodological potential for the research process by recognising fluidity along the insider–outsider continuum. This, they argue, involves movement from detached theory to the bridge between theory and practice and, finally, to the co-construction of conclusions. Thus, when participants own the research outcomes, they are more likely to use them in their own professional contexts. In the final contribution, chapter 13, Raveaud argues that although much cultural knowledge and behaviour is acquired informally through participation in social activities, few research initiatives have tapped the potential for teacher professional development through the use of video, which can capture classroom practice across national and cultural boundaries. This chapter develops a case for harnessing the insights from international comparative studies using video for cross-cultural classroom observations, to promote teachers' reflective thinking. In a pilot study, video data were gathered in both a French and an English infant classroom. This provided a mediating object to create a sense of dissonance, and to challenge the taken-for-granted beliefs of teachers in the two countries. Situations which at first appeared strange, incomprehensible or shocking became opportunities for practitioners to critically revisit their practice, assumptions and values with a renewed eye, akin to generating an outsider's perspective on their own education system.

Much as these chapters present original findings that we believe have substance and value in their own right, we hope their collective impact offers a challenging, innovative and helpful contribution to the methodological literature within and beyond the field of comparative and international education.

References

Alexander, R. (2000) *Culture and Pedagogy: international comparisons in primary education*. Oxford: Blackwell.

Alexander, R. (2010) World Class Schools – Noble Aspiration or Globalised Hokum?, *Compare*, 40(6), 801-817. http://dx.doi.org/10.1080/03057925.2010.523252

Arthur, L. (2001) Bits of Baggage and Wanderers' Tales: towards the construction of a new theoretical framework for comparative adult education, *Studies in the Education of Adults*, 33(2), 100-108.

ArtNews (2015) Reopen Christoph Buechel's Mosque Project in Venice. 27 May. http://www.artnews.com

Bauman, Z. (1995) Making and Unmaking of Strangers, *Thesis Eleven*, 43, 1-16. Massachusetts Institute of Technology. http://the.sagepub.com/content/43/1/1.citation

Bereday, G.Z.F. (1964) *Comparative Methods in Education*. New York: Holt Rinehart & Winston.

Bhabha, H.K. (1994) *The Location of Culture*. London: Routledge.

Castells, M. (1996) The Rise of the Network Society, in *The Information Age. Economy, Society and Culture*, vol. 1. Cambridge: Blackwell.

Crossley, M. (2000) Bridging Cultures and Traditions in the Reconceptualisation of Comparative and International Education, *Comparative Education*, 36(3), 319-332. http://dx.doi.org/10.1080/713656615

Crossley, M. (2014) Global League Tables, Big Data and the International Transfer of Educational Research Modalities, *Comparative Education*, 50(1), 15-26. http://dx.doi.org/10.1080/03050068.2013.871438

Guo, S. (2010) Lifelong Learning in the Age of Transnational Migration, *International Journal of Lifelong Education*, 29(2), 143-147. http://dx.doi.org/10.1080/02601371003616509

Hans, N. (1949) *Comparative Education*. London: Routledge.

Hellawell, D. (2006) Inside-Out: analysis of the insider-outsider concept as a heuristic device to develop reflexivity in students doing qualitative research, *Teaching in Higher Education*, 11(4), 483-494. http://dx.doi.org/10.1080/13562510600874292

Mallinson, V. (1975) *The Introduction to the Study of Comparative Education*, 4th edn. London: Heinemann.

McNess, E., Arthur, L. & Crossley, M. (2015) 'Ethnographic Dazzle' and the Construction of the 'Other': revisiting dimensions of insider and outsider research for international and comparative education, *Compare*, 45(2), 295-316. http://dx.doi.org/10.1080/03057925.2013.854616

Merton, R.K. (1972) Insiders and Outsiders: a chapter in the sociology of knowledge, *American Journal of Sociology*, 78(1), 9-47. http://dx.doi.org/10.1086/225294

Pike, K. (1990) On the Emics and Etics of Pike and Harris, in T. Headland, K. Pike & M. Harris (Eds) *Emics and Etics: the insider/outsider debate. Frontiers of Anthropology*, vol. 7. London: SAGE.

Schuetz, A. (1944) The Stranger: an essay in social psychology, *American Journal of Sociology*, 50(5), 369-376. http://dx.doi.org/10.1086/219654

Simmel, G. (1908 [1958]) *Soziology, Untersuchungen ueber Formen der Vergesellschaftung* [Sociology, Studies in the Forms of Socialisation], 4th edn. Berlin: Ducker Humboldt.

CHAPTER 1

'Ethnographic Dazzle' and the Construction of the 'Other': shifting boundaries between the insider and the outsider

ELIZABETH McNESS, LORE ARTHUR
& MICHAEL CROSSLEY

Introduction

In this chapter we present some initial ideas on how the theoretical concepts of the 'insider' and the 'outsider' might be re-examined in an era where advances in comparative, qualitative research methodologies seek to be more inclusive, collaborative, participatory, reflexive and nuanced. Earlier essentialist definitions of the outsider as detached and objective, and the insider as culturally embedded and subjective, are re-examined and set within an international research and teaching context which recognises the increased migration of people, ideas and educational policies. We argue that, in the context of such change, it has become more difficult to categorise and label groups and individuals as being 'inside' or 'outside' systems, professional communities, or research environments. We recognise that individual and group identities can be multiple, flexible and changing such that the boundary between the inside and the outside is permeable, less stable and less easy to draw.

Social constructivist epistemologies, for example, regard identity as multiple, shifting and constantly in the process of formation. This challenges essentialist dualisms such as the insider/outsider, the researcher/researched, and questions the distinctions that have been drawn between the ethnographical 'emic', which seeks to understand a culture from the inside, and the comparative 'etic', which seeks to compare across different cultures (Pike, 1967; Morris et al, 1999). A predisposition to accept such dualisms, and position ourselves as outsiders, has dangers as it can entice us to place more emphasis on that which is unfamiliar and strange, rather than on that which is familiar. The American ethnographer Fox (1989, p. 18) has referred to this tendency as 'ethnographic dazzle', which can distract us from more subtle comparisons and meaning making and lead us to draw simplistic causal relationships – for instance, between student outcome and classroom practice, as demonstrated in much media and policy reaction to the publication of international league tables (Rautalin & Alasuutari, 2009; Ringarp & Rothland, 2010). Thus, it is important to avoid polarisation – of the insider or the outsider, the 'social constructionist' versus the overly fixed 'essentialist' in terms of different societies and communities – but, instead, to recognise that neither the researcher nor the subjects of analysis are fixed, stable and coherent but constantly shifting, incomplete, fragmented, and contradictory in relation to both collective and personal existence (Calhoun, 1995). Thomson and Gunter (2011, p. 26) have used Bauman's notion of 'liquid identities' to recognise how boundaries in the research process can be 'messily blurred in particular places and times'. Other researchers have sought to resolve insider/outsider tensions, relating to the place of outsider judgement, by developing research procedures that ask insiders to verify such judgements before finalising conclusions (Tobin et al, 1989).

We recognise that, within the field of international and comparative education, new methodologies are being employed to develop more contextually relevant understandings when working cross-culturally. The active development of collaborative and inter-disciplinary international research teams has sought to harness the strengths of combining multiple linguistic and cultural perspectives, not only in the collection and analysis of data, but also, importantly, in identifying key issues and appropriate research designs. Such collaborations make it possible to investigate phenomena across national and cultural boundaries, addressing issues of conceptual and linguistic significance from both the inside and the outside and, in so doing, seek to enhance contextual relevance.

In recognising these and other contemporary methodological trends we accept that, in practice, insider–outsider boundaries can and do occur, sometimes as fixed, immoveable entities with obstacles to overcome, and at other times as something more fluid, almost invisible, but nevertheless difficult to penetrate or negotiate. The following section thus draws on a historical perspective to examine the intellectual origins of 'otherness' as a foundation for the subsequent re-examination of the implications for contemporary forms of cross-cultural and comparative investigation.

Some Theoretical Positions in Relation to the Insider/Outsider

Insider/outsider perspectives have been discussed, theorised and researched across many academic disciplines over several decades: in anthropology from the perspective of the observer studying different cultures; in sociology with regard to social groupings and class, the dynamics of power relationships and social mobility; in psychology with regard to group behaviour and interaction; in linguistics and intercultural studies in the context of second language acquisition and cultural integration; and in philosophy in terms of the individual, the self, phenomenology and reflexivity. All these perspectives have left their mark on research theories, methodologies and methods – including in the field of international and cross-cultural comparative education.

On a broader level, being inside or outside is often part of everyday language and consciousness. For thousands of years human beings have erected boundaries to protect their own against 'outsiders'. In many societies, as Arnot (2012) points out, individuals and groups have strong loyalties to their own communities in which they have a role and a contribution to make, and a set of relationships that they can draw upon when in need. These civic identities are often outside the nation-state, being located within, for example, ethnic or family structures. Not surprisingly, it is usual for people to define who they are in relation to who they are not. In some ancient cultures the monstrous 'Other', such as the Chimaera, defines and makes clear the civilised self. In modern culture, the song 'Baby it's Cold Outside' (Loesser, 1944) seductively invites the listener to stay indoors where it is warm and welcoming. Being an insider can make one feel comfortable and ensure a sense of belonging. On the other hand, a person can be an insider, while feeling like an outsider. Differentiated groups from within the 'inner' circle can exercise power, sometimes beyond what can be expected, just as outsiders can be powerful oppressors – the strangers who are not really part of us. Some outsiders may just be travellers, newcomers, migrants or settlers trying hard to become part of the insider majority (Gudykunst, 1983). As teachers and researchers we often assume that drawing learners inside the learning community is, indeed, a good thing. We aim to create a sense of safety and belonging, though this can also lead to the imposition of one set of values and norms over another, something that we will return to later.

This sense of belonging, of wanting to be part of a community, has been explored by many scholars, including early social scientists such as Ferdinand Toennies (1855-1936) against the background of increasing modernity, industrialisation, urbanisation and isolation. Toennies theorised about *Gemeinschaft* (community), which offered intimacy and warmth, as opposed to *Gesellschaft* (society), which was seen as unwelcoming to outsiders. He argued, well over a hundred years ago, that modern society was caught in an irresistible process of disintegration. Its very progress was doomed. It was the community that would offer comfort, while the outside world was inevitably strange and somewhat hostile (Lindenfeld, 1988).

The German sociologist Georg Simmel (1858-1928) also considered the role of the outsider from the perspective of the individual migrant. This was set in the context of a Germany where, by 1907, 5% of its working population (12 million) were migrants (Bade, 1983). The resulting fear of foreigners/outsiders became emotive and widespread, and this was coupled with the desire to preserve one's own cultural heritage or insiderness. Paradoxically perhaps, Simmel also explored the notion of the newcomer or wanderer who does not mind being an outsider. Indeed, his stranger is strong and self-sufficient. Simmel's sociology was informed by the dialectic approach which characterises the individual and society. He argued that there is no such thing as a harmonious group because any social relationship needs to include both harmony and conflict, attraction and repulsion, love and hatred:

> The stranger thus is not to be considered here in the usual sense of the term, as the wanderer who comes today and goes tomorrow, but rather as the man who comes today and stays tomorrow – the potential wanderer, so to speak, who, although he has gone no further, has not quite got over the freedom of coming and going. (Simmel, cited in Levine, 1971, p. 143)

Simmel's understanding of the stranger is that of an objective outsider arguing that, because the stranger is not bound by roots and traditions, they can confront the group with a distinctly objective attitude. Simmel's stranger is an expert who views the new environment with a degree of objectivity, bringing with it a freedom to understand more clearly, without the filter of the cultural prejudices of the insider:

> Objectivity may also be defined as freedom: The objective man is not bound by the ties which could prejudice his perception, his understanding, and his assessment of data. (Simmel, cited in Levine, 1971, p. 146)

Simmel, however, did agree that this objectivity could also be seen as partial because, he argued, 'Objectivity is by no means non-participation, it is a positive and definitive kind of participation' (Simmel, cited in Levine, 1971, p. 145). Insiders may confide in outsiders on issues they would not discuss with those on the inside. This type of stranger, or outsider, is seen in a positive light, as the expert who sees things clearly and has much to contribute. The contemporary researcher, too, can experience that sense of being the knowledgeable outsider, the objective one, who can observe and perceive matters more clearly than a subjective insider. The methodological limitations and 'political' implications of such dualistic thinking underpin the significance of our renewed analysis and reconsideration.

Alfred Schuetz, (1899-1959) took an altogether different stance when considering the role of the individual outsider, the stranger. Schuetz was an Austrian migrant to the USA from Nazi Germany in 1938. This had a bearing on much of his writings. His equally seminal paper 'The Stranger' (1944) concerns an individual who tries to be at least tolerated by the insider group that s/he approaches. Insiders are viewed as the dominant group to which the newcomer, or stranger, tries to become accepted by seeking to gain cultural knowledge of the insider group. Such new knowledge may remain incoherent, inconsistent and lacking in clarity, but for members of the in-group it may offer sufficient coherence to allow the stranger to be admitted.

> The stranger, therefore, approaches the other group as a newcomer in the true meaning of the term. At best he may be able to share the present and the future ... however he remains excluded from such experiences of its past. Seen from the point of view of the approached group, he is a man without history. (Schuetz, 1944, p. 502)

This idea of a 'past', or history, is also important in terms of interpreting meaning and understanding when we look across cultures. It is noteworthy that the strangers of both Simmel and Schuetz perform a different function with regard to conflict within the group: Simmel's stranger observes conflict situations within the local group from the outside, while Schuetz's stranger is in conflict from within. A comparison between these two concepts shows that Simmel's stranger is credited with objectivity because the locals are seen to need the outsider perspective, while Schuetz's stranger needs to work hard to seek acceptance from within the new community in order to become an insider.

It is not difficult to see how these two opposing perspectives of the insider and outsider have relevance for the field of international and comparative education. Concepts such as objectivity and subjectivity are central to all research deliberations. In one sense we are all newcomers, strangers or outsiders though, as researchers, we are rarely entirely on one side or the other – and in practice, we are often somewhere in between. This tension is developed by Schuetz (1945) through his concept of the 'homecomer' who is, simultaneously, both insider and outsider. The homecomer is someone who has been away for a prolonged period of time and is about to rejoin a group even though s/he may feel like an outsider to it. Homecomers expect to return to an environment of which they think they still have intimate knowledge – although the home environment may have changed. The Chinese have a nickname for such a returnee: 'sea turtle' (*hai-gui* in Mandarin), which refers to someone who was born on a shore but has been across the sea, and is now returning to that same shore (Gill, 2010). This ambiguity – of being both inside and outside – affects many who have spent a prolonged period in a different culture and who experience a sense of not quite belonging in either culture. The following quotation, from an international student based in the UK, illustrates this:

> I have got two sets of values: one is for here [the UK] and one is for China ... I think they are just natural ... I am grown-up here. When I went back to China, I just went back to being the same – who I was before I came here ... but it [England] is not my place. I am a guest and the guest is always less powerful. (Gu et al, 2010, p. 17)

This is important because it raises the relative power of insiders and outsiders, which can have profound effects on all involved in the research process. It is interesting to note that, in this situation, the student sees himself/herself as less powerful as an outsider because of his/her status as a 'guest'.

The researcher Merton (1972) examines the insider/outsider concept, not from the perspective of the individual, but from that of social groupings such as suppressed black communities in a predominantly white American society. He argues that researchers should look at power relationships beyond their own organisations and their own contexts; being an insider does not necessarily mean the same as being a member of the community being researched. Merton goes on to say that in structural terms, we are all insiders and outsiders, members of some groups and, sometimes, not of others. He writes about distrust between social groupings and of extreme insiderism. He argues that this can lead to a mistaken assumption that, for example, only black scholars can understand black issues, or only women can understand women's issues. Following this logic, the outsider would be characterised as having a structurally imposed incapacity to comprehend alien groups. This can set up essentialist views of one group being superior to the other, or some knowledge being more relevant or valuable than others. Merton argues that there is no need to be Caesar in order to understand Caesar though, referring back to Fox (1989), without a detailed understanding of the history and cultural underpinning of a group, outsiders may be distracted by what they see as different and so focus on certain aspects, such as collectivism or individualism, without real depth of analysis or deep understanding. Researchers, and policy makers, beware!

Sociologically, of course, we might consider that we are all both insiders and outsiders: members of some groups and not of others by reason of gender, language, cultural/professional background, nationality, ethnicity and age, adding to the fluidity of such terms. Katyal and King (2011) describe their educational research carried out in Hong Kong, a city in which they had each lived and worked for a long time. At one level, they regarded themselves as insiders, since they had a degree of familiarity with the city and were researching their own professional environment. However, neither was ethnically Chinese (one an Indian woman and the other an American man), and this became an important factor while collecting data in a number of Hong Kong schools. Here there were elements of outsiderness within a dominant Chinese culture where different understandings of what is meant by leadership and management in a Confucian context constantly challenged their own western cultural values and sensitivities.

Soudien (2009) also usefully explores the concepts of insider and outsiderness by examining two dominant critiques of globalisation – that is, the 'delinkers' who stand outside globalisation and its educational cultures, as opposed to the 'subverters', who call for the reform of structures from within. With reference to the developing world and the developed world, he links the term 'outsiderness' to rationality and individualism, the 'white' hegemony, on the one hand, and to power and oppression within globalisation discourses on the other.

> Evident in the variety of these outsider approaches to globalisation, it needs to be said, is a serious and sustained critique of the hierarchylising and ranking, the dividing, and indeed the 'othering' proclivities of globalisation. (Soudien, 2009, p. 40)

Soudien extends his analysis in ways that directly relate to our own theoretical and methodological concerns by arguing that what is important is to recognise the impact that insider/outsider perspectives have had on educational practice around the world.

> Critically, as inclusive educational policy has attempted to be in most countries, it has come to settle around normative markers – literacy and competence in the global economy – that advantages the English-speaking middle class groupings and disadvantages those who do not fit this profile or who struggle to obtain the attributes of English-speaking middle-class groupings and middle-class behaviour. (Soudien, 2009, p. 43)

However, such polarisation, in Soudien's view, does not reflect the realities of the gap, the third space, the in-between which is a feature of everyday life. The third space is neither inside nor outside but pivots across the the difference between being outside and being inside. The old and the new can live side by side. Different cultural traditions can be accommodated with the more powerful discourses of the new.

Mediating Cultural and Linguistic Meaning in the 'Third' Space

If we move beyond the bipolar and essentialist constructs of insider/outsiderness we must acknowledge the space and tensions between – just as individual migrants are not just immigrants/outsiders but also newcomers. To some extent their own culture, their own ideas and belief systems travel with them, and this allows them to create new understandings and interpretations within the host communities (Cowen, 2009). Researchers also have multiple identities which can play out differently in different situations. Moreover, they have past histories and what the German philosopher Gadamer (2012) refers to as 'prejudices', or pre-judgement (*prae-judicium*), creating a 'historically-effected consciousness' (*wirkungsgeschichtliches Bewußtsein)*, which Gadamer sees as a positive attribute. It is through our historically effected consciousnesses that we understand and interpret the world. For Gadamer, the past has a truly pervasive power in the phenomenon of understanding. The past cannot be restricted to merely supplying the texts or events that make up the objects of interpretation, but it is what creates our horizon (*Horizont*) of understanding. Thus Gadamer develops a concept of understanding that takes the interpreter's present participation in history into account, when he says:

> The real power of hermeneutical consciousness is our ability to see what is questionable. Now if what we have before our eyes is not only the artistic tradition of a people, or a historical tradition, or the principles of modern science in its hermeneutical precondition but rather the whole of our experience, then we have succeeded, I think, in joining the experiences to our own universal and human experience of life. (Gadamer, 1976, p. 13)

So, as researchers, we cannot escape our past histories, but Gadamer sees that as a strength which enables us to have a deeper and more nuanced understanding of new situations and experience. He goes on to argue that in seeking to interpret the world we should create a 'fusion of horizons' (*Horizontverschmelzung*) which enables us to mediate between the familiar and the strange, or the inside and the outside, in a way which leaves neither unaffected. However, he is referring not to a compromise of understanding but to what Warnke (1987, p. 169) argues is a conversation in which 'all participants are led beyond their initial positions towards a consensus that is more differentiated and articulated than the separate views with which the conversation-partners began'. Gadamer himself argues that the aim is not necessarily to agree with other points of view but to understand them:

> In a conversation, when we have discovered the other person's standpoint and horizon, his ideas become intelligible without

> our necessarily having to agree with him; so also when someone thinks historically, he comes to understand the meaning of what has been handed down without necessarily agreeing with it or seeing himself in it. (Gadamer, 2012, p. 302)

The ENCOMPASS project, which looked at pupils' experience of schooling in England, France and Denmark (Osborn et al, 2003; McNess, 2006), illustrates such a process of 'fusing horizons' without seeking consensus or, in more current discourse, 'best practice'. It involved researchers from all three countries who each wrote about their initial reactions when visiting project schools in a different national context. The result was illuminating, producing not only an informative outsider's perspective of a different national system, but also an insider's re-evaluation of those 'taken-for-granted' elements in the researcher's own national context. The way in which the researchers described practices within a different national context gave a clear indication of the underlying assumptions which operated within their own context, as this extract from a Danish researcher describing a French school shows:

> What first strikes a Danish visitor to a French school is its clinical and strictly functional environment, which seems to have little connection with young people's lives and their learning ... Pupils do not have the opportunity to create their own physical space where they can express and stamp their individuality. (Osborn et al, 2003, p. 51)

It is clear that the researcher recognises the contrast with the collaborative and community-based assumptions of schooling within Denmark. Similarly, the French researcher drew attention to the 'branding' evident in English secondary schools with their uniforms and entrance-hall displays of sporting and creative arts achievements. This was seen in opposition to the French ideal of a common and equitable school experience for all. The English researcher drew attention to the relatively small, unhurried and less fragmented nature of the Danish *folkskole*, in contrast to the larger comprehensive schools in England where curriculum subject boundaries and academic/pastoral boundaries are more clearly drawn. Such observations, when discussed within international teams of researchers, can enable a more contextualised and nuanced way of understanding the influence and consequences of such difference in terms of policy and practice.

In a similar vein, the cultural theorist Bhabha draws attention to a 'Third Space' which can be seen as between the insider and outsider. Communication between the two requires the 'production of meaning', which relies not only on a general understanding of the use of language, but on an understanding of the 'performance' of language in a particular context, which might not be fully understood on either side:

> The pact of interpretation is never simply an act of communication between the I and the You designated in the statement. The production of meaning requires that these two places be mobilized in the passage through a Third Space, which represents both the general conditions of language and the specific implication of the utterance in a performative and institutional strategy of which it cannot 'in itself' be conscious. What this unconscious relation introduces is an ambivalence in the act of interpretation ... The meaning of the utterance is quite literally neither the one nor the other. (Bhabha, 1994, p. 53)

This draws into the discussion the role of language in mediating meaning. As outsiders we need to be able to understand and interpret not only what is said in a literal sense, but also the underlying meaning of historically and culturally embedded discourse. There is a growing body of literature from cultural and activity theorists, and others, which argues that, in the process of intercultural communication, there is a third perspective which is constructed when the insider and outsider meet. This liminal space of in-betweenness can be an area of hostility, but also one of great creativity, mutual understanding and new wisdom. As Bakhtin suggests:

> A meaning only reveals its depths once it has encountered and come into contact with another, foreign meaning ... We raise new questions for a foreign culture, ones that it did not raise itself; we see answers to our questions in it; and the foreign culture responds to us by revealing to us its new aspects and new semantic depths ... such a dialogic encounter of two cultures does not result in merging or mixing. Each retains its own unity and open totality, but they are mutually enriched. (1986, p. 7)

Bakhtin refers to this as 'stranger knowledge' and argues that this new awareness is not necessarily vocalised but can involve hearing what has not been said. This requires what psychologists refer to as cognitive empathy, and Sennet (2012) argues that this requires a curiosity and openness to new understandings and a dialogic form of communication which is subjunctive and tentative, rather than declarative. This can be difficult if you enter the research space as the 'expert' outsider, with opinions and values developed elsewhere.

However, international and comparative researchers can often be found working within this third space, whether as individual researchers who have knowledge of more than one cultural and linguistic context, or as cross-cultural teams which include both cultural and linguistic insiders/outsiders. This would include North/South collaborative research which draws upon post-colonial perspectives and critical theory to create more equitable and participatory approaches to comparative research that highlight local voice, as well as the increased recognition and inclusion of indigenous knowledge (Bainton & Crossley, 2009; Tikly & Barrett, 2011). This can present problems, and Louisy (1997) describes tensions in relation to being an inside researcher working within a small island state where communities are close-knit and where 'everybody knows everyone'. Other researchers, having begun work as total outsiders, have then been drawn into insider positions, making it increasingly difficult to maintain a degree of intellectual distance. Crossley and Vulliamy (1984, 1997) have written extensively about such dilemmas with reference to their own fieldwork in Papua New Guinea. They demonstrate the strengths of well-grounded multi-level case studies that combine both insider and outsider perspectives. They argue that this can facilitate research that is more sensitive to local context, while retaining systematic rigour and an important degree of detachment from the culture and world view being studied. Such work is seen as holding the potential for improving the impact of research upon policy and practice within diverse cultural contexts, and for stimulating local research capacity building in ways that do much to challenge traditional insider/outsider relationships (Barrett et al, 2011).

Searching for linguistic and conceptual equivalence is a fundamental aspiration for cross-cultural researchers, but it can be both time consuming and difficult to realise, whether working across national boundaries or across cultural borders within the same national context. Arthur (Arthur et al, 2007), for example, has undertaken a number of studies where her German background, native language competence and biculturalism did much to strengthen the depth of understanding. As a member of a European-wide higher education project involving several countries and a variety of languages called the REFLEX study, she was at times an insider as well as an outsider, with shifting perceptions and understandings. REFLEX was a qualitative study which also involved a large-scale survey of fifteen European countries and Japan, focusing on university graduates, their higher education experiences and subsequent employment five years after graduation. This work challenged the large team of researchers' essentialist notions of cross-cultural knowledge and understanding. The extensive questionnaire comprised eleven sections which included educational and related experiences, transition from study to work, employment history since graduation, current work, competences needed for work and evaluation of study programme. Designing and implementing the survey was anything but a straightforward process. The countries involved collected graduates' data differently, depending on the availability of central databases containing graduates' contact details. Researchers in Switzerland and the Netherlands were able to use a national register from which to draw their sample. But in many other countries (e.g. Finland, Germany and the UK) researchers had to rely on the cooperation of individual higher education institutions, and their interpretations of data protection issues, to access graduates' contact details. These various interpretations of 'data protection' challenged preconceived notions of what is ethically right or wrong. Similarly, survey questions concerning ethnicity, common practice in many countries, were inconceivable on grounds of a troubled history in Germany and Austria, yet this point is not easily understood by outsiders. Furthermore, reciprocal explanations of terminology were time consuming and difficult to realise. Words such as 'job' or 'occupation', even 'profession', or poor translations leading to expressions such as 'on the job', carry different meaning in different cultural contexts. The term 'profession', for example, is complex because in the Anglo-Saxon meaning it often refers to a qualification accredited by, and providing entry to, professional bodies, usually after graduation, while in many other countries this accreditation role is assigned to the universities. Over the course of the project, such cross-cultural distinctions became blurred, revealing the limitations of overly simplistic and essentialist conceptualisations (Arthur, 2006; Arthur et al, 2007; Little & Arthur, 2010).

Theories of representation, which might help clarify these points, distinguish between the following approaches: the reflective approach, in which language functions like a mirror to reflect the true meaning as it already exists in the world; the intentional approach, where, as individuals, we use language to convey meaning or to communicate things which are special and unique to us; and the constructivist approach, in which meaning and language operate through symbolic practices and processes. The relationship between language, knowledge and culture is a complex one. After all, language must mean something, in the sense of mental representation. In other words, representation is the production of meaning of the concepts in our mind through language. As Hall (1997, p. 24) explains, the main point is that meaning does not inhere in things, in the world. It is constructed, produced. It is the result of a signifying practice – a practice that produces meaning – which is culturally moulded. Meanings change, adapt or fade away in the course of time and from one location to another. In the constructivist sense, there is a social, public aspect to language. Things carry no meaning in themselves. People construct meaning using representational systems, such as concepts and signs, within the context of their own cultural environment. However, paradigms of culture pose a multitude of questions yet offer few answers. Their interpretation rests on one's own understanding and perception of a given context or situation. Cultural understanding is therefore not readily transferable from one country to another or from one community to another, particularly if language barriers intervene. This is where simplistic or aggregated understandings of different educational practices and their influence on pupil attainment, such as 'whole class teaching', 'rote learning', 'personalised learning' or 'assessment for learning', can lead to distortions within education policy making.

Making New Meaning in International and Comparative Research

We have moved into a new global intellectual context where research partnerships require insiders and outsiders to work together in new ways. Those who have engaged in research across different cultures and linguistic communities know how complex and, at the same time, exciting such ventures can be. However, research is not an aim in itself, a goal to be reached for individual satisfaction. Researchers must seek to communicate with others; findings are to be shared with communities similar to or different from one's own. Researchers are concerned with creating mutual understanding and sharing cross-cultural meaning – what Crossley (2008, 2009) has referred to as a 'bridging of cultures and traditions'. In other words, scholars construct meaning out of their own situation, and then mediate that meaning to others in a spirit of mutuality and cooperation. In this case there are two meanings – the primary meaning, which is constructed in relation to the self and its cultural context, and the secondary meaning, which is collectively constructed by the group. Shotter (1993) agrees with much that has been argued above by suggesting that both sets of meanings lead to newly created knowledge which he refers to as a third kind of knowledge. This third kind of knowledge is derived from within a shared situation, a social institution or society, or, in this instance, from collaborative comparative research. In this case individual researchers cannot come to a shared understanding of the phenomenon under investigation on their own. They are dependent on processes of negotiation within the group. Recognising the potential of this 'third' space to generate new insights for both the individual researcher and the cross-cultural research team has important theoretical and methodological implications for international and comparative education. Moreover, such contextually situated analysis, which draws on a Sadlerian tradition which sees education as contextually situated and a product of social systems which are culturally, historically and politically determined by 'forgotten struggles and difficulties' and 'battles long ago', has the potential to counterbalance current preoccupations with the comparison of large, cross-national datasets where meaning is often attributed to aggregated identities and categories.

Conclusion

So, to conclude, factors that include ethnicity, language, gender, age, academic status, and personal and professional experience all shape and influence insider/outsider perspectives on the research process – and these in turn influence methodological approaches, research designs, data analysis and evaluation. Questions that arise from this generate important implications for all researchers, and for long-held assumptions about the benefits of working as an objective outsider to 'make the familiar strange'. How can outsiders, without the detailed historical and cultural understanding of the insider, interpret what they see? Is it possible, or appropriate, to objectify the subjective and, bearing the researcher's reflexivity in mind, to subjectify what seems to be at first glance objective? Do international and comparative researchers have to have teaching experience in order to research teachers? Do they have to speak the language of those being researched, as has long been argued? Indeed, what can be learned by the increasingly mobile research community of the twenty-first century from the literature relating to insider and outsiderness?

Being an insider or outsider, we argue, has much to do with our own constantly evolving lives, academic scholarship, previous experiences, and prior knowledge of the context to be researched. It has much to do with how we each perceive the world, and how we interpret what we see and experience. As Hellawell maintains, there are then:

> subtly varying shades of 'insiderism' and 'outsiderism'. The more important point has to do with empathy, trying to understand the other person, or the other context, rather than closeness or distance. Moreover, it can sometimes become apparent that the same researcher can slide along more than one insider–outsider continuum and in both directions during the research process. (Hellawell, 2006, p. 489)

A key word here is 'empathy'; this means the capacity to recognise and share thoughts or feelings that are being experienced by others. International comparativists often aim to build bridges, to mediate between different cultural communities, between those on the inside and those outside – and to construct intercultural meaning. Researchers are both inside and outside the learning environment, and inside and outside the phenomena under investigation. Research may require us to distance ourselves and yet at the same time to become immersed. We are neither complete observers nor complete participants but often working in that 'third space' in between. Important, too, is the interactive process shaped by the researcher's personal history and biography, gender and ethnicity. Here, reflexivity and situated ethics increasingly matter. The researcher, as the mediator of meaning, seeks a new body of ethical directiveness fitted for our contemporary world. In this, mutual understanding and shared meaning are important. While Habermas (1984) suggests that our goal should be finding agreement rather than just understanding, Gadamer (2012) recognises that, at least in the historical sense, understanding may not always bring agreement. We can understand the past without agreeing with its precepts. Bhabha (1994) takes this a stage further by arguing that it is by moving through the 'third space' of intercultural dialogue, beyond the concepts of the insider and the outsider, that we can produce new meaning that does not result in 'merging or mixing' but mutually enriches understanding. Certainly, all researchers need to come to terms with their own position within the research process and engage with a diversity of expectations and perspectives – many of which may be fragmented, imaginary, or even contradictory and divisive. For those working in higher education it is important to see this as part of a developmental process.

Acknowledgements

This chapter is an amended version of an article first published in *Compare* (McNess et al, 2015). We thank the publishers, Taylor & Francis, and the editors of *Compare*, for permission to rework this material here.

References

Arnot, M. (2012) Youth Citizenship and the Politics of Belonging: introducing contexts, voices, imaginaries, *Comparative Education*, 48(1), 1-10. http://dx.doi.org/10.1080/03050068.2011.637759

Arthur, L. (2006) Higher Education and the Knowledge Society: issues, challenges and responses in Norway and Germany, *Research into Comparative and International Education*, 1(3), 241-252. http://dx.doi.org/10.2304/rcie.2006.1.3.241

Arthur, L., Brennan, J. & de Weert, E. (2007) *Employer and Higher Education Perspectives on Graduates in the Knowledge Society*. Milton Keynes: Centre for Higher Education Research and Information, The Open University.

Bade, K. (1983) *Vom Auswanderungsland zum Einwanderungsland? Deutschland 1880-1980*. Berlin: Colloquium Verlag.

Bainton, D. & Crossley, M. (2009) Lessons from Comparative and International Education, in C. Fourali, S. Issler & G. Elliott (Eds) *Education and Social Change: connecting local and global perspectives*, pp. 15-26. London: Continuum.

Bakhtin, M.M. (1986) Response to a Question from *Novy Mir* Editorial Staff, in C. Emerson and M. Holquist (Eds) *Speech Genres and Other Late Essays*, trans. V.W. McGee. Austin: University of Texas Press.

Barrett, A., Crossley, M. & Dachi, H. (2011) International Collaboration and Research Capacity Building: learning from the EdQual experience, *Comparative Education*, 47(1), 25-43. http://dx.doi.org/10.1080/03050068.2011.541674

Bhabha, H.K. (1994) *The Location of Culture*. London: Routledge.

Calhoun, C. (1995) Critical Social Theory, in *Culture, History and the Challenge of Difference*. Oxford: Blackwell.

Cowen, R. (2009) The Transfer, Translation and Transformation Processes: and their shape-shifting, *Comparative Education*, 45(3), 315-327. http://dx.doi.org/10.1080/03050060903184916

Crossley, M. (2008) Bridging Cultures and Traditions for Educational and International Development: comparative research, dialogue and difference, *International Review of Education*, 54(3-4), 319-336.

Crossley, M. (2009) Rethinking Context in Comparative Education, in R. Cowen & A.M. Kazamias (Eds) *International Handbook of Comparative Education*, pp. 1173-1187. http://dx.doi.org/10.1007/978-1-4020-6403-6_73

Crossley, M. & Vulliamy, G. (1984) Case-study Research Methods and Comparative Education, *Comparative Education*, 20(2), 193-207. Republished in A. Sica (Ed.) (2006) *Comparative Methods in Social Science*. New Delhi: SAGE.

Crossley, M. & Vulliamy, G. (Eds) (1997) *Qualitative Educational Research in Developing Countries*. London: Garland.

Fox, R. (1989) *The Search for Society: quest for a biosocial science and morality*. New Brunswick, NJ: Rutgers University Press.

Gadamer, H.-G. (1976) *Truth and Method*, 2nd edn. London: Sheed & Ward.

Gadamer, H.-G. (2012) *Truth and Method*, 2nd rev. edn. London: Continuum.

Gill, S. (2010) The Homecoming: an investigation into the effect that studying overseas had on Chinese postgraduates' life and work in their return to China, *Compare*, 40(3), 359-376. http://dx.doi.org/10.1080/03057920903464555

Gu, Q., Schweisfurth, M. & Day, C. (2010) Learning and Growing in a 'Foreign' Context: intercultural experiences of international students, *Compare*, 40(1), 7-23. http://dx.doi.org/10.1080/03057920903115983

Gudykunst, W.B. (1983) Towards a Typology of Stranger–Host Relationships, *International Journal of Intercultural Relationships*, 7(4), 401-413. http://dx.doi.org/10.1016/0147-1767(83)90046-9

Habermas, J. (1984) *The Theory of Communicative Action. Vol. 1: Reason and Rationalisation of Society*. London: Heinemann.

Hall, S. (Ed.) (1997) *Representation: cultural representations and signifying practices*. London: SAGE Publications in association with the Open University.

Hellawell, D. (2006) Inside-out: analysis of the insider–outsider concept as a heuristic device to develop reflexivity in students doing qualitative research, *Teaching in Higher Education*, 11(4), 483-494. http://dx.doi.org/10.1080/13562510600874292

Katyal, K.R. & King, M. (2011) 'Outsiderness' and 'Insiderness' in a Confucian Society: complexity in context, *Comparative Education*, 47(3), 327-341. http://dx.doi.org/10.1080/03050068.2011.586765

Levine, D. (Ed.) (1971) *Georg Simmel on Individuality and Social Forms.* Chicago: University of Chicago Press. http://dx.doi.org/10.7208/chicago/9780226924694.001.0001

Lindenfeld, D. (1988) Toennies, the Mandarins and Materialism, *German Studies Review*, 11(1), 57-81. http://dx.doi.org/10.2307/1430834

Little, B. & Arthur, L. (2010) Less Time to Study, Less Well Prepared for Work, Yet Satisfied with Higher Education: a UK perspective on links between higher education and the labour market, *Journal of Education and Work*, 23(3), 275-296. http://dx.doi.org/10.1080/13639080.2010.484415

Loesser, F. (1944) Baby it's Cold Outside (words and music), recorded by many artists, including Ray Charles with Betty Carter.

Louisy, P. (1997) Dilemmas of Insider Research in a Small-country Setting: tertiary education in St. Lucia, in M. Crossley & G. Vulliamy (Eds) *Qualitative Educational Research in Developing Countries*. London: Routledge.

McNess, E. (2006) Nous écouter, nous soutenir, nous apprendre: a comparative study of pupils' perceptions of the pedagogic process, *Comparative Education*, 42(4), 517-532. http://dx.doi.org/10.1080/03050060600988403

McNess, E., Arthur, L. & Crossley, M. (2015) 'Ethnographic Dazzle' and the Construction of the 'Other': revisiting dimensions of insider and outsider research for international and comparative education, *Compare*, 45(2), 295-316. http://dx.doi.org/10.1080/03057925.2013.854616

Merton, R.K. (1972) Insiders and Outsiders: a chapter in the sociology of knowledge, *American Journal of Sociology*, 78(1), 9-47. http://dx.doi.org/10.1086/225294

Morris, M.W., Leung, K., Ames, D. & Lickel, B. (1999) Views from Inside and Outside: integrating emic and etic insights about culture and justice judgement, *Academy of Management Review*, 24(4), 781-796.

Osborn, M., Broadfoot, P., McNess, E., Planel, C., Ravn, B. & Triggs, P. (2003) *A World of Difference? Comparing Learners across Europe*. Maidenhead: Open University Press.

Pike, K.L. (1967) *Language in Relation to a Unified Theory of the Structure of Human Behaviour*. The Hague: Mouton. http://dx.doi.org/10.1037/14786-000

Rautalin, M. & Alasuutari, P. (2009) The Uses of the National PISA Results by Finnish Officials in Central Government, *Journal of Education Policy*, 24(5), 539-556. http://dx.doi.org/10.1080/02680930903131267

Ringarp, J. & Rothland, M. (2010) Is the Grass Always Greener? The Effect of the PISA Results on Education Debates in Sweden and Germany, *European Educational Research Journal*, 9(3), 422-430. http://dx.doi.org/10.2304/eerj.2010.9.3.422

Schuetz, A. (1944) The Stranger: an essay in social psychology, *American Journal of Sociology*, 49(6), 499-507. http://dx.doi.org/10.1086/219472

Schuetz, A. (1945) The Homecomer, *American Journal of Sociology*, 50(5), 369-376. http://dx.doi.org/10.1086/219654

Sennet, R. (2012) *Together: the rituals, pleasures and politics of cooperation.* London: Penguin.

Shotter, J. (1993) *Conversational Realities: constructing life through language.* London: SAGE.

Simmel, G. ([1908] 1958) *Soziologie, Untersuchungen über Formen der Vergesellschaftung*, 4th edn. Berlin: Duncker & Humboldt.

Soudien, C. (2009) Globalisation and Its Malcontexts: in pursuit of the promise of education, in J. Zajda & V. Rust (Eds) *Globalisation, Policy and Comparative Research*, pp. 35-49. Dordrecht: Springer.

Thomson, P. & Gunter, H. (2011) Inside, Outside, Upside Down: the fluidity of academic researcher 'identity' in working with/in school, *International Journal of Research & Method in Education*, 34(1), 17-30. http://dx.doi.org/10.1080/1743727X.2011.552309

Tikly, L. & Barrett, A.M. (Eds) (2011) Researching Education Quality in Low-income Countries: politics, processes and practice, *Comparative Education Special Issue*, 47(1).

Tobin, J., Wu, D.Y.H. & Davidson, D.H. (1989) *Preschool in Three Cultures: Japan, China and the United States.* New Haven, CT: Yale University Press.

Warnke, G. (1987) *Gadamer: hermeneutics, tradition and reason.* Cambridge: Polity Press.

CHAPTER 2

Exploring the Concept of Insider–Outsider in Comparative and International Research: essentialising culture or culturally essential?

ANNA ROBINSON-PANT

Introduction

From the title of this book based on the BAICE-funded series of seminars we gain a sense of the distance travelled since this idea was first introduced to the field of comparative and international education. The comparative method is implicit in the terms 'outsider/insider', and in the early days of comparative education there would have been no need to ask 'inside and outside of *what*?' Sadler's seminal speech in 1900 provides the answer: 'The practical value of studying ... the working of foreign systems of education is it will result in our being better fitted to study and to understand our own' (Sadler, 1900). The binaries of us/them, English and 'foreign' systems of education provided the basis for comparison, and the purpose was to learn and develop through this analytical process.

Over the past century, the field of comparative education has changed in response to rapid globalisation, in terms of problematising the nation-state and turning to other units of comparison, including 'culture'. Also influenced by processes of globalisation, the growing field of international education has been shaped by the activity of international organisations, such as league tables produced by the Organisation for Economic Co-operation and Development (OECD), the World Bank and donor agencies to compare educational performance across and within continents. Arnove (2010, p. 829) notes how education is increasingly viewed in 'economistic' rather than 'humanistic' terms, and Alexander (2010) points to the politicisation of this kind of research activity. The current purpose of such comparative analysis thus stands in stark contrast to Sadler's original notion of learning and professional development.

As a researcher and teacher in comparative and international education today – influenced by developments in postcolonial theory – I have tended to see 'outsider/insider' perspectives as a useful starting point for facilitating intercultural learning and dialogue. But as an analytical tool within research studies, I have found the terms more problematic. As I hinted above, there is much ambiguity in the concept. Although in the thematic forum discussions on which this book is based, we narrowed outsider/insider down to 'perspectives' (rather than also considering outsider/insider roles), the question of 'inside and outside what?' remains. Even if we see this ambiguity in meaning more positively, as potential flexibility, the dualism set up here seems to be informed by a reductive goal – rather than aiming to analyse, identify and generate new patterns. Like other dualisms common in this field (such as researcher/researched, informal/formal, quantitative/qualitative, literate/illiterate), the insider/outsider distinction pushes us to categorise and polarise people's identities, roles and knowledges. It can close down rather than open up debate and investigation. Recognising the limitations of the outsider–insider dualism, researchers have proposed adaptations: the model of a continuum between outsider and insider perspectives (Hellawell, 2006), and building on Bhabha's notion of the 'Third Space' as a way of responding to fluid and dynamic identities and boundaries (McNess et al, 2013). However, as I will explore in the next section on the emic/etic dialectic, these alternative models also seem to rely on an initial notion of separation between outsider and insider positions.

My main area of concern, however, is not about what kind of model or framework is constructed (whether polarised, continuum or three-part model), but is around the dominant assumptions underpinning the outsider/insider dichotomy: unitary fixed identities, bounded communities and, above all, an essentialised notion of 'culture'. Within the field of comparative and international education (CIE) today, it seems to me that these assumptions are our greatest challenge: we either have too much or too little 'culture'! The case of too much culture can be seen in research on the internationalisation of higher education and teaching international students, which is still often shaped by a strong discourse around cultural difference (also expressed in dualisms such as Confucian versus western pedagogy, collectivist versus individualist values). Turning to the current policy trend within international education for comparing educational success across nations – the most recent being the OECD (2013) survey of adult skills – attention tends to be focused on explaining differences in institutional structures, assessment systems and curriculum, rather than on exploring or even explaining 'Culture'.

Both examples above are dependent on a similar understanding of culture – even the apparent lack of attention to 'culture' in comparative surveys is due to an assumption of there being essential differences between, say, English and Taiwanese people/societies. The starting point appears to be that as the essential cultural characteristics of a nation cannot be changed, policy makers have to identify instead the non-cultural/neutral ingredient from Taiwan that might make a difference to education in the UK.

This brings to mind again Sadler's warning against uncritical transfer of educational systems/curriculum/approaches in 1900: 'We cannot wander at pleasure among the educational systems of the world, like a child strolling through a garden, and pick off a flower from one bush and some leaves from another, and then expect that if we stick what we have gathered into the soil at home, we shall have a living plant' (Sadler, 1900). Fast-forward to the present, and our current contexts of educational reform and comparative research suggest that the bushes in Sadler's garden may already be hybrid and that 'we' are a diverse group, perhaps a cross-cultural and interdisciplinary team of researchers and educational policy makers (see McNess et al, 2013). How can the concept of outsider/insider help us to respond to these increasingly complex issues around cross-cultural transfer? More formalised procedures around research governance mean that the individual researcher/researched relationship is now mediated by different agencies. How does the simple dichotomy of insider/outsider map on to the multiple and sometimes fragmented roles, relationships and identities performed by the various actors in an applied educational research study?

In everyday life, I am often influenced by a sense that I am an insider or an outsider. Sometimes it helps me to make sense of change – identifying the way in which my institution is being transformed by new managerial discourses, for instance. I also find myself and other parents essentialising culture in our conversations when we talk about girls' behaviour as compared with boys', or when I explain English culture to my students in terms of common characteristics. So what is going on? I have found Spivak's (1986) term 'operational essentialism' (in relation to feminism) useful to explain the ways in which we have to resort to such binaries and essentialism in order to move beyond them.

In this chapter, I aim to investigate how the insider/outsider concept can be used to enhance our understanding about processes of learning and the kind of knowledge being constructed in comparative and international educational research. Coming from the field of ethnographic research on adult learning, literacy and development, I have been struck by how outsider/insider debates engage with issues that have long been the concern of educators within anthropology and of theorists on informal learning. I will turn to writers in these fields first to consider how we might counter what I have identified above as the limitations of the outsider/insider concept as an analytical tool.

Emic/Etic and Insider/Outsider: is there a difference?

Since being coined by the linguist Pike in 1970, the terms emic/etic have permeated anthropological accounts of fieldwork and are often considered as synonymous with insider/outsider. For this reason, I began to explore how the distinction between emic/etic had evolved within anthropology as a way of understanding processes of knowledge construction. The terms originated in linguistic analysis as 'phonetic' (representing 'the set of possible distinctions that might be used in the characterisation of human speech' [Agar, 1980, p. 190]) and 'phonemic' ('the subset of those distinctions useful in describing the sound differences that are perceived as significant by speakers of a particular language' [Agar, 1980, p. 190]). In a series of dialogues with Pike, which form the basis of a book published in 1990, Harris makes a strong case for the analytical superiority of emic/etic over insider/outsider:

> This distinction [insider/outsider] lacks clarity because it does not specify whether the outsider's point of view leads to emic or etic knowledge based respectively on emic or etic operations ... the distinction between insider and outsider does not come to grips with the epistemologically salient meaning of the emic/etic contrast. (Harris, 1990, p. 51)

Throughout their book, the authors argue that 'emics and etics are first, last and always epistemological constructs' (Lett, 1990, p. 132). The various definitions of emic and etic all refer to the construction of knowledge: 'etics denotes an approach by an outsider to an inside system, in which the outsider brings his own structure – his own emics – and partly superimposes his observations on the inside view, interpreting the inside in reference to his outside starting point' (Harris, 1990, p. 49). It is our understanding of the phenomenon, not the phenomenon itself, that is emic or etic. The writers in the book differ mainly with respect to the purpose of (etic analysis as a means of entering emic systems as opposed to being an end in itself [Lett, 1990, p. 127]) and what they refer to as the 'procedures' of research, which transform observations into accounts. What comes across strongly in these discussions is the detailed analysis of experiential learning and knowledge construction. Pike draws on Polyani's (1967) theory of tacit knowledge to discuss how people learn to act as insiders without knowing why and emphasises that the learning is two-way: 'But just as the outsider can learn to act like an insider, so the insider can learn to analyse like an outsider' (Pike, 1990, p. 34).

What seems different from the polarisation associated with outsider/insider is the interconnectedness and 'blending' (Agar, 1980, p. 191) of emic and etic. Agar discusses these terms in terms of how difficult it would be construct an ethnographic statement that is not a blend: 'A statement would almost always contain some assumptions about perception or intent on the part of group members, but it would also be constructed by the ethnographer in terms of his own professional context and goals' (Agar, 1980, p. 191).

Pike captured these synergies and the 'involved nature of emics leading to etics, and etics leading to emics ... some phases of this paradoxical problem' (Pike, 1990, p. 45) in a poem:

> EMIC CIRCLE
> See, and know.
> Know, and be.
> Be, and do.
> Do, and see.
> See, and know.

Dell Hymes (1990, p. 123) discusses the process as the 'three step sequence', emphasising that that 'etic–emic–etic constitute not a dichotomy but a dialectic'. All these writers contrast the linear process associated with outsider/insider with the complexity of knowledge construction through etic–emic–etic and through textualisation. Looking at the ways in which knowledge is constructed through text, Clifford (1983, p. 120) emphasises that 'ethnography is from beginning to end enmeshed in writing. This writing includes, minimally, a translation of experience into textual form.' Lett's (1990, p. 130) definition of emic constructs as 'accounts, descriptions and analyses expressed in terms of the conceptual schemes and categories regarded as meaningful and appropriate by the native members of the culture' gives an insight into the 'procedures' through which data are transformed into text. Agar's metaphor of anthropological fieldwork as a 'funnel' (starting broad and narrowing down) conveys how the process of constructing knowledge is interconnected with the researcher's changing relationship with informants: 'One first takes an involved, humanitarian position, striving for breadth of understanding in a student-child-apprentice position. As the fieldwork progresses, one in part takes a detached scientific view, focuses on some specific issues, and designs systematic approaches to formally document the experience from the perspective of a stranger' (Agar, 1980, p. 204).

A key difference between outsider/insider and emic/etic lies in this sense of progression in learning and the dynamic, complex nature of research relationships. While the outsider/insider concept focuses our attention on micro-level relationships and roles, we need to look elsewhere to find a framework for analysing the processes of knowledge construction and learning that take place through cross-cultural fieldwork.

Learning through Doing: the ethnographic experience

Reading anthropological literature about fieldwork as a rite of passage, I have been struck by how much explicit discussion there is about the process of learning (and sometimes teaching) through emic/etic knowledge construction. Clifford (1983, p. 127) describes participant observation as 'shorthand for continuous tacking between the "inside" and "outside" of events: on the one hand grasping the sense of specific occurrences and gestures empathetically, on the other stepping back to situate these meanings in wider contexts'. Agar (1980) sees ethnography as being about the learning/teaching of rapport in the research context, describing the 'student-child-apprentice role' of the researcher. Developing distance and proximity are central to this process, as Todorov (1988) suggests, and Street (2001, p. 93) describes the 'essence' of the ethnographic experience as 'proximity and distance held in tension simultaneously'. The dialectical notion of knowledge construction associated with etic–emic–etic comes through Todorov's discussion of such learning: 'The climax of this anthropological education is thus not distancing (in relation to others) but detachment (in relation to oneself).' Street's (2001) chapter 'Ethnography for Linguists' identifies three concepts involved in learning ethnography: epistemological relativity ('recognising one's assumptions about knowledge'), reflexivity ('ability to reflect critically on the way in which one's own cultural background and standpoint influences one's view of other cultures' and critical consciousness ('viewing ethnography not simply as a convenient tool for researching but as itself a product of particular dominant societies at a particular period') (Street, 2001, p. 95). All these writers are going a step further than describing how the researcher can compare insider–outsider perspectives, to provide conceptual tools for analysing the shifts and growth in their understanding.

These insights into how people learn to become ethnographers all emphasise the importance of informal learning as compared with formal training in research methods. Agar's idea of the researcher as 'apprentice' is important here, as he explains: 'by its very nature, an apprentice's role cannot be done for you. Besides, with an ethnographer's sensitivity to the importance of relationship in the learning process, it is difficult to allow another screen between yourself and the person from whom you are supposedly learning' (Agar, 1980, p. 195). The ethnographer learns experientially through human relationships, as Tonkin (1984, p. 219) discusses: 'Fieldwork is the experiential teaching of what "social" means.'

Writing on insider/outsider perspectives in CIE has rarely focused on how researchers learn through the etic–emic–etic dialectic. Instead we may read more about what differences and similarities emerge from comparative analysis of educational experiences, systems or practices. By contrast, within ethnography, informal learning through researcher/ researched interaction is recognised and discussed as central not only to gaining access or developing rapport but to the generation of research data and analysis. Holy (1984, p. 32) points to the 'social relationship between the researcher and subject' as having the status of a research method: 'the interaction between anthropologist and host ... can be used as the method of yielding data and developed into the main research tool'. This interaction is not just about getting to know each other, but about dialectical construction of knowledge, getting to know and share "each other's" cognitive maps' (Holy, 1984, p. 32).

I am suggesting above that the attention given to analysing and identifying informal learning within the anthropological literature has emerged from the recognition of the importance of emic/etic as an analytical tool. There is also the potential for 'outsider/insider perspectives' to serve a similar educational purpose in research – particularly if conceptualised as a dialectic process, rather than emphasising the contrasting perspectives of insider and outsider. In the next section I will look at how we might use the concept of insider/ outsider to question and transform dominant discourses on culture within international policy-focused research and higher education institutions.

Essentialising Culture or Culturally Essential?

Now I will turn to the tricky question of 'culture' – which really has been the subject of the earlier part of this chapter too. 'Learning culture' is the main challenge faced not only by ethnographers, but by all those working in the field of comparative and international education. As I have suggested above, anthropologists have written more explicitly about how they learn culture, and Agar (1980, p. 190) draws on a metaphor of linguistic competence to capture this: 'culture is the name for the grammar and vocabulary of the language ethnographers use when they describe their ability to give accounts'. Today's ethnographers also share an understanding of culture as a 'deliberate abstraction ... to help anthropologists conceptualise that ever-changing whole' (Baumann, 1996, p. 11, cited in Holliday, 1999, p. 254). Holliday (1999) goes on to discuss the difficulties of this definition, saying that 'culture is an abstraction yet everything else suggests it is a concrete reality'. This could be seen as the tension that I described earlier between the ways in which we talk about culture in everyday life and the recognition of what Holliday (1999) calls a 'small culture' paradigm. Within applied linguistics, he described how 'a "small culture" approach attempts to liberate "culture" from notions of ethnicity and nation' as compared with 'a large culture approach [which] results in reductionist overgeneralisation, otherization of foreign educators' (Holliday, 1999, p. 238). Particularly relevant to the two meanings of 'culture' that I am identifying in this chapter, Holliday insisted that 'It is not my intention to argue that culture really means X rather than Y but to clarify what we mean when we use the word in different ways for different things' (Holliday, 1999, p. 238).

Unlike today's anthropologists, comparative and international educational researchers (as a more diverse group in terms of disciplines and aims) seem to lack a shared reference point on 'culture', and the default position (particularly in policy contexts) is often the 'large culture' paradigm. In particular, the field has been influenced by Hofstede's (2003) work in management studies on cultural characteristics and norms of behaviour. His research involved collecting information about how people behave in specific countries in order to provide 'measurable behavioural formula' (Holliday, 2011, p. 14) for cross-cultural training in commercial companies. Looking from an educational perspective at how we 'learn culture', Holliday suggests ways of shifting from the 'neo-essentialism' informed by Hoftstede to 'critical cosmopolitanism' – from us comparing our culture with theirs 'to all parties looking critically at cultural texts everywhere' (Holliday, 2011, p. 14). Although aspiring to the ideal of 'critical cosmopolitanism', I am interested in the role that 'neo-essentialism' contributes to learning culture (Spivak's 'operational essentialism'). Returning to the etic–emic–etic dynamic, I suspect that it is the constant movement between 'large' and 'small' culture paradigms that helps us to develop the skills of 'critical cosmopolitanism'.

Learning Culture through Adopting an Insider–Outsider Lens

At the beginning of this chapter, I suggested that we no longer know how to answer 'insider and outsider of what?' However, the insights from etic–emic–etic debates on learning culture suggest that the answer could be 'culture'. I will now turn to see how the insider–outsider concept can be used to investigate and compare assumptions about culture and support intercultural dialogue within research. I will draw on three examples from research that I have conducted in the field of international and comparative education. I have chosen vignettes where the participants were engaging directly with insider/outsider discourses about culture. The three examples are from different areas of CIE (internationalisation of UK higher education; international development; and internationalising research methodology), and point to differing implications for research and policy. I am interested to look at the implications of the insider–outsider concept for learning, not only within educational institutions (as Hellawell [2006] has explored in relation to teaching reflexivity to doctoral students), but also within development organisations/programmes.

Intercultural Learning in Universities

I have been conducting research with and on international students across my university for several years. The following extract comes from a research project with doctoral students who discussed their experience of moving from their home country to the UK university. Mohammed was studying in the School of Medicine and described the transition from Malaysia to the UK:

> We believe we should pay respect to our teachers, that is what we are taught traditionally. But as time goes by, we know how things work here. We value how to argue ... so we are getting on to it. We can discuss in an openly manner. There's different idea about politeness. For example, we are taught that our teachers, our supervisors, they are equivalent to our parents. So we don't argue with them, whatever they say, we obey. We will do it. We will make sure it happens at whatever cost. But in here there is lots of freedom. You can discuss ... it's a friend relationship.

In this interview, Mohammed spoke with great certainty about the contrasts between Malaysia and the UK (i.e. 'here'). By framing his comments in terms of insider/outsider perspectives ('we' refers to Malaysian students), he was able to move back and forth between the practices of teacher and student in Malaysia and the new ideas he has encountered about relationships with his supervisors in the UK. On first reading, Mohammed appears to adopt a 'big culture' approach, essentialising the differences, particularly around the culture of 'respect' and the 'different idea about politeness'. However, he could also be seen to adopt a 'small culture' approach as he analyses his own learning, explaining how he is taking on certain practices and how he is 'making culture' too ('we value how to argue'). In other discussions, Mohammed had challenged his own use of 'we' to represent Malaysian students, saying that they were not a homogeneous group and that some students, like him, were mature mid-career professionals, unlike the 'fresh graduates'.

Holliday et al (2004, p. 15) advise: 'while respecting whatever people say about their own culture, take what they say as evidence of what they wish to project rather than as information about where they come from'. The quote from Mohammed above was extracted from a DVD which we produced for supervisor training programmes (Magyar &

Robinson-Pant, 2010). The students participating in this research project felt that their views and perspectives were not always taken on board by supervisors and were keen to contribute to developing resources for professional development. This probably influenced how Mohammed set out to explain Malaysian culture to an outside teacher.

As part of the original project, we held regular meetings with a smaller group of respondents to discuss their experiences during their first year of a PhD course. We explored how we positioned ourselves within the conversations (including myself and my colleague Anna Magyar as 'outsiders', being supervisors rather than students). Students defined their identities in terms of their country origins at the beginning of this process (and sometimes they identified strongly with a certain discipline too). However, as their experiences converged and different identities emerged, we/they rarely generalised about 'us Malaysians'. Discussions became more focused on the shared experiences of 'us international students'.

Looking at the potential of insider/outsider to facilitate intercultural learning and analysis within this context, I would suggest that both the 'essentialised' concept of culture and the 'small culture' approach helped to move us forward in this project. If we had dismissed the 'large culture' descriptions that students often used to define themselves by (and which we researchers also adopted as a useful shorthand when we explained 'English' ways of giving feedback, etc.), I suspect that we would not have begun to work together as a group. However, it was important that the 'large culture' approach and an essentialised approach to insider/outsider perspectives was only our starting point, rather than the outcome of the project – which might be seen by some as an intercultural learning process rather than as 'research'.

Women's Literacy and Development

I will move now to discuss ethnographic research with two women's literacy programmes in Nepal, which I conducted as part of my PhD. Figure 1 is from a flipchart used by NGO staff to help women to form and run savings and credit groups. The picture depicts a women's group meeting being chaired by a man because none of the women were literate. The women are all talking in pairs or not paying attention and the caption reads that because they are illiterate, they are not disciplined and do not run the group in an orderly fashion.

The next page of the flipchart shows the same group of women sitting in a circle with a woman chairing and taking minutes as they had all now learned to write at a literacy class. During the year I spent with this development programme, I attended many women's group meetings where I heard lectures about the advantages of being in a group, as in this account from my field notes:

> Sahana (NGO staff): It's an objective ... that means?
> Facilitator of group: Desire
> Sahana: You should have one desire in a group, not many. If you throw stones in the dark, you don't know where they will go ... Now, what is a group?
> Woman (in the group): If many people sit in one place
> Sahana: what are the advantages of a group?
> Ramesh (NGO staff, starts reading the list): You can take advantage from Care or other NGOs if you have a group. If you need water or agriculture, go to Care. If you need education or a clinic, go to Save ... If you have a group, then if one person goes from the group, the skill is not lost. (Extracted from Robinson-Pant, 2001, p. 121)

Figure 1. Illustration from an NGO flipchart for women's groups in Nepal.

Although the NGO staff, Sahana and Ramesh, knew the women in this community well, they adopted an outsider role whenever they joined a meeting like this. Here they were formally teaching the women what was expected if they registered as an official women's group – using manuals and flipcharts to test them on the list of advantages of joining a group. The NGO staff saw themselves (as development insiders) as conveying to the women the messages from their organisation. There was a strong ideology that development activities should be conducted as a group not just as individuals, and that women needed to be literate in order to run and participate effectively in a group. This approach informed the way that the programme was planned – with literacy classes provided as an entry point to savings and credit women's groups.

Although this example is from over ten years ago, the 'literacy first' approach (critiqued by Rogers, 1999) to women's literacy is still dominant in many development programmes in Nepal and elsewhere. I suggest that this is due to an essentialised approach to culture being promoted by development agencies (and here the 'big' culture seemed to be that of development, with a dichotomy between developed and undeveloped women). Although as a researcher, I aimed to develop an insider–outsider perspective on this programme – through learning about how the women participants viewed and engaged with this dominant development discourse – I found it difficult to share these insights with my NGO colleagues. Instead, I was aware of adopting a dual role. As a developer, I shared my findings with NGO staff and the central office about how to improve the programme in the form of regular bullet-pointed reports. Yet as a researcher, I was writing a thesis that challenged the dominant cultural assumptions informing this area of women's development. I felt limited in how far the insider–outsider dialectic could become an approach to enhance intercultural understanding within this programme – although it was the main source of my own learning as an ethnographer.

The Quantitative/Qualitative Divide

My last example comes from recent experience of working on a policy-focused research project in Cambodia (funded by an international development agency). Unlike the other research discussed above where I conducted research myself, my role was to support a research team in Cambodia on an ethnographic study investigating adult learning. The project involved a workshop at the beginning and end of the research process in Phnom Penh to discuss the research design and policy implications from the findings with a larger group of stakeholders.

As an academic researcher, I was already aware of shifting between 'outsider' and 'insider' perspectives in terms of policy and research cultures – not least with regard to the dichotomising of literacy and illiteracy in development discourses. From previous work with international development organisations, I have accepted that adopting this terminology and dualism between 'literate' and 'illiterate' people is often a necessary starting point (similar to essentialising about culture in higher education discussions). However, I was surprised that the research workshops in Cambodia became focused on the polarisation of quantitative and qualitative research methodology. A leading economist at the workshop put forward a strong argument that a small-scale ethnographic study alone could not inform government policy:

> Quotes are important as they represent the perspectives of people. It is not only about the number. But this should be combined with representative sample survey data. A small sample based qualitative research study is like pepper and garlic – you can add it to soup to make it more tasty, but you need the meat. Without the meat, you cannot survive. We are just discussing about the spices here. We need the bigger picture. Ethnography is just about the study of minority people only and researchers write about how they farm etc. It is a human story and it sounds interesting. Sometimes foreigners study in Siem Reap and they find it interesting to read in Sweden. It is not relevant to the policy discussion here.

The metaphor of the soup, which emphasised that ethnographic data were useless without large-scale surveys, was later referred to by other participants as the 'Cambodian soup' – perhaps because ethnography had been associated with 'foreigners'. As with Mohammed's account earlier, this extract needs to be read as a performance in a specific context with particular aims. This was a contribution at a workshop about an internationally funded research study where the only researcher with ethnographic experience was a foreigner (me). It was interesting that through the ensuing discussion, research cultures became essentialised, not only in terms of the quantitative/qualitative divide, but also through associating ethnography with the West and with information that was more useful for outsiders like me (and possibly the international development agency directing the project), than for Cambodians. By constructing his critique around insider/outsider perspectives on research, the speaker here appeared to set up an opposition between two research approaches and communities. Afterwards, he explained to me that he believed in the power of using both quantitative and qualitative methods for policy making and that his reference was intended to contrast survey with small-scale qualitative research, rather than qualitative versus quantitative 'as a whole'. However, some workshop participants later spoke out to identify themselves as 'economists' rather than 'ethnographers', to be clear which side they were on.

As a doctoral supervisor with many students over the years who have told me they had to adopt quantitative methods to satisfy colleagues or sponsors, this exchange was in some ways familiar to me. However, since the workshop I have reflected more on my role as a foreign consultant through learning about these complex cultural relationships in this project – not only between Cambodia/West, but also about the policy/research cultures being constructed, and the assumed epistemological divide between quantitative/qualitative methods. As the above extract illustrates, by adopting an oppositional positioning as outsider (foreigner, ethnographer, academic researcher) versus insider (Cambodian, economist, policy maker), we were unable to take the discussion of policy implications further in this workshop. Perhaps the next step could be to introduce the insider/outsider concept explicitly to the discussion as a way of disentangling some of these embedded assumptions about culture/s. In his account of research on comparative pedagogy, Kelly (2013, p. 12) describes how the team 'tried to form a "third space" where the interpretations and worldviews of researchers bringing different preferred ways of knowing were shared in an open and inclusive manner'. The latter two examples above demonstrate the difficulty of beginning this dialogue in policy contexts.

Conclusion: drawing out the implications for comparative and international education

My aim in exploring these three contrasting vignettes from different areas of my own research in CIE was to investigate how the concept of insider/outsider perspectives could help to support intercultural dialogue and learning. Within all three contexts, the challenge seemed to be around how to move beyond essentialising culture or the static dichotomy of outsider/insider. The example from research with international students illustrates how such cultural generalisation can be a starting point to build up a dialogue that later takes account of more complex understandings of culture. I associate this process with the etic–emic–etic dialectic explored earlier. The other two examples began from similar assumed binaries (literate/illiterate, developed/undeveloped, qualitative/quantitative) which shaped the interaction between participants. However, perhaps because these discussions took place in development policy/programme contexts rather than within an educational institution, there seemed to be less opportunity to create a dialogic space (as we had done through the research project in the UK university). In terms of my own learning, the experience of constantly shifting between outsider and insider perspectives gave me greater understanding into the intersection of cultures within policy-focused and policy-shaped research.

Comparing the etic–emic construct has pointed to the value of focusing on how knowledge is constructed through the insider–outsider perspectives within comparative research, rather than only on the knowledge itself. I have argued in this chapter that we need to find ways of harnessing the educational potential of the insider–outsider concept as a way of bringing 'culture' more centrally into research on comparative and international education. It is also about recognising the importance of informal learning in the professional development of educational researchers. I see similarities with earlier debates in the literature on case study as an educational approach (see Platt's [1988] notion of learning vicariously through case study). In response to comparativists who suggested that the use of case study implied a move away from comparison, Crossley and Vulliamy (1984, p. 204) argued: 'Case study need not be purely descriptive; it need not be limited to the micro level; and it need not ignore comparative analysis itself.' In other words, the focus can be on conveying the dynamic construction of knowledge through the case study, rather than simply presenting the case. Taking the analogy of insider–outsider perspectives, I suggest that there is potential to examine how we can move from a description of outsider or insider insights into a certain phenomenon at the micro level, to develop greater understanding of the processes of comparative analysis. Rather than using insider–outsider as a descriptor, we can use it as an educational tool to enhance intercultural learning and challenge the supposedly neutral 'technicist' approaches that currently dominate research and evaluation in many policy, programme and research institutions.

References

Agar, M. (1980) *The Professional Stranger*. New York: Academic Press.

Alexander, R. (2010) 'World Class Schools' – Noble Aspiration or Globalised Hokum? BAICE Presidential Address at the 10th UKFIET Conference on Education and Development 2009, *Compare*, 40(6), 801-817. http://dx.doi.org/10.1080/03057925.2010.523252

Arnove, R. (2010) Reflections on Comparative Education and International Development, *Compare*, 40(6), 827-830. http://dx.doi.org/10.1080/03057925.2010.523258

Baumann, G. (1996) *Contesting Culture*. Cambridge: Cambridge University Press.

Clifford, J. (1983) On Ethnographic Authority, *Representations*, 2 (Spring), 118-146.

Crossley, M. & Vulliamy, G. (1984) Case-study Research Methods and Comparative Education, *Comparative Education*, 20(2), 193-207. http://dx.doi.org/10.1080/0305006840200202

Harris, M. (1990) Emics and Etics Revisited, in T. Headland, K. Pike & M. Harris (Eds) *Emics and Etics: the insider/outsider debate. Frontiers of Anthropology*, vol. 7. London: SAGE.

Hellawell, D. (2006) Inside-out: analysis of the insider–outsider concept as a heuristic device to develop reflexivity in students doing qualitative research, *Teaching in Higher Education*, 11(4), 483-494. http://dx.doi.org/10.1080/13562510600874292

Hofstede, G. (2003) *Culture's Consequences: comparing values, behaviours, institutions and organisations across nations*. London: SAGE.

Holliday, A. (1999) Small Cultures, *Applied Linguistics*, 20(2), 237-264. http://dx.doi.org/10.1093/applin/20.2.237

Holliday, A. (2011) *Intercultural Communication and Ideology*. London: SAGE.

Holliday, A., Hyde, M. & Kullman, J. (2004) Intercultural Communication: an advanced resource book. London: Routledge.

Holy, L. (1984) Theory, Methodology and the Research Process, in R. Ellen (Ed.) *Ethnographic Research: a guide to general conduct*. London: Academic Press.

Hymes, D. (1990) Emics, Etics and Openness: an ecumenical approach, in T. Headland, K. Pike & M. Harris (Eds) *Emics and Etics: the insider/outsider debate. Frontiers of Anthropology*, vol. 7. London: SAGE.

Kelly, P. (2013) Researcher Positionality in Comparative Pedagogy: a relational account. Paper prepared for BAICE Insider/Outsider Forum.

Lett, J. (1990) Emics and Etics: notes on the epistemology of anthropology, in T. Headland, K. Pike & M. Harris (Eds) *Emics and Etics: the insider/outsider debate. Frontiers of Anthropology*, vol. 7. London: SAGE.

Magyar, A. & Robinson-Pant, A. (2010) International Research Students: reflections on PhD supervision. DVD and guide produced for University of East Anglia's Centre for Staff Educational Development. Available from a robinson-pant@uea.ac.uk

McNess, E., Arthur, L. & Crossley, M. (2013) 'Ethnographic Dazzle' and the Construction of the 'Other': revisiting dimensions of insider–outsider research for international and comparative education, *Compare*, 45(2), 295-316. http://dx.doi.org/10.1080/03057925.2013.854616

Organisation for Economic Co-operation and Development (OECD) (2013) Skilled for Life? Key Findings from the Survey of Adult Skills. Paris: OECD.

Pike, K. (1990) On the Emics and Etics of Pike and Harris, in T. Headland, K. Pike & M. Harris (Eds) *Emics and Etics: the insider/outsider debate. Frontiers of Anthropology*, vol. 7. London: SAGE.

Platt, J. (1988) What Can Case Studies Do? *Studies in Qualitative Methodology*, 1, 1-23.

Polyani, M. (1967) *The Tacit Dimension*. New York: Doubleday.

Robinson-Pant, A. (2001) *Why Eat Green Cucumber at the Time of Dying? Exploring the Link between Women's Literacy and Development in Nepal*. Hamburg: UNESCO Institute of Education.

Rogers, A. (1999) Improving the Quality of Adult Literacy Programmes in Developing Countries: the 'real literacies' approach, *International Journal of Educational Development*, 19, 219-234. http://dx.doi.org/10.1016/S0738-0593(99)00015-2

Sadler, M. (1900) How Far Can We Learn Anything of Practical Value from the Study of Foreign Systems of Education? Quoted in J. Higginson (Ed.) (1979) *Selections from Michael Sadler: Studies in World Citizenship*, p. 49. Liverpool: Dejall & Meyorre.

Spivak, G. (1986) Imperialism and Sexual Difference, *Oxford Literary Review*, 8, 225-244. http://dx.doi.org/10.3366/olr.1986.028

Street, B. (2001) Ethnography for Linguists (Chapter 3), in C. Roberts, M. Byram, A. Barro, S. Jordan & B. Street (2001) *Language Learners as Ethnographers.* Clevedon: Multilingual Matters.

Todorov, T. (1988) Knowledge in Social Anthropology: distancing and universality, *Anthropology Today*, 4(2), 2-5. http://dx.doi.org/10.2307/3033229

Tonkin, E. (1984) Producing Data, in R. Ellen (Ed.) *Ethnographic Research: a guide to general conduct.* London: Academic Press.

CHAPTER 3

Constructing the Insider and Outsider in Comparative Research

PETER KELLY

Introduction

This chapter seeks to explore the power relations that help to construct 'insiders' and 'outsiders' within research groups. It identifies three idealised collectives – emergent, established and exclusive – and discusses how each of these constructs the insider and outsider and the implications of this for comparative researchers.

For Dorothy Holland and Jean Lave (2009), life is comparative, and as people contrast their expectations and experiences (their histories-in-person) which they bring to their current undertakings (as persons-in-process) they are transformed. In this relational account, capability and expertise are adaptive processes within the many fluid and dynamic cultures and communities in which people participate. When formalised, as in critical ethnography (Lave, 2011), comparative adaptation allows researchers to unpick their taken-for-granted assumptions. If they were, say, to consider in two countries the effect of objectifications like 'gender', 'ethnicity' or 'class' on other objectifications like 'students', 'progress' and 'attainment' in further objectifications like 'mathematics' 'lessons' in 'school' 'classrooms', they might begin by questioning the common-sense assumption that each of these words carries the same meaning in each context. For example, what does it mean to be constructed as a white, working-class boy in terms of what you can and can't do? While the temptation may be to treat whiteness, working-classness and boyness as the same across cultures, comparison can uncover whether different processes lie behind each and the extent to which such processes are contingent, thus allowing an exploration of power relations.

There is another way in which life is comparative. In Edward Said's (1978) account of orientalism, people define themselves through comparison with others. Ambivalence or even antipathy towards the presumed values, expectations, rules, meanings and ways of acting of others is coupled to identification with particular norms, discourses and practices, and identification as members of the cultures, communities or groups which share these. Such common-sense perspectives take for granted reifications or objectifications of cultures, communities or groups, imbuing them with essentialist pre-given meaning which helps maintain the insider–outsider binary, exposed in phrases like, 'she's not one of us', 'what would you expect from someone like that', 'I know your sort' and 'men – you can't trust them – they're all as bad as each other'. Inside the warm embrace of social collectives, people may feel comfort, ease and belonging, or that embrace can be chastening and controlling. Outsiders might feel excluded, but then again may cherish the freedom this brings.

Holland and Lave's and Said's accounts differ in emphasis, but both share the view that comparison is not, as common-sense accounts would have us believe, a benign activity; rather, it is largely a political act. I have written elsewhere (Kelly, 2014) about how common-sense accounts of the insider and outsider are unsettled when behaviours deemed inside or outside cultures are inconsistent, blurring the limits between cultures (Nederveen Pieterse, 2004). If cultures are fluid, forever changing, mixing and adapting as people with multiple affiliations move in and out of them, perhaps, as McNess et al (2013) suggest, it would be more appropriate to refer to the degree of insiderness and outsiderness which individuals experience. In comparative research, their solution is to encourage inclusive spaces where researchers, irrespective of their relative positioning, regard constructed cultural boundaries as transitional as they collaborate in the construction of new meaning. I accept this (Kelly, 2014), but argue that those engaged in such endeavours must also seek to moderate power across different researcher positions. Yet it is also important for comparativists to explore processes of constructing cultures, communities, groups, identities, boundaries and the other, so as to expose further the workings of power. So, in this chapter I turn to how people are positioned as inside or outside cultures, communities or groups before considering implications for comparative research. But first I must briefly clarify what I take each of these to mean.

For du Gay et al (1997), culture is the process by which meaning is produced, circulated, consumed, commodified and endlessly reproduced and renegotiated in society. As Hall, one of du Gay's colleagues, writes:

> To say that two people belong to the same culture is to say that they interpret the world in roughly the same ways and can express their ideas, their thoughts and feelings about the world in ways which will be understood by each other. (Hall, 1997, p. 2)

Cultures are to be found in the views and behaviours – that is, the ways of being – common to groups of people, which can be called cultural practices to emphasise their processual basis. Wenger (1998) describes communities of practice as sharing norms, discourses and practices, crucially, in pursuit of common goals or interests. Thus we might say communities of practice are cultures with a purpose. Finally, in this article, I will use the term 'groups' to refer to those subject to common stratifications based on objectified constructs like ethnicity, gender, nationality or social class. Together I refer to cultures, communities and groups as collectives.

Why Account for Collective Activity?

We can view collectives in common-sense or relational terms. Most comparative research is set in the first and so fails to analyse its relation to the working of power; it is this relation which is the focus of the second.

Common-sense accounts privilege the individual. Some do this by focusing on those psychological explanations which reify individual selves and identities. But it is possible for sociocultural accounts to do this as well, if, for example, they objectify cultures and communities and see them as acting on and thereby transforming participating individuals. From individualised common-sense perspectives like these, insiders and outsiders are personal identities developed through our engagement with largely benign practices in taken-for-granted social worlds. As such, insiderness and outsiderness are things we possess as individuals; their degree depends on our lived experiences, although they can be transformed with new experiences.

Relational accounts attempt to expose power dynamics which are often masked in common-sense accounts. These consider positioning, identification and boundary work as reciprocal social processes that privilege the participation of some over others, who may even be excluded. From this relational perspective, insiders and outsiders are contingent and socially useful identity constructions which reify positions within arenas of competing interests. As such, the labels 'insider' and 'outsider' or our sense of insiderness or outsiderness say something about us, our relation to the social world, the opportunities we enjoy and the benefits we can access.

For Bourdieu, people gain influence in different social contexts or fields through their deployment of capitals (Bourdieu, 1986). Economic capital concerns money or things which can be immediately and directly convertible into money. Cultural capital comprises the knowledge and ways of behaving which are socially acceptable and valorised within specific contexts, although this may be institutionalised in the forms of educational qualifications. Finally, social capital indicates the networks of social obligation and thus the connections which one has to others and through which one may be able to gain some advantage. So, in Bourdieusian terms, the degree of insiderness and outsiderness we feel in relation to the spaces we inhabit (our habitus) indicates the capitals we have and their currency within the fields in which we participate.

Relational research can aim to support the transiting of boundaries between such fields by increasing an awareness of their architecture and purpose and, where appropriate, challenging them in order to encourage their reconstruction or demolition. Boundaries are constructed or maintained when people take for granted that which is bounded. Challenging this and attempting to cross, reconstruct or demolish such boundaries also troubles what it means to be inside or outside. So, when I question the category 'man' by asking, for example, 'What is manness?', 'What can and what can't men say and do?', 'When does manness become not manness?', 'Is this the same as womanness?' and 'Is this always the same everywhere?', I am considering the construction of people as men and how that construction is culturally bounded. But whether I accept or challenge such boundaries, I am engaged in identity work which is, to some extent, transformational. And in questioning such objectifications as man or woman, I am also challenging those who categorise and the assumptions they bring with their implicit power imbalances.

While supporting individual reflexivity to challenge social convention is important, such work is inevitably limited if it privileges the agent while ignoring the social relations in which they exist. Therefore, in this chapter, I consider how comparativists can contribute to a wider social analysis which exposes the workings of power and those who are favoured by these processes. With this in mind, I will now turn to consider how collectives can be analysed to expose boundaries between and the relation of individuals to fields and their capital currencies. Specifically, I will ask, 'How are insiders and outsiders constructed in each of these collectives, and how does this construction relate to their capitals in the field?'

Categorising Collectives

Weber proposed that patterns in social practice can be identified as 'ideal types' in order to make comparisons across contexts without losing the richness and messiness of real life (Weber, 1949; Crotty, 1998). In this, ideal does not refer to perfect things, moral ideals or statistical averages; it refers to the world of ideas, and ideal types are idea-constructs that help put the chaos of social reality in order (Weber, 1949). They are formed by describing and interpreting the characteristics of a given phenomenon and so stress elements common to most cases rather than corresponding to all of the characteristics of any one particular case. In the following section I suggest three ideal types of collectives: emergent, established and exclusive. These are intended to be neither comprehensive nor distinct; rather, they may apply partially or in combination in everyday contexts.

Emergent Collectives

Most of the activities people engage in, such as train travel, eating in a restaurant, going to the cinema or attending a football match, are, to some extent, collectively shaped. In this section I will draw on the example of shopping, but the reflections which follow apply across similar emergent collectives. When going shopping they may observe mutual norms or expectations of, say, the politeness they expect from shop assistants; they may share a discourse, allowing them to understand the significance of words like check-out or the notion that a reduced item will probably be at a lower price than normal because of some imperfection, while an offer will be at a lower price without such qualification; and they may engage in common practices like queueing or, in some stores, taking tickets to indicate a place in a queue. Together, these shared ways of being a shopper can be referred to as shopping culture, and this may vary slightly between localities and even between shops. People may even feel a shared commitment to some shops over others, and shops may try to encourage shoppers' identification with them through constructing themselves and their shoppers as a community with a common goal, be it, for example, one of a shared concept of affordability (an aspect of economic capital), a shared likeness of a particular style (an aspect of cultural capital) or a shared demographic (an aspect of social capital). These are all factors in constructing the field of shopping, and thereby who is able to participate most fully by having the capital resource which allows this.

We learn how to do collective activities like shopping through participation, and Wenger (1998) describes the process of participative learning as one of moving from peripheral to expert as we become better at negotiating its various components. Thus our knowledge of shopping is largely implicit; we are aware neither of what we need to know to be able to shop, nor of how we came to know it. Implicit knowledge like that required for shopping is set within what Bernstein (1999) calls a horizontal discourse.

The unwritten expectations, understandings and rules of shopping allow people to pursue their own interests in a social context with many others also pursuing related but different personal interests. But there is also a shared interest in maintaining these expectations, understandings and rules, and people have many ways to demonstrate their disapproval when, as with rudeness or queue jumping, these are ignored. Indeed, we may say that the norms, discourses and practices of shopping are informally policed by the collective of shoppers and shop assistants. And while, for the most part, membership of such collectives comes with being there, the degree of insiderness or outsiderness people experience most likely depends on their acceptance of these shared understandings.

I have called such social activities 'emergent collectives' to emphasise their fluid, sometimes transient and indistinct, and yet overtly inclusive nature. Their components seem to pertain as we enter a shop, where other shoppers may be coming and going all the time, while aspects also apply to online shopping, cafés and restaurants, and other real and virtual spaces. They are also subject to change, as new groups of shoppers are attracted – say, younger customers – while others go elsewhere, and as practices associated with, say, technological developments or fashionable trends and their associated discourses emerge, so others decline.

There are many ways in which people unable to meet expected norms, discourses and practices are excluded from or marginalised within emergent collectives, but mostly their lack of capital resource restricts their full participation. When wheelchair users experience poor access, we might see them as lacking physical capital in the field of traditional shopping architecture. When some elderly shoppers lack the capacity to engage in online collectives, we can point to their lack of cultural capital in IT. While some may consider it an individual's responsibility to integrate in such circumstances, others may demand that society does more to raise awareness of and challenge such barriers to full inclusion by changing the nature of fields. Important here is whether individuals are seen as being in deficit to norms (lacking the capitals to engage in the field), or whether norms are seen as being unfairly restrictive (the field unfairly restricts the range of utilisable capitals). More generally, many lack the economic capital to shop at exclusive stores or the cultural capital to know what the latest fashions dictate, otherwise retail activity would not be such a strong indicator of social position, and clearly such demarcations can apply to socially stratified groups; together, such processes are complicit in the construction of insiders and outsiders.

Established Collectives

There are occasions when people come together in more formal ways than those of the loose communities encouraged, for example, by commerce and discussed in the last section, not only because the collective helps them to follow their personal interests, but because they have a common shared interest or investment. Clubs and societies are examples, but so might be workplaces or, indeed, towns, villages or localities with established groups of residents (Hogenstijn et al, 2008). While joining a club shows, at the initial stage at least, an acceptance of its norms, discourses and practices, getting a new job or moving into a residential community may not necessarily carry such a commitment. Hence there may need to be a period of negotiation to establish respect for traditions and recognition of the rights and responsibilities which acceptance into the establishment may bring, even if the newcomer might wish to bring about change. We can describe such established collectives as having shared (although also subject to change, albeit often regulated) cultures or ways of being a member, employee or resident; and, as in the last section, we can look at how, as communities, they encourage identification with their common goals and shared norms, discourses and practices. Again, we can describe these established collectives as fields by looking at the capital resource which can be exchanged for influence within them. So, some hobbies require an investment in expensive equipment which may not otherwise be available for public use, and this requires economic capital. Certainly there is a need to look the part, an aspect of cultural capital, to be successful in getting some jobs. And the need for references, a facet of social capital, may exclude some from certain tenancies. The possession of capital resource, sometimes closely associated with different groups, contributes to the social demarcation of those eligible to become established insiders and those remaining as outsiders.

Such collectives are policed informally, like emergent collectives, and more formally. Formal policing proceeds where there are explicit norms with accompanying sanctions for not meeting these and constructed boundaries from entry requiring gatekeepers. Change to these is normally regulated by formal processes. For example, professional bodies often adhere to standards of conduct. Failure to meet these can be linked to training and development requirements and even expulsion from the profession where misconduct is considered severe enough. Even club membership is often conditional on the acceptance of club rules, although informal processes of social acceptance probably play a larger part, as they might in residential communities. Together this means established collectives are often more open to traditionalism and conservatism aimed at maintaining the status quo. They are also vulnerable to the recycling of prejudice and bias in processes of 'othering' (Said, 1978), and, as a result, may be self-sustaining by attracting, in particular, those who share their worldview.

Exclusive Collectives

Some collectives require a degree of expertise of members, but they can also offer a material or cultural capital benefit, and there may be symbolic value to belonging as well. This is not really a separate type of collective, as both emergent and established collectives can be exclusive. For example, for the non-native language speaker many emergent collective activities are exclusive because they do not have the cultural capital in terms of language expertise to participate. Similarly, participation in community sport or music requires a degree of competence. In terms of established collectives such as workplaces, many jobs require certified expertise, a form of cultural capital called symbolic capital, and various professions use their recognition and endorsement of qualifications to restrict entry and rigorously police professional standards. Properties in some residential areas demand extensive economic capital, in terms of both rent or purchase and ongoing maintenance.

Requirements for high economic capital, specialist cultural capital, expert symbolic capital or elite social capital provide a barrier to inclusion, while the acquisition of each of these capitals is fraught with difficulty. For example, the specialist cultural capital which leads to high-status qualifications is set within what Bernstein (1999) refers to as a vertical discourse which privileges the access of some, often those from more advantaged socio-economic backgrounds, over others. So, youngsters who grow up in poorer homes may have less access to books, less experience of mature conversations and less opportunity to form and express their opinions, and together these may restrict their capacity to deal with the unfamiliar and sometime esoteric and abstract knowledge required for the development of those academic understandings required for high grades in school-leaving exams.

Allied to this, as well as applying more widely, this exclusivity can take many other forms: opportunities for work experience may depend on who you know, access to privileged institutions may depend on what you're worth, and, indeed, despite legislation, many continue to face discrimination on the basis of their age, ethnicity, gender and sexuality.

Through webs of capital exchange such as those described above, at times involving multiple processes acting together or in opposition to each other, there arises a fluid interplay of insiderness and outsiderness with people sometimes positioned as inside and sometimes as outside different aspects of collective social activity.

Categorising Comparative Research as a Collective Activity

Finally in this chapter I will turn to comparative research activity and consider relations between three fields: comparative research collectives; the contexts they research; and the research communities in which their findings are legitimated and disseminated. I will then look at how each of these separate fields is influenced by the capital currencies brought by researchers and participants. Finally, I will discuss implications. I will illustrate each of these by focusing on three broad categories of comparative research: colonial, international and relational.

Colonial

Colonial approaches to comparative research are those where interpretations are biased towards those of one cultural group and the values and agendas of one cultural group dominate. In *L'Étranger* (1942 [2013]), Albert Camus provides us with a picture of a meaningless world onto which meaning is imposed by people, depending on their life experiences. The novel centres on the narrator's colonialist worldview; ethnic Algerians are treated at best with indifference, at worst, contempt. This centring can be read alongside Edward Said's (1978) notion of 'othering', mentioned earlier, where the weaknesses of one group are emphasised in relation to the values and norms of a second more powerful group, so that the first are seen as in deficit and in need of improvement. Such perspectives are rooted in a common-sense, taken-for-granted view of the world which hides the working of power.

Researchers who bring a single worldview uncritically to bear in seeking to understand diverse situations are similarly culpable. In one stark example, the English government inspection agency Ofsted has carried out a number of evaluations of teaching in countries successful on the PISA international surveys (e.g. Ofsted, 2010). These have typically involved a small number of Her Majesty's Inspectors visiting schools and educational institutions using their own inspection framework designed for use in English schools to gather evidence of what works. Their purpose is to identify factors that have the potential to aid improvement in England. Here the research collective, Ofsted, is also the arbiter of legitimacy for the research process, and so the knowledge production field and the legitimating field are almost one and the same. Further, these fields are highly regulated and slow to change. As such, this is both an established and an exclusive collective. In this situation, valorised cultural capitals will be those aligned with current versions of the Ofsted inspection framework, most likely including the ability to interpret school and student performance data, to carry out and analyse structured observations and to discuss 'best practice' and 'what works', while symbolic capitals contributing to the influence of individual inspectors in the research process might include the extent of their experience in education and reliability of their previous inspection work as ascertained through moderation exercises with colleagues. Combined, these capitals will help delimit insider inspectors from outsider others and, clearly, outsiders will include those subject to the gaze of the research process.

International

International approaches are also common-sense in that they either take for granted or objectify cultures, masking the work of power. In so doing, they purport to be part of a progressive movement towards universal conceptualisations of human activity. The hegemony of western worldviews has led some to claim they are universally applicable. This was seen with the ascendancy of neo-liberal economics and democratic political models leading to 'the end of history' hypotheses in the 1990s. As such they are similar to westernisation or homogenisation models of globalisation (Nederveen Pieterse, 2004). Given the political and economic troubles of the last decade, it is clear in retrospect that such claims should be treated with extreme caution.

Rather than describing global convergence on a shared way of viewing the world, such perspectives again provide for the domination of minority worldviews by a single hegemonic worldview. As such they seek unity rather than plurality or diversity; they assume worldviews can be culturally neutral and do not depend on value positions and that it is possible to construct a single way of adequately describing the world. They do not see descriptions and analyses as contingent and situated within particular ideologies.

Examples of internationalist perspectives and research include the work of supranational organisations like the Organisation for Economic Co-operation and Development (OECD), whose *Education at a Glance* presents its analyses of PISA data often as undisguised policy advocacy, and UNESCO, whose *Education for All Global Monitoring Reports* are similarly replete with policy advice; and of edu-businesses like Pearson, who, with the *Economist*, a weekly current affairs publication, developed *The Learning Curve*, which they describe as an online resource of social and education data from which they draw lessons for policymakers. Documents such as these take a standpoint of objective expertise and make sweeping claims. Theirs is a modernist perspective; analyses are reductionist and seek causality, and recommendations are linear and instrumental and apply universally. And by thus privileging Anglo-Saxon explanations and solutions they are little different from the colonialist perspective of Ofsted: the field of each research collective, established and exclusive in its delimitation of insiders and outsiders, is very similar to that of the legitimating community, while research contexts are clearly outside but subject to the gaze of this field.

Objectivist thinking sees cultures acting on people, and thereby favours a simple insider–outsider binary. For example, Döbert et al (2004) survey the conditions of school performance in seven countries using a multi-level systems analysis. Bronfenbrenner (1977) suggests that those inside such systems are 'inscribed' by them and bring 'inscribed' national assumptions and worldviews to bear on their subsequent activities. Applying this reasoning to researchers, each member of an international team brings their own perspective. But negotiation with their partner researchers allows a new and more generally applicable worldview consensus to emerge. The linguistic, disciplinary and other cultural skills of the team can then allow this new consensus worldview to be objectified and applied to a range of different cultural situations. Certainly, in such an analysis, there is space for teams to recognise and address some inequalities, including any tendency towards colonialism. But in focusing on seeking commonality and generating consensus, researchers might not fully attend to their differing underpinning discursive positions and value systems within the research collective.

Approaches like this carry the pretence of plurality, but all too often ignore the structural inequalities in voice lent by differences in capital to access these exclusive collectives. For example, English is the primary international medium for communication; if left unchallenged, this can increase the access that researchers whose cultural capital includes confidence in English have to participate in international conferences and to publish their work, and, in terms of the wider research community, can privilege the English language literature as a common base in the field of international and cross-national work, from which literature not available in English is marginalised. Also, researchers who have symbolic capital in being recognised as successful in the established collective endeavour of international research might be allowed or indeed expected to drive the agenda in international teams. With no analysis of these potential power dynamics, research teams run the risk of supporting the colonisation of international and cross-national research by a small number of majority worldviews.

Finally, the relationship between researchers and those who are the subject of the research gaze is one-dimensional, ignoring situated and contingent cultural complexity by assuming common values, purposes and meanings. Because it is value-blind, one of the problems with this perspective in comparative education research is its tendency to valorise what works over what is important to different cultures. 'What works' studies of schooling concern identifying similarities and differences in curriculum content, activities, forms of organisation, and so on, and in so doing they take values for granted. Yet to understand we need to go deeper, beyond what works, and look at the reasons why different cultures value schooling and how this affects what teachers say and do. We need, in fact, to explore variations in the meanings and ways of being which bind classroom cultures: pedagogy. To take a simple example, very similar content or activities may differ in the way of coming to know or knowing which they serve, and this may only be discernible from a wider perspective. But international researchers engaged in cultural borrowing across schools objectify the practices of teachers and students in classrooms and appropriate them for their own cultural capital as researchers. In so doing they strip the act of teaching of its embodied, tacit meanings, taking it from the cultures and discourses in which it is situated. This is why 'what works' research studies lack substance and have been much criticised (Alexander, 2000, 2009), with many (Goldstein, 1996; Gorard, 2001; Bonnet, 2002; Osborn et al, 2003) ascribing their failure to deliver on what they promise to the naivety of context and value-neutral perspectives.

Relational

Whereas colonial and international research ignores power relations within research teams and their legitimising community and maintains the separation of researcher and research subject by treating those subject to their gaze as others or outsiders, relational accounts acknowledge that comparative research is a political endeavour. As such, they attend: (1) substantively to power relations between participants within the contexts they research; and (2) methodologically to the influence on research of power relations between researchers, between researchers and research participants, and between researchers and the wider research community. This is because in relational terms research is held to be a process of learning by adapting in collective activity (Lave, 2011) which is enhanced by including a wide range of researchers and participants (Holland & Lave, 2009). This makes it important to analyse the extent to which people lie within or outside emergent, established and exclusive collectives in research contexts and to think of who is included and who is marginalised in each methodological relation and, where appropriate, try to democratise these.

Examples given earlier illustrate how an analysis of collectives can aid the uncovering of power relations in research contexts. I will give one further example. I have been involved in comparing classroom interactions in low and high mathematics sets in English secondary schools (we actually compared them with Danish mathematics classrooms for students of the same age as well). Such sets are established collectives, with higher sets being exclusive collectives requiring specialist cultural capital, including an understanding of abstraction, and the symbolic certification of this through test success. But within both types of sets there may be peer groupings at work, forming emergent collectives from time to time which may influence the course of lessons. Our analysis considered how capitals with currency in emergent peer groups have less worth in established lower sets than they do in higher sets, and indicated how the development of specialist capitals which would allow movement through sets is, in part, inhibited by peer group activity in lower sets (Kelly et al, 2013).

Turning to methodology, adopting a democratic ethic suggests people should be free to participate equally in making decisions on matters which affect them or in holding to account those who represent them (Swift, 2006). So, democratic research activity, first and foremost, ought to be inclusive and discursive, attempting to equalise the voices of researchers and research participants and, to aid this, be transparent and open to challenge from those represented, be they the views of those within the team or the views of research participants on whose behalf decisions and recommendations are made.

I will not discuss here the many ways which are used to ensure that research participants and contexts are represented faithfully, nor how processes like participant validation can allow them to see and, if they need to, to challenge how they are represented in research findings. It is important, however, that findings reflect the complexity of people and contexts without oversimplification, which I will return to shortly, while also being presented in ways which allow participants, if need be, to challenge them.

In terms of varied perspectives within research teams, while some social research approaches remain geographically located, as with the US and European phenomenological traditions, more often research is bounded by ontological or epistemological distinctions, disciplinary cultures, allegiance to specific theoretical or methodological frames or work within specific fields of inquiry. Each potentially forms the basis for exclusivity in research collectives, hence restricting the participation of researchers bringing different cultural capital to international collaborations, even within research collectives conducting inter-disciplinary research. Further, when work on specific inquiries is set within disciplinary cultures, the activities of different researchers most likely are influenced strongly by their own national and local research agendas as well as by the differences they bring in experience, interpretation and understanding of theorisations and related empirical findings.

International teams can, however, provide a 'third space' that 'enables other positions to emerge' (Rutherford, 1990, p. 211). This is a productive space for negotiation across worldviews; for renewal, creativity and innovation in ways which cannot be imagined separately by the individuals involved (Bhabha, 1996). It is not a space in which to seek consensus, but rather one in which to open up possibilities. In doing so, new perspectives are sought which undermine claims to cultural totalisation through 'the collision between differing points of view on the world that are embedded in [different voices] ... pregnant with potential for new world views' (Bakhtin, 1981, p. 360). Indeed, collaborations of diverse researchers on shared projects providing an opportunity to unleash such creative processes.

Open dialogue within international research teams can go some way to creating a 'third space' and avoiding the imposition of a single hegemonic worldview across contexts. While pragmatically English does provide a shared language and common literature to act as a basis for cross-national research collaborations, researchers should try to counteract the ways English privileges access for some and particular worldviews, increasing their capital worth. The important point here is that neither language nor literature should be limiting. Nor should there be an assumption that researchers and research ideas, which increasingly move freely across countries, are converging on a single worldview. This belief in cultural homogenisation ignores how widely available ideas are adapted to and hybridised in different circumstances. Hence within the shared culture of an international team there needs to be recognition of difference, allowing for negotiation without closing down possibilities of interpretation and analysis and working in an open and transparent manner to allow for the identification of power relations. Wider literature in the different languages relevant to the research contexts should be sought, differences in translation examined, and differences in interpretation considered as part of the research process. Throughout, members of international teams should explore, in their own understandings, cross-national similarities and differences and develop new or hybrid perspectives.

Second, in seeking fairer representations, democratic research should challenge the normative hegemony of taken-for-granted commonsense perspectives, exposing the influence of power relations. Researchers should, as Schreiwer (2010) suggests, maintain a critical distance from a preoccupation with normative, prescriptive and positivist methodologies; from research biased towards reform and advice, policy improvement and learning from others. Instead, as indicated earlier, research should seek authentic and inclusive accounts of the research context and debates within and between researchers and participants, attempting to maintain an appreciation of situated complexity and include any tensions between competing and incommensurate values and aims. Larsen (2010) suggests this may include: (1) new thinking on time, challenging linearity and emphasising contingency and reciprocity; (2) new thinking on space, challenging globalisation as homogenisation, and essentialism with nation-states, cultures, identities, and so on; and (3) new thinking on mobility, challenging policy borrowing and transfer. And as a consequence of the difficulties inherent in seeking fairer representations, the theorisations, findings and solutions constructed through research may at times be seen as partial and provisional, and therefore researchers should acknowledge when reaching a consensus has not been possible.

Finally, in each of these, democratic research activity also needs to acknowledge and openly account for the influence the wider legitimating research community brings. This requires openness and honesty on the part of researchers both with their research colleagues who may be subject to different national and institutional demands, and between researchers and participants in terms of, for example, the constraints of writing for publication.

Conclusion

In this chapter I have argued that being an insider or an outsider is not about occupying an objective position on one side or another of a social boundary. Rather, it is the mixture of feelings people have as they participate in various social collectives (be they emergent or established, apparently inclusive or exclusive); sometimes participation is comfortable, perhaps improving through interaction with others, while at other times it seems clumsy and partially or wholly restricted. To explain this I have linked the capitals people bring and their currency in different social collective fields. As such, the terms insider and outsider are shorthand for those privileged or marginalised in social collectives.

At the outset I suggested that is only those afforded some of the privileges of insiders in social collectives who can learn by and transform through participation (Holland & Lave, 2009); as critical researchers (Lave, 2011), such insiders can unpick taken-for-granted assumptions to explore power relations. Power relations are implicit in social collectives as people define themselves through comparison with others (Said, 1978), be they inside their warm embrace or chastening grip, or outside in the cold or grateful to be free.

Comparative education research is an unavoidably political endeavour. Colonial and international approaches ignore these power relations. It is only by adopting a relational stance that researchers can explore power relations, as expressed through notions of insiders and outsiders, within their research groups, in the wider research community which legitimates their research and in the contexts they research.

Finally, I have indicated how democratic approaches can guide ways of working relationally by suggesting opportunities for wider participation and influence in decision making, although these must be accompanied by an awareness of how such participation is limited by different circumstances. An account of emergent, established and exclusive collectives can aid this.

References

Alexander, R. (2000) *Culture and Pedagogy: international comparisons in primary education*. Oxford: Blackwell.

Alexander, R. (2009) Pedagogy, Culture and the Power of Comparison, in H. Daniels, H. Lauder & J. Porter (Eds) *Educational Theories, Cultures and Learning: a critical perspective*. London: Routledge.

Bakhtin, M. (1981) Discourse in the Novel, in M. Holquist (Ed.) *The Dialogic Imagination*. Austin: University of Texas Press.

Bernstein, B. (1999) Vertical and Horizontal Discourse: an essay, *British Journal of Sociology of Education*, 20(2), 157-173. http://dx.doi.org/10.1080/01425699995380

Bhabha, H.K. (1996) Culture's In-between, in S. Hall & P. DuGay (Eds) *Questions of Cultural Identity*. London: SAGE.

Bonnet, G. (2002) Reflections in a Critical Eye: on the pitfalls of international assessment; knowledge and skills for life: first results from PISA 2000, *Assessment in Education*, 9(3), 387-401. http://dx.doi.org/10.1080/0969594022000027690a

Bourdieu, P. (1986) Forms of Capital, in J. Richardson (Ed.) *Handbook of Theory and Research for the Sociology of Education*. New York: Greenwood Press.

Bronfenbrenner, U. (1977) Towards an Experimental Ecology of Human Development, *American Psychologist*, 32, 513-531. http://dx.doi.org/10.1037/0003-066X.32.7.513

Camus, A. (1942 [2013]) *L'Étranger* [The Outsider]. London: Penguin.

Crotty, M. (1998) *The Foundations of Social Research: meaning and perspective in the research process*. London: SAGE.

Döbert, H., Klieme, E. & Sroka, W. (Eds) (2004) *Conditions of School Performance in Seven Countries*. Münster: Waxmann.

du Gay, P., Hall, S., Janes, L., Mackay, H. & Negus, K. (1997) *Doing Cultural Studies: the story of the Sony Walkman*. London: SAGE.

Goldstein, H. (1996) Introduction, *Assessment in Education*, 3(2), 125-129. http://dx.doi.org/10.1080/0969594960030201

Gorard, S. (2001) International Comparisons of School Effectiveness: the second component of the 'crisis account' in England?, *Comparative Education*, 37(3), 279-296. http://dx.doi.org/10.1080/03050060120067785

Hall, S. (Ed.) (1997) *Representation: cultural representation and signifying practices*. Milton Keynes: The Open University.

Hogenstijn, M., van Middelkoop, D. & Terlouw, K. (2008) The Established, the Outsiders and Scale Strategies: studying local power conflicts, *Sociological Review*, 56(1), 144-161. http://dx.doi.org/10.1111/j.1467-954X.2008.00780.x

Holland, D. & Lave, J. (2009) Social Practice Theory and the Historical Production of Persons, *Actio: an international journal of human activity theory*, 2, 1-15.

Kelly, P. (2014) Intercultural Comparative Research: rethinking insider and outsider perspectives, *Oxford Review of Education*, 40(2), 1-20. http://dx.doi.org/10.1080/03054985.2014.900484

Kelly, P., Pratt, N., Dorf, H. & Hohmann, U. (2013) Comparing Pedagogy in Mathematics in Denmark and England, *European Education Research Journal*, 12(4), 553-567. http://dx.doi.org/10.2304/eerj.2013.12.4.553

Larsen, M. (2010) New Thinking in Comparative Education, in M. Larsen (Ed.) *New Thinking in Comparative Education: honouring Robert Cowan*. Rotterdam: Sense Publishers.

Lave, J. (2011) *Apprenticeship in Critical Ethnographic Practice*. Chicago: University of Chicago Press. http://dx.doi.org/10.7208/chicago/9780226470733.001.0001

McNess, E., Arthur, L. & Crossley, M. (2013) 'Ethnographic Dazzle' and the Construction of the 'Other': revisiting dimensions of insider and outsider research for international and comparative education, *Compare*, 45(2), 295-316. http://dx.doi.org/10.1080/03057925.2013.854616

Nederveen Pieterse, J. (2004) *Globalisation and Culture: global mélange*. Lanham, MD: Rowman & Littlefield.

Office for Standards in Education (Ofsted) (2010) Finnish Pupils' Success in Mathematics. https://www.ofsted.gov (accessed 10 July 2012).

Osborn, M.J., Broadfoot, P., McNess, E., Planel, C., Ravn, B. & Triggs, P. (2003) *A World of Difference? Comparing Learners across Europe*. Maidenhead: Open University Press.

Rutherford, J. (1990) The Third Space: interview with Homi Bhabha, in J. Rutherford (Ed.) *Identity, Community, Culture, Difference*, pp. 207-221. London: Lawrence & Wishart.

Said, E. (1978) *Orientalism*. London: Penguin.

Schreiwer, J. (2010) An Enlightenment Scholar in English Robes, in M. Larson (Ed.) *New Thinking in Comparative Education: honouring Robert Cowan*. Rotterdam: Sense Publishers.

Swift, A. (2006) *Political Philosophy*. Cambridge: Polity Press.

Weber, M. (1949) Objectivity in the Social Sciences and Social Policy, in E.A. Shils & H.A. Sinch (Eds) *The Methodology of the Social Sciences*. New York: Free Press.

Wenger, E. (1998) *Communities of Practice: learning, meaning and identity*. New York: Cambridge University Press. http://dx.doi.org/10.1017/CBO9780511803932

CHAPTER 4

Beyond 'Insiders' and 'Outsiders' in Research for Education Policy-making? The Discursive Positioning of the Researcher in International and Comparative Education

NILOU M. HAWTHORNE

> Us and them, Self and Other, the drawing of demarcation lines in culture and academia, and the reactions of those who are kept outside have been familiar topics for a long time, and scholarship has gradually started to take this history into account. (Schipper, 1997, p. 122)

Introduction

There are many ways of viewing 'insiders' and 'outsiders' and the underlying conceptions of 'insiderness' and 'outsiderness', though I was drawn into the imagery of the 'drawing of demarcation lines in culture and academia' of the above citation: the discursive construction of otherness as being 'kept outside', excluded, and on the other side of 'lines in culture and academia'. It is the main contention of this chapter that not only is the discourse of 'insiders' and 'outsiders' in social research descriptive of perceived states of affairs in the social world, it also constructs and partially constitutes those same social realities. It follows from this that there are no 'insiders' or 'outsiders' in social relations apart from those constructed, and that the lines in culture and academia that have been drawn are not fixed or permanent.

The aims of this chapter are twofold. In the first place, it uses a discursive perspective to revisit the insider/outsider binary, considers some its conceptual limits, and re-examines the features that are typically captured in the use of insider/outsider constructs. In the second place, it seeks to support the opening of discursive space for researchers to actively participate in the re-positioning of researcher subjectivities; and this is treated as an intrinsic aspect of the development of the international and comparative education research field. Both of these aims are grounded in the observation that education researchers are actors in the education systems which are the object or site of their research activity, and so are not immune from the processes and practices through which researcher roles, identities and subjectivities are being reformulated and reformed. The relative positioning of the researcher within the research activity, and how it may be changing due to the dynamic context in which contemporary education research takes place, is a current issue of concern for international and comparative education research (McNess et al, 2013). McNess et al also emphasise that the insider/outsider construct, as applied to 'researchers and the researched' in international and comparative education, requires a more nuanced understanding of the relationship between these two groupings and how individuals might situate themselves through insider conceptions. A critical approach to discourse analysis as presented in this chapter provides an analytical method for reconceptualising these relationships.

The chapter is in three parts. In the following section I introduce some of the theoretical issues underpinning the critical approach adopted, starting with some of the more salient conceptual features of discourse analysis, and then focusing on discursive subject positioning and how it applies to insider/outsider and similar binary constructs. In the second section I look at the broader landscapes in which researcher roles, identities and subjectivities are situated and positioned by considering how discursive imaginaries influence education policy-making processes. The third section is a response to two critical junctures that have been reached in the field of international and comparative education. The first of these concerns the influence of the 'global knowledge economy' imaginary and the comparative approach favoured by exponents of this narrative. The second is the potential threat to the presence of an independent academic voice on educational matters within the public sphere created by some forms of research for education (Crossley, 2014; Barrett & Crossley, 2015).

The international sustainable development agenda for 2015 to 2030, which includes a number of education for sustainable development targets, was agreed by the United Nations in September 2015 under the title 'Transforming Our World: the 2030 Agenda for Sustainable Development'. The establishment of frameworks for the implementation and follow-up of the 2030 agenda, as well as the continued assessments of the outcomes of the Education for All initiative and the Millennium Development Goals, all provide a transitional bridge and a timely opportunity to take measure of the changing landscape of comparative education research. This chapter is a preliminary step in applying discursive tools in that direction, guided by the understanding that many of the most significant changes to educational governance are being initiated discursively.

Positioning the Researcher in International and Comparative Education

Discourses and Texts

A critical approach to discourse analysis provides an analytic method of distinguishing between the 'imaginaries' or ideational aspects of the socio-cultural world and its material aspects. I treat discourse as an ideational or semiotic constellation or landscape of objects through which social identities, social relations, social institutions and other social phenomena may be examined. Consequently the use of language and other semiotic practices in and through discourses is understood as creating socio-cultural meanings that have identifiable social and cultural effects and which it is the purpose of analysis to explicate. This is not simply about the use of rhetorical features in texts to persuade audiences to particular opinions or courses of action; rather, it concerns how characterisations and other discursive objects are specified and scripted in the production of discourses, in and through texts, and the constitutive effects on social life. Texts provide the empirical data on which critical analyses of discourse can rely 'for grounding claims about social structures, relations and processes' (Fairclough, 1992, p. 211), and, since text production is an integral activity within the matrix of networks and institutions involved in education policy processes, policy processes leave a textual history that provides material objects (texts) for analysis.

Subject Positions and Discursive Characterisations

A subject position is a discursively delineated way of being and acting, or a scripting of subjects in a discursive framework. The term subject is used on account of its double senses as 'one who is affected' (subjected) and 'one who has agency' (following Fairclough, 1985). A discourse subject is then a special form of discourse object whose agentive attributes are indicated within texts and produced and reproduced in and through discourses. The subject and the discursive positioning of the subject are both constructs of discourse and as such may be evidenced from text analysis; Fairclough (1989) encapsulates this in referring to an 'ideal subject' – that is, a subject as they are positioned by the implied author of a text. Furthermore, a discourse subject when provided with distinct traits which individualise them within discourses represents a character. The use of characterisation in discourse production operates by making plausible the relationship between an imagined character and their imagined actions:

> Character entails an illusion in which the reader is a creative accomplice. Out of words we make a person. A variety of descriptions of some posited individual, together with descriptions – implicit or explicit – of that individual's actions and reactions, suffice to lead most readers to conceive of a person of whom these references and insights are just glimpses. (Toolan, 2001, pp. 80-81)

In English, 'the researcher' (as it is used in the chapter title, for example) is understood in specific textual contexts as 'any and all researchers'. This is an example of homophoric reference, in which the referent (researcher) is considered as representative of the whole class, although this is not specifically indicated in the text (Halliday & Hasan, 1976). In this syntactic structure the use of the definite article indicates that there is a linguistically embedded form of characterisation that positions a discourse subject who typifies and embodies group membership (Hawthorne, 2014). This type of 'part-for-whole' device is typically described in rhetoric as a particularising synecdoche. Other linguistic and textual devices that can be used to position subjects in discourses include the use of modality indicators, indexicals, imperatives, and argumentation strategies (Luke, 1995). 'Text and talk' is one formulation of the two areas in which subjectivities are formed and intersubjective relations are discursively mediated: Luke, for example, notes that it is in the dynamics of everyday life that 'subjectivities are strategically constructed and contested through textual practices' (1995, p. 14), while Davies and Harré (1990) identify 'talk' as a discursive practice in which subjective positioning constitutes speakers and listeners, and at the same time, is a discursive resource through which new positions may be negotiated.

The characterisation of 'the researcher' can be extended by considering some of the subject positions that occur in discourses that valorise social science researcher subjectivities through their activities or practices, such as 'teacher', 'scholar', 'academic', 'manager', 'scientist' or 'expert'. In these examples we see the teacher as positioned in the discourses of higher learning in a liberal democracy, the scholar or academic as positioned in discourses of the academy, the manager as positioned in the discourses of public management, the scientist as positioned in scientific discourses and the expert as positioned in discourses of scientific management. Each of these discourses constellates relations of objects, including, as well as theories, themes and epistemological presuppositions, both the prototypical characterisation of a discursive subject, and the practices associated with its discursive positioning.

'Insider' and 'Outsider' as Discursive Subject Positions

The use of binary oppositions like 'outsider' and 'insider', 'other' and 'self', 'them' and 'us' in social research, as in social life, can be interpreted as socio-cultural expressions of social relations that privilege one half of the binary over the other. Three potential consequences arise from this. First, the use of the binary construct emphasises discursive and material differences between 'insider' and 'outsider' groupings where there may also be similarities; second, the complexity of contingent historical and geopolitical processes is easily disguised or taken for granted in their use; third, and most important, the constructing and constitutive properties of discourses and texts suggest that the use of binary oppositions may construct and script, and thereby partially constitute, the same differences that it is their purpose to understand. As one example, in the discourses of access and diversity categories of insider/outsider, majority/minority, sameness/difference have been shown to reinforce exclusionary and inequitable practices in campus relations in the United States (Iverson, 2012). From a linguistic perspective binaries are neutral, but once conditioned by contexts of use, once used in discourse, this neutrality is negated. Consequently, when viewed from a discursive perspective, binary constructs such as 'insider/outsider' are intrinsically constructs that delineate discursive subject positions.

Merton's proposal concerning a sociological understanding of the 'insider' provides two important insights: firstly, that any claims to 'monopolistic or privileged access to social truth' are epistemological claims, and secondly that such claims 'develop under particular social and historical conditions' (1972, p. 19). An 'insider' community is therefore not necessarily bound by or to a social formation (institution, ethnic community, nation, etc.) but rather to organised knowledge, beliefs and values; consequently, the shared epistemological claims of its members are a significant delineating property of an insider community. 'Insiderness' or 'outsiderness' from this perspective can be reconsidered in discourse terms as constructs that specify the attributes or partial characterisations of a discourse subject and a subject position that discursively indicates an individual social actor's relation to a group that is both historically and socially constituted and bound through epistemological or other knowledge claims. Nevertheless, the fundamental problem with the use of binaries as markers of social identity still remains in this reconceptualisation, and this is that only two subject positions are admissible to an individual member or potential member – either 'inside' or 'outside'; there are no degrees of 'insiderness' or 'outsiderness'. The insider/outsider binary, even taking into account the significance of its base in the epistemological claims of communities, cannot easily be used to deal with the complexities inherent in how these epistemological claims are made or sustained or altered; or with partial claims to group membership, or changes to claims through time.

In the context of the changing formations and practices of international and comparative research some of the inadequacies of binary constructs in conceptualising social and community relations have been brought into sharp relief; conceptualising and identifying the 'inside' or 'outside' of systems, professional communities or research environments has become increasingly difficult (McNess et al, 2013). The discourse community construct developed by Swales (1987, 1990) provides an alternative and multifaceted theoretical apparatus from which to analyse groups formed from the epistemological claims common among group members while also allowing for the social and historical contingencies of group formation that the sociological formulation captures.

Discourse Communities and Epistemic Communities

The first feature of a discourse community is that it has an identifiable 'communality of interest' through a shared common public goal or goals. The public aspect of this feature is important even though in Swales' account it is not necessary that it be explicit. The second feature is that there are means and mechanisms for intercommunication between members. Related to these two features, members of a discourse community have expectations (primarily discursive) that may include the appropriateness of its topics, and the role that documentation or forms of communication have in the functioning of the community. According to Swales (1987, p. 6), a discourse community has 'an inbuilt dynamic towards an increasingly shared and specialized terminology' and a 'critical mass' of members with a suitable degree of knowledge and expertise. Other properties that add to the flexibility of its use as an analytic construct are that a discourse community is unconstrained by space or time and is media-neutral; it may or may not be connected to what members perceive as their main day-to-day concerns; and it does not presuppose, or exclude, high levels of personal involvement among its members.

Discourse community analyses have been used extensively for the purposes of understanding the use of academic genres, and for analysing academic writing and other academic discourse practices (Swales, 1990; Hyland, 2009). By considering a disciplinary research community as a discourse community, the delineating features of its constitution as an insider community are preserved, but with some advantages. This is because it is through the discursive contexts of text production and knowledge production, and specifically the practices in which researchers engage, that epistemological claims are made, agreed and shared as part of the development of the research field. An additional step in moving beyond the conceptual limits of the insider/outsider binary can be taken by further specifying one of the features of a discourse community. A discourse community that has the production of socially validated knowledge as its shared common public goal can be conceptualised as an epistemic community. The constraint on this use of 'epistemic community' that distinguishes it from other applications of the term is that the use of historically constituted and socially validated practices for the production of a field of knowledge is essential, so that an ad hoc community formed to address a social issue would not in this frame be considered as an epistemic community (although it may meet discourse community criteria).

In a social constructivist frame the researcher comes into view both as observing social practices and relations, and as being a participating-subject in social practices and social relations. With regard to the practices of research activity, the researcher as observing-subject is located in a discursively mediated environment of social relations from which subjectivities are positioned, negotiated and re-negotiated (Ainsworth & Hardy, 2006; Iverson, 2012), or 'inculcated' through the non-reflexive adoption of practices (Fairclough, 2003). A researcher may, though, occupy numerous other positions in the education field: as parent, school governor, employee, trade union member, etc., a researcher may therefore be involved in educational practices which all have their own discursively mediated socio-cultural environments through which a researcher is positioned as a participating-subject. The distinction between the observing-subject and participating-subject thus provides a heuristic device for analysing different sets of relations and practices within the education field. While the observing-subject position is limited to the members of an epistemic community, which in the international and comparative field is a community that transcends national and regional boundaries and institutional affiliations, the participating-subject discursive position is one that is shared with other participating-subjects in the field, in which may be included various communities of 'the researched'.

One advantage of this framework is that it facilitates understanding the ways in which different aspects of researcher subjectivities are formed; for example, the activities of the 'teacher-researcher' and 'expert-researcher' and 'expert-teacher-researcher' can be described, contrasted and explained in terms of discourse community memberships. Another advantage is that the discourse community framework provides a structured flexibility for treating complex research environments like cross-national research collaboration. As an example, within a multi-national and/or multi-lingual research group, while the research group as an entity can be treated as a primary discourse community, this does not preclude recognising other discourse community memberships that may or may not be directly relevant to the research activity, but the discourse community framework facilitates explicit consideration of these types of issue as part of research design.

The 'Global Knowledge Economy' and Educational Policy-making

Background

The discursive subject positioning of researchers has to be understood within the broad socio-cultural context in which education research takes place, and in relation to education policy-making. This is the case whether research supports the production of policy, is for policy analysis, or is for policy critique as part of broader social critiques. The functioning of globalising economic discourses and their impacts within educational governance now form part of the discursive landscape in which researcher discursive subject positions are situated as objects of discourse. One of the features of the contemporary education policy-making environment is the effect of an economically driven agenda acting as steering mechanism on the path of educational development and improvement at an international level. In this context I understand education policy-making as a dynamic process that produces discursive and material changes in the education field and through which changes are activated and maintained in the field from the interactions between a networked complex of institutions and the interrelated discursive practices and material experiences of social actors within it.

International organisations such as the Organization for Economic Cooperation and Development (OECD), the World Bank Group (World Bank), the World Trade Organisation (WTO) and the International Monetary Fund (IMF), despite not having an explicit mandate for education, conceptualise it in economic terms impacting all scales of policy-making: international, regional, state, sub-state regional and local levels (Carnoy & Rhoten, 2002, Torres & Schugurensky, 2002; Robertson et al, 2002; Ball 2012b, Lingard et al, 2013). These organisations have created a discursive framework for education that limits the conception of problems and their solutions to the logics of economics, and in which education systems and their practices are perceived and conceptualised in global economic terms. This network of organisations has a fundamental adherence to the ethos of the free market in the provision of education services and in consequence presupposes benefits in privatising public assets and expanding private market relations in the education field.

The World Bank Group Education Strategy 2020, *Learning for All: investing in people's knowledge and skills to promote development* (World Bank, 2011) (hereafter Education Sector Strategy 2020), acknowledges that 'that the world as a whole is emerging from the global financial crisis at a modest rate' (p. 21), referring to the 2008 collapse of the international banking system, but throughout the document the World Bank sustains its belief in the self-correcting nature of markets despite this view being undermined by the effects of market failures. The World Bank Strategy 2020, while claiming that it merely *recognises* the 'the growing role of the private sector in education' (p. 3), actively supports commercial and profit-seeking interests in the development of national education provisions.

The 'global' in economic narratives acts as a geospatial indicator that is distanced from the specificities of local sites of education policy-making processes and educational practices, and in these sites I include regional, national and sub-national environments. Invoking 'the global economic' in education policy-making is most evident in the assumption that there is a single 'global' knowledge economy, rather than an alternative conception in which knowledge production plays a complex and varied role in the economic, social and political life of different social formations. This view of the global as economic is compounded by the implicit acceptance of the idea of a global consensus which echoes a common assumption of positivist thinking that consensus, by whatever means it is achieved, is the natural path of progress. It is for these reasons that I treat the 'global knowledge economy' as a discursive object and economic imaginary (see also Sum & Jessop, 2014).

The Education Sector Strategy 2020 (World Bank, 2011, p. 1) makes passing reference to both the Universal Declaration of Human Rights (1948) and the United Nations Convention on the Rights of the Child (1989) in relation to access to education as a basic human right and, in so doing, confirms organisational awareness that education provisions arranged through national states and regional bodies fall within the framework of international law: international law thus provides a social, cultural and political framework, and global context, for education improvement and development. In contrast, the consensus assumed for globalising processes in the economic discourses of educational change appear almost exclusively in economic-technological forms that cannot recognise those aspects of globalisation, the social, cultural and political, that involve 'progressive spatial segregation, separation and exclusion' (Bauman, 1998, p. 3). The programme outlined within the Education Sector Strategy 2020 for education systems 'around the world' – systems improvements and the development of a global knowledge-base (World Bank, 2011, pp. 1, 5-7) – suggests that understanding the relations between education and social inclusion and social justice does not feature highly in its priorities. The OECD, in contrast, does address the issue of fairness in education, but isolates educational equality from the issue of social inequality and social justice (Bøyum, 2014). The 'global knowledge economy' as imagined is a distinct and distant world from that in which educational processes and practices are understood as aspects of socialisation, sociality, and community or social interests in common with others; education as an exercise of and for citizenship, or the concept of education as cooperation, 'ushirikiano' or 'learning with and from each other', are significant exclusions from its discursive frame.

Forms of Distance in International Education Policy-making Discourses

A remarkable feature of the textual output of organisations that privilege economic discourses in education policy-making contexts is the extent to which it is ahistorical and decontextualised, and depopulates the discursive landscape in which education policy processes take place, thereby limiting the terms in which discussion and investigation of education practices and policy-making processes take place (Torres & Shugurensky, 2002; Connell, 2013). The worldview presented in the World Bank's Education Sector Strategy 2020 is not only spatially distant from the sites of education practices and the places where policy is mediated and translated into strategies, plans, operations and procedures, desired outcomes and practices – it is also a worldview that is distanced from the past, and from the present. In the imaginary of the 'global knowledge economy' on which this worldview relies and through which the strategy is projected into the future (Nordtveit, 2012), education is divorced not only from the local situatedness of teaching and learning, but also from the historically realised institutions, interests and processes of the wider socio-cultural contexts that have created, and that maintain, national education systems.

The distance between the discursive positioning of social actors as they appear in the frame of economic educational governance and that of those who actually exercise agency from different positions in the social field of education is marked, and is relatable to the discursive construction of the rational actor. Within the discourses that have developed from neoclassical economic thought, the figure of the 'rational actor' as a prototypical characterisation of the individual in society scripts the actions of all social actors in the social field of education. The self-interested individual of these discourses is a fictive figure formed from intertextual and interdiscursive borrowings: the character is male, individualistic, enterprising and entrepreneurial, has private rather than public interests, and applies an instrumental rationality to all education market transactions (Ball, 2012a).

Given the central position of knowledge production, which is especially evident in the Education Sector Strategy 2020, as framed both for economic development and for producing a knowledge-base for education policy-making, the positioning of the academic researcher in universities and other institutions of higher education is noticeable from its absence. An OECD thematic review of higher education, 'Tertiary Education for the Knowledge Society' (OECD, 2008), includes 'academic career' as one of the facets of its 'international investigation of tertiary education policy' (p. 1), and the policy directions for the academic career use a human resources perspective, positioning 'the academic' as a human capital resource. The Education Sector Strategy 2020 makes reference only to 'academic luminaries' and 'distinguished academics' (p. 11) whom it has consulted. This is consistent with the findings that the use of soft governance and its regimes of regulation have created a form of policy process that is characterised by its hierarchical nature and strategic and tactical operations which displace or marginalise specific groups of educational professionals and experts (Gunter, 2011). Both the World Bank and the OECD constructs and discourse positions for 'the academic' align with the prototypical characterisation of the 'rational actor' that scripts the constitution of the individualistic academic entrepreneur. Nevertheless, the OECD does identify research activity as an academic activity and emphasises the importance of academic freedom and accountability (OECD, 2008).

While education research communities are distant through absence from these policy texts, the World Bank positions itself as a key actor in the knowledge-based economy discourses that it imagines. Its self-perception of its role in education policy-making as a 'knowledge bank' is described thus:

> the Bank thinks of itself as a 'knowledge bank' and aspires to be both a *generator* of new knowledge and a *synthesizer* of existing knowledge. (World Bank, 2011, p. 53, emphasis in original)

On the surface, the World Bank utilises the established discursive practices of academic and disciplinary text publication as vehicles for the production of knowledge, and these credentials are essential if its self-positioning as a key actor in the production of knowledge is to be sustained and legitimised. However, the self-referential nature of the knowledge production from the World Bank is problematic (Steiner-Khamsi, 2012).

The OECD as part of its organizational strategy has 'strengthened its hand as a centre of technical expertise, data collection and data analysis, at a time when data have become central to governance at both global and national level' (Sellar & Lingard, 2013, p. 715). This can be seen as being directly related on one side to its organisational interests, and on the other, to the importance given to constituting the knowledge(-based) economy after having accepted it as a discursive object of the economic imaginary. The OECD in particular, as the author and publisher of PISA (Programme for International Student Assessment) survey data (OECD, 2001, 2004, 2007, 2010, 2014), has discursively constructed 'data' as being of central importance in policy formation within the orthodoxies of economic soft governance, and this can be traced back through the

OECD's authorship and publication of *The Knowledge-based Economy* (OECD, 1996), where it states:

> Human capital indicators, particularly those relating to education and employment, are central measures for the knowledge-based economy. (p. 43)

PISA data are widely treated as an economic indicator and proxy for national human capital resource because that is the purpose of their production. The World Bank claims that PISA and TIMMS (Trends in International Mathematics and Science Study) provide a measure of workplace skills that can be used to predict economic growth rates, and uses national performance rankings within its methodology (World Bank, 2011, p. 3). But the scope of PISA data provides a limited assessment of student competencies that is unrelated to school curricula. They decontextualise teaching and learning from their school-based local institutional contexts (Keating, 2011) and from the particulars of their national context, and at the same time, despite their limited scope, may be used in national and sub-national contexts to provide a technical rationale and justification for politically driven education reforms (Bonal & Tarabini, 2013).

Cross-national surveys producing curriculum-based data-sets for monitoring country trends specifically to support teaching, learning and curriculum development are theoretically an indispensable tool for comparative education research. This is what it is claimed both TIMMS and PIRLS (Progress in International Reading Literacy Study) are designed to provide. But there is a need for a clear distinction to be preserved, just as in other scales of student assessment, between those assessments that are for the monitoring and evaluation of students' learning and progression, and the improvement of pedagogy, and those that are treated as a performative measure of systems.

This underlines the importance of understanding the contexts of use of research data, as their interpretation and value vary according to how they are contextualised and the uses to which they are put – hence the range of purposes to which they are suited or fit for purpose. This aspect of comparative education research is clearly recognised in the cross-cultural, mixed-methods and multi-disciplinary approach of the academic comparative research field and is evident not only in its critiques of the use of large-scale assessment data but also in critiques of cross-national education policy transfer. The use of statistical methods and other quantitative research to produce economic indicators for constituting the imaginary of a 'global knowledge economy' highlights the need for sustained evidence and argument concerning their contexts of use.

'Insiders' and 'Outsiders' in the Domain of Education Research for Policy-making

Beyond 'Insiders' and 'Outsiders'

The World Bank frames its interventions in national education systems as an offer of technical assistance, aid and support (World Bank, 2011), an intervention strategy also used by the IMF (Popke, 1994). Since integrating the 'global knowledge economy' imaginary within its discursive production it has repositioned itself as a key actor in the provision of research and knowledge on education and educational development. Within the 'global knowledge economy' worldview, the use of economic discourses as expert or technical knowledge, presupposing that there are economic 'truths' in a positivist sense, is dissociated from how these discourses are used by, for example, the World Bank, IMF and OECD to produce and reproduce the socio-cultural conditions required for legitimising their own influence. The absence of autonomous voices, historical perspectives and appreciation of the local contexts of education provision in the texts from the World Bank and OECD is therefore unsurprising given the nature of the discursive space that their imaginaries create. Furthermore, as the prevalence of economic discourses of the role of education in society increases, so the scope within the public sphere for democratic debate about how relations between education and societies may be understood, developed, reformed or transformed decreases.

The contemporary discursive policy-making environment is complicated by multi-scalar patterns of governance, and this includes the impact of the organisations that position themselves as key actors in international education governance: the World Bank explicitly positions itself as a centre of knowledge for education policy-making, and the OECD does this implicitly through the production and publication of survey data. In this environment, insider/outsider notions and similarly constructed binaries of the us/them, selves/'others' etc. fail to capture some of the most salient features of the matrix of interests, processes, practices, institutions and discourses that now comprise the educational policy-making arena. Transcending the limits of these binary constructions and the manner in which they position social actors in various education contexts and communities is not a simple or straightforward task. However, the discursive context of much policy reform suggests that an effective way of moving beyond insider/outsider positions is for researchers to actively, and collectively, position social actors differently, as part of the effort to re-script the framework of possibilities for education reforms; and this includes the positioning of 'the researcher'. Researcher subjectivities that are formed from the positive values of the epistemic community and that position the researcher as a public intellectual who provides an independent voice within the public sphere are not 'commonsensical' within the rationalities that advocate free-market economics and so cannot appear in their associated discourses; but, in spite of limiting factors (such as institutional and funding restraints and the constraints on research publication and dissemination media), this does not imply that discursive space for the positive values of the epistemic community and the researcher position as a public intellectual have entirely disappeared from the social world, or can be made to do so.

Critical Junctures

Both of the critical junctures identified above as of current concern to the international and comparative research community can be related to the discursive impact of the imaginary of the 'global knowledge economy' and the worldview of which it is a part. The absence of epistemic communities from this worldview and of particular characteristics or attributes that may constitute researcher subjectivities, as well as the utilisation of forms of education research that produce the indicators required as a warrant for human capital measurement, are all indicative of the application of an economic rationality that is blind to all but its own interests. Yet, despite the undoubted power of the use of economic governmentality to impact and produce new policy forms in education, the pervasiveness of free-market discourses and the weight given to them in new and emerging forms of education policy-making, the public sphere still maintains resilience to their effects. It is still the case that 'dominant strategies do not occupy an empty landscape' (Clarke, 2004, p. 44).

Within this landscape are the communities, school systems and individual schools which have their own assumptions and practices that may include the positive institutionalised values of social good, social objectives and ethics based in social understanding (Keating, 2011). As well as academic communities and traditional national policy forums, trade unions and social movements are among the forms of social organisation through which the economically motivated ambitions of a globalising agenda are mediated, re-contextualised and contested (Ozga et al, 2006). The regional scale of education policy-making is also an area in which significant mediation of the market agenda is evident. As just one example, the Organization of Ibero-American States for Education, Science and Culture (Organización de Estados Iberoamericanos; OEI) in its *2021 Metas Educativas* ('2021 Education Goals') (OEI, 2010) has called for continued international cooperation and collaboration in supporting its commitment to the transformative power of education. Critical junctures such as those arising from the forms of distance created by dominating economic discourses in education research for policy-making can be met by applying intellectual imagination to the opportunities that exist for exposing and mediating their effects. The use of quantitative measures and other statistical research may lend itself to providing headline comparisons of educational outcomes, but the use of such research in constituting the 'global knowledge economy' and in positioning international and transnational institutions as key actors in the education policy field merits continued inquiry.

Closing Comments

The specific issue of 'insider/outsider' conceptions within the academy suggests that applying reflexivity in the exercise of practice is necessary for the individual researcher with appreciation of how researcher positions, including one's own, fit within the design of research activities (Doyle, 2013) and with awareness, for example, of how personal history and professional trajectory privilege certain subjects in the research field over others. Nevertheless, professional subjectivities are negotiated, re-negotiated or 'inculcated' in the context of professional practices, and so it is primarily through research activity that these subjectivities are constituted. It is from the application of intellectual imagination to research design and planning, developing research methodologies, advancing theory and critical perspectives, extending the availability of options for the publication and dissemination of research findings, and creating new forms of international collaboration and cooperation that the strength of the field, and ultimately the position of the researcher, will be decided.

The academic voice of comparativists ought to be among those whose educational priorities maintain a balanced and empirically grounded view of the relation between sociality, economics and politics in the conduct of social life; and the responsibility for re-constructing and re-positioning researcher subjectivities and maintaining the distinctiveness of comparative scholarship clearly lies within the international epistemic community. This is a call not for irrationalism as a response to the characterisation of the 'rational actor', but for the application of a humane rationality. There is that form of rationality that is not singularly self-interested and through which awareness of historical and geopolitical perspectives becomes necessary, if sometimes unpleasant, for understanding the multitude of different experiences, circumstances and realities that have constituted our contemporary global present. Finally, reaffirming the position of the researcher as a public intellectual grounded within the ethics of an epistemic community can help to strengthen a specifically international public sphere, not only as an adaptation to changed scales and modes of educational governance, but because this time of transition into what could be a transformative era for social justice in education worldwide calls for careful consideration of how lines in culture and academia are redrawn.

References

Ainsworth, S. & Hardy, C. (2006) Critical Discourse Analysis and Identity: why bother? *Critical Discourse Studies*, 1(2), 225-259. http://dx.doi.org/10.1080/1740590042000302085

Ball, S.J. (2012a) *Foucault, Power, and Education*. London: Routledge.

Ball, S.J. (2012b) *Global Education Inc.: new policy networks and the neo-liberal imaginary*. London: Routledge.

Barrett, A. & Crossley, M. (2015) The Power and Politics of International Comparisons: editorial, *Compare*, 45(3), 467-470. http://dx.doi.org/10.1080/03057925.2015.1027509

Bauman, Z. (1998) On Glocalization: or globalization for some, localization for some others, *Thesis 11: critical theory and historical sociology*, 54(1), 137-149.

Bonal, X. & Tarabini, A. (2013) The Role of PISA in Shaping Hegemonic Educational Discourses, Policies, Practices: the case of Spain, *Research in Comparative and International Education*, 8(3), 335-341. http://dx.doi.org/10.2304/rcie.2013.8.3.335

Bøyum, S. (2014) Fairness in Education – A Normative Analysis of OECD Policy Documents, *Journal of Education* Policy, 29(6), 856-870. http://dx.doi.org/10.1080/02680939.2014.899396

Carnoy, M. & Rhoten, D. (2002) The Meanings of Globalization for Educational Change, *Comparative Education Review*, 46(1), 1-9. http://dx.doi.org/10.1086/324053

Clarke, J. (2004) Dissolving the Public Realm? The Logics and Limits of Neo-liberalism, *Journal of Social Policy*, 33(1), 27-48. http://dx.doi.org/10.1017/S0047279403007244

Connell, R. (2013) The Neoliberal Cascade and Education: an essay on the market agenda and its consequences, *Critical Studies in Education*, 54(2), 99-112. http://dx.doi.org/10.1080/17508487.2013.776990

Crossley, M. (2014) Global League Tables, Big Data and the International Transfer of Educational Research Modalities, *Comparative Education*, 50(1), 15-26. http://dx.doi.org/10.1080/03050068.2013.871438

Davies, B. & Harré, R. (1990) Subject Positioning, *Journal for the Theory of Social Behaviour*, 20(1), 43-65.

Doyle, S. (2013) Reflexivity and the Capacity to Think, *Qualitative Health Research*, 23(2), 248-257. http://dx.doi.org/10.1177/1049732312467854

Fairclough, N. (1985) Critical and Descriptive Goals in Discourse Analysis, *Journal of Pragmatics*, 9, 739-763. http://dx.doi.org/10.1016/0378-2166(85)90002-5

Fairclough, N. (1989) *Language and Power*. New York: Longman.

Fairclough, N. (1992) Discourse and Text: linguistic and intertextual analysis within discourse analysis, *Discourse & Society*, 3(2), 193-217. http://dx.doi.org/10.1177/0957926592003002004

Fairclough, N. (2003) *Analysing Discourse: textual analysis for social research.* Abingdon: Routledge.

Gunter, H.M. (2011) Governance and Education in England, *Italian Journal of Sociology of Education*, 2, 31-45.

Halliday, M.A.K. & Hasan, R. (1976) *Cohesion in English.* London: Longman.

Hawthorne, N.M. (2014) The Discursive Construction of the 'Communication Engineer' in *The Bell System Technical Journal* Foreword. Paper presented to the Centre of Research in Language and Linguistics, University of Roehampton, 2 February.

Hyland, K. (2009) Corpus Information Discourse Analysis: the case of academic engagement, in Maggie Charles, Susan Hunston & Diane Pecorari (Eds) *Academic Writing: at the interface of corpus and discourse*, pp. 110-128. London: Continuum.

Iverson, S.V. (2012) Constructing Outsiders: the discursive framing of access in university diversity policies, *Review of Higher Education*, 35(2), 149-177. http://dx.doi.org/10.1353/rhe.2012.0013

Keating, J. (2011) New Forms of Policy in Australia. Paper presented at International Sociology of Education Conference, London, 4-6 November.

Lingard, B., Martino, W. & Rezai-Rashti, G. (2013) Testing Regimes, Accountabilities and Education Policy: commensurate global and national developments, *Journal of Education Policy*, 28(5), 539-556. http://dx.doi.org/10.1080/02680939.2013.820042

Luke, A. (1995) Text and Discourse in Education: an introduction to critical discourse analysis, *Review of Research in Education*, 21, 3-48.

McNess, E., Arthur, L. & Crossley, M. (2013) 'Ethnographic Dazzle' and the Construction of the 'Other': revisiting dimensions of insider and outsider research for international and comparative education, *Compare: a journal of comparative and international education*, 45(2), 295-316. http://dx.doi.org/10.1080/03057925.2013.85461.

Merton, R.K. (1972) Insiders and Outsiders: a chapter in the sociology of knowledge, *American Journal of Sociology*, 78(1), 9-47. http://dx.doi.org/10.1086/225294

Nordtveit, B.H. (2012) World Bank Poetry: how the Education Strategy 2020 imagines the world, in Steven J. Klees, Joel Samoff & Nelly P. Stromquist (Eds) *The World Bank and Education Critiques and Alternatives*, pp. 21-32. Rotterdam: Sense Publishers. http://dx.doi.org/10.1007/978-94-6091-903-9_2

Organisation for Economic Co-operation and Development (OECD) (1996) *The Knowledge-based Economy.* Paris: OECD Publishing.

Organisation for Economic Co-operation and Development (OECD) (2001) *Knowledge and Skills for Life: first results from PISA.* Paris: OECD Publishing.

Organisation for Economic Co-operation and Development (OECD) (2004) *Learning for Tomorrow's World: first results from PISA 2003*. Paris: OECD Publishing.

Organisation for Economic Co-operation and Development (OECD) (2007) *PISA 2006: science competencies for tomorrow's world*. Paris: OECD Publishing.

Organisation for Economic Co-operation and Development (OECD) (2008) Tertiary Education for the Knowledge Society. OECD Thematic Review of Tertiary Education: Synthesis Report. Paris: OECD. http://www.oecd.org/education/skills-beyond-school/40345176.pdf

Organisation for Economic Co-operation and Development (OECD) (2010) *PISA 2009 Results*. Vol. II. *Overcoming Social Background: equity in learning, opportunities and outcomes*. Paris: OECD Publishing.

Organisation for Economic Co-operation and Development (OECD) (2014) *PISA 2012 Results*. Vol. I, rev. edn. *What Students Know and Can Do*. Paris: OECD Publishing.

Organización de Estados Iberoamericanos (OEI) (2010) *2021 Metas Educativas: La Educación Que Queremos Para La Generación De Los Bicentenarios*. Madrid: OEI. http://www.oei.es/metas2021.pdf

Ozga, J., Seddon, T. & Popkewitz, T. (2006) Introduction: education research and policy – steering the knowledge-based economy, in Jenny Ozga, Terri Seddon & Thomas S. Popkewitz (Eds) *World Yearbook of Education 2006. Education Research and Policy: steering the knowledge-based economy*, pp. 1-14. Abingdon: Routledge.

Popke, E.J. (1994) Recasting Geopolitics: the discursive scripting of the International Monetary Fund, *Political Geography*, 13(3), 255-269. http://dx.doi.org/10.1016/0962-6298(94)90030-2

Robertson, S., Bonal, X. & Dale, R. (2002) GATS and the Education Service Industry: the politics of scale and global reterritorialization, *Comparative Education Review*, 46(4), 472-495. http://dx.doi.org/10.1086/343122

Schipper, M. (1997) Knowledge Is Like an Ocean: insiders, outsiders and the academy, *Research in African Literatures*, 28(4), 121-141.

Sellar, S. & Lingard, B. (2013) The OECD and Global Governance in Education, *Journal of Education Policy*, 28(5), 710-772. http://dx.doi.org/10.1080/02680939.2013.779791

Steiner-Khamsi, G. (2012) For All by All? The World Bank's Global Framework for Education, in Steven J. Klees, Joel Samoff & Nelly P. Stromquist (Eds) *The World Bank and Education: Critiques and Alternatives*, pp. 3-20. Rotterdam: Sense Publishers. http://dx.doi.org/10.1007/978-94-6091-903-9_1

Sum, N.-L. & Jessop, B. (2014) *Towards a Cultural Political Economy: putting culture in its place in political economy*. Cheltenham: Edward Elgar.

Swales, J. (1987) Approaching the Concept of a Discourse Community. Paper presented at the 38th Annual Meeting of the Conference on College Composition and Communication, Atlanta, GA, 19-21 March. http://Files.Eric.Ed.Gov/Fulltext/ED286184.pdf

Swales, J. (1990) *Genre Analysis: English in academic and research settings.* Cambridge: Cambridge University Press.

Toolan, M. (2001) *Narrative: a critical linguistic introduction*, 2nd edn. Abingdon: Routledge.

Torres, C.A. & Schugurensky, D. (2002) The Political Economy of Higher Education in the Era of Neoliberal Globalization: Latin America in comparative perspective, *Higher Education*, 43(4), 429-455. http://dx.doi.org/10.1023/A:1015292413037

World Bank (2011) *Learning for All: investing in people's knowledge and skills to promote development. Education Sector Strategy 2020.* Washington, DC: World Bank. http://siteresources.worldbank.org/EDUCATION/Resources/ESSU/Education_Strategy_4_12_2011.pdf

CHAPTER 5

Mind the Gap: reflections on boundaries and positioning in research in international and comparative education

CLAIRE PLANEL

Introduction

The gaps between classificatory systems can be powerful and creative in aiding our understanding of cultural phenomena. This chapter will explore how the concept of a 'third space', working in a classification gap, can be applied to research in international and comparative education. Reflecting back over five cross-cultural research studies, this chapter will look at the boundaries between education in different countries and compare the positioning of researchers and participants, to explore the complex and fluid areas where cultures, research and research parties can cross these national boundaries in the 'third space'.

The origins of the term derive from Bhabha's (1994) demonstration of how boundaries between unequal social groups can be a positive force in creating new genres in literature. Bhabha opened a new perspective on gaps, boundaries, frontiers and borders, which are grey areas often with more negative associations: taboos in anthropology (Leach, 1964; Douglas, 1966), and wars and humanitarian crises in politics. This new way of thinking has been taken up in different areas: art (British Council, 2015); language and communication (Kelly, 2009); trans-professional intercommunication (Hulme, 2009); and identity in cross-cultural adoption (Hübinette, 2004). It has been applied in educational research (Levy, 2008; Stein & Coburn 2007; Gutiérrez, 2008), and more particularly and saliently to this chapter, in international and comparative education (McNess et al, 2013).

National contexts are bounded entities (Broadfoot et al, 2000, pp. 42-51). The 'third space' is defined here as research in the boundaries between national contexts where differences can be explored, resulting in increased understanding not only about national contexts but about education more generally. Relativity in meanings becomes apparent, and is most pronounced, in the gaps between the value systems of different cultural groups; 'it is the "inter" – the cutting edge of translation and negotiation, the in between space – that carries the burden of the meaning of culture' (Bhabha, 1994, p. 38). Negotiation and meaning are key words in the research presented here.

Comparisons across national contexts carry with them concepts of duality and identity – them/us, self/the other(s), insider(s)/outsider(s) – which researchers have to address (Serrant-Green, 2002; Ganga, in Ganga & Scott, 2006; Mercer, 2007). For some (Merton, 1972) there are two discrete insider–outsider doctrines; for others (Banks, 1998), the situation is more complex and requires a four-part classification. It is argued here that positioning of researchers is more fluid (McNess et al, 2013; Milligan, 2014) and that new terms such as inside–outsider are needed to capture the fluidity and relativity of the role – terms which relate to factors of situation, location, time and perceptions.

The terms insider and outsider in educational research are often associated with two distinct epistemologies, philosophies and methodologies: quantitative research based on objectivism, positivism and the use of large statistical methodology uses an outsider approach; and qualitative research, based on subjectivism, interpretivism and the use of small in-depth research methods is more associated with the term insider. This rigid dualism of classification is not always helpful. It is perhaps more useful to see these two traditions as a continuum rather than an 'either/or' paradigm, with research positioned at any point between the two extremes of quantitative and qualitative research. The point on the continuum at which research in education is situated depends upon the nature of the questions the research is attempting to answer. Quantitative research gives a broad picture of trends in education; qualitative research can explain meanings through contexts. Although the extremes are clear, research often uses mixed methods (Miles & Huberman, 1994; Cresswell, 2003) to give both a broader picture from the outside and a deeper understanding of meanings from the inside. Three of the research projects described here used mixed methods. While there may be validity in associating one extremity of a theoretical and methodological continuum with an outsider perspective, and the other end of the continuum with an insider perspective, it will be seen that positioning is more complex and needs more methodological development.

This chapter will consider five research projects in which the author was a researcher who explored the embedded cultural values of several European countries. The studies are not representative of research in international and comparative education. The chapter is 'reflective', as the concept of the 'third space' is applied after the completion of the original research projects. The boundaries and meeting points between national cultures of education where national values met were explored by researchers with varied positioning, in different locations, methodologies, areas and stages of research. The parties involved were multinational researchers and, in limited cases, the participants themselves.

Study 1

The first study was the author's doctoral thesis (Planel, 2000b), which was an ethnographic comparison of primary schooling in two countries. The aim was to understand the underlying values of English and French classrooms and see how these impacted on learning. In terms of theory and methodology the study was towards the qualitative end of the scale but validity, generalisability and reproducibility were built into the research design. The conclusions were important as they highlighted the importance of context in pedagogy; the role played by the sharing of cultural understandings between teachers, pupils and parents about education in each country, that made learning effective. England and France were chosen for biographic reasons, and also because despite their geographical proximity and entwined histories the cultural values of the two countries are very different. With a single researcher who was bilingual and bicultural, the point at which the two sets of cultural values met was the researcher herself. The boundary between English and French educational values was located in the reflexivity required by ethnographic research where the researcher was the research instrument. This boundary was where national values about learning met: collectivism, teacher authoritarianism, intellectualism, rationality and negative assessment in the French context, and the individualism, empiricism, creativity and positive assessment of the English context. Teacher and pupil discourse in the classroom showed in the English context that there was less teacher dominance, pupils were expected to 'find out' for themselves, there was an emphasis on practical work and there was less structure and sequence in teaching and learning. By contrast, there was strong teacher 'scaffolding' in the French classrooms around a *leçon* (lesson); there was more emphasis on 'thinking' than on 'doing'; and more importance was given to following a structure of simple to complex in learning, with priority given to logic, method and rules. Data from pupils' perceptions showed how pupils had internalised these cultural values. It was the boundary between the two sets of values, where they confronted each other, that had made these values visible.

The bilingual bicultural researcher occupies a privileged place with one foot in each cultural system of values. Hoogvelt (1997, p. 158) describes this cultural hybridity as 'a kind of superior cultural intelligence owing to the advantage of in-betweenness, the straddling of two cultures and the consequent ability to negotiate the difference'.

When bilingualism and biculturalism do occur together, which is not a sine qua non, individuals vary in how they psychologically manage their identities and languages (Benet-Martinez et al, 2002). Bicultural individuals have to learn to be both insiders and outsiders. For the author, switching culture was similar to code switching in language; as context dictated choice of language so context dictated choice of culture – 'It is possible and acceptable to participate in two different cultures or to use two different languages, perhaps for different purposes, by alternating one's behaviour according to the situation' (Ogbu, in Ogbu & Matute-Bianchi, 1986, p. 89). Thus there was an insider identity in a French classroom as the language and context were French and there was an insider identity in an English classroom as the language and culture were English. However, it was also necessary at times to think outside the actual context and reflect as an outsider, in order to compare what was seen and heard with the context of the other country – Would what was being observed in a French classroom happen in an English classroom? Or, how would an English child have reacted to the French teacher's comment? This fluidity between functioning as an insider and an outsider became an essential research tool, developing in finesse through the five different research projects. However, true bilingualism and biculturalism are rare, as an individual's language competence may vary in different topics and registers. Thiery (1978) defines bilingualism according to the perceptions of others about social and cultural equivalence. There was not therefore a clear boundary between insider and outsider for the bicultural ethnographic researcher. Whilst biculturalism can lead negatively to psychological neurosis, particularly when set in the context of migration, it can conversely act as a positive research tool in comparative education.

Study 2

The second international and comparative study was the QUEST (Quality of Educational Systems Transnationally) project (Broadfoot et al, 2000). Again involving England and France, this was an innovative and larger study using quantitative and qualitative methodology carried out by five researchers, to explore how different national educational provision can affect children's learning and achievement. It was trying to do what large-scale international assessment studies cannot do, and link pupil achievement to context, look at the qualitative differences in achievement between national samples of pupils and answer the 'Why?' questions that are raised by large-scale studies. Researchers worked between the boundaries of national and cultural values at all stages of the research process.

A fundamental part of the design of the research instruments was the negotiation required in the gap between English national culture in education and French national culture in education, to create interview schedules and assessments in language (English or French) and maths which would have national contextual validity. In both assessment and interview schedule design it is important to note that unlike PISA surveys (OECD, 2012), which are conceived in English, translated into French, then use double language translation, neither was developed in one language and then translated into another, but they were conceived in joint understanding or 'parallel development' of conceptual and language differences (Poortinga 1993; Williams, 1994). First, looking at the pupil questionnaire, researchers had to negotiate in the gap between two sets of cultural values to resolve the problem of how to formulate a question that would elicit pupil perceptions about pupils' relative achievements in class. At the time, English cultural values were still influenced by the idea that achievement was based on an individual child's perceived abilities; each child should do their best but it was understood that some children would do better than others. Contrastingly in France, all children were expected to reach a certain level each year, leading in a succession of steps to Baccalaureate pass or fail selection at the end of secondary schooling. Researcher negotiation in this boundary between different cultural understandings led to formulating a normative assessment question in English – 'Why do you think some children do better at school than others?' and a criterion-referenced assessment question in French – '*A ton avis pourquoi certains élèves réussisent-ils mieux que d'autres a l'école?*' ('Why do you think some children succeed more than others?')

Looking at the design of the language and maths assessments, researchers explored how the cultural values of the two countries were embedded in the national curricula and assessments. Stein and Coburn (2007, p. 7), in their work on fostering similar pedagogy across different education districts in the United States, have developed Wenger's (1998) concept of 'reification' to describe the ideas inherent in district policy documents: 'We use reification to mean a concrete object that embodies a set of ideas or processes.' Here, reification is extended and developed to mean national educational texts which embody national cultural values about education. Thus the English and French curricula and the national assessments carried out in each country towards the end of primary schooling are reifications. They contain not only the content of what is to be studied, but also cultural values about what is important in education (Planel, 2000a). The analysis of curricula showed that English education valued width and 'openness' to learning and that French education valued more depth and relative 'closedness'. For example, in the maths assessments English questions were often not straightforward. They often required good language skills, and a combination of different maths skills in one item. French questions were more straightforward. In the testing of computational skills, a French item was clearly testing multiplication, whereas in the English equivalent, the item was set out as a division item with a missing number, so that pupils had to use more extended mathematical skills to understand that what was required was multiplication. Similarly in the language papers the French paper was more 'closed' in the sense that items in the reading comprehensions were more factual and contextual, and writing tasks required pupils to follow structural guidelines. In contrast, items in English reading comprehension were more co-textual and inferential, and writing tasks gave more encouragement to pupils to create their own ideas. The results of the assessments showed that each national sample performed better at their own national test items. Thus, reification in the content and presentation of national assessments is important as it suggests that international tests will lack equal cultural validity.

Another term, 'boundary object', also from Stein and Coburn (2007, p. 6), is useful to describe national curricula and assessment data. Stein and Coburn use the term to describe reifications that cross educational districts to develop the sharing of ideas and practices. Boundary objects are redefined here as reifications from one national context that come into contact with reifications from a different national context. Thus a comparative analysis of boundary objects – for example, national assessments – allows researchers in international and comparative research to explore meanings in different national contexts.

Whereas in the first study the 'third space' took place in the reflexivity of one researcher who was both an insider and an outsider, the positioning of researchers in the QUEST project was more complex. Schratz (1992, p. 3) argues that using insider–outsiders provides 'a three way' understanding of culture. The two bilingual research assistants occupied two roles: first, the same positioning as the researcher in the PhD project; and second, as mediators in the QUEST research team. Terms such as 'hybrid' (Hooguelt 1997) and 'broker' (Stein & Coburn, 2007) have been used to describe the function that individuals who are both insiders and outsiders have in interpreting meaning and understanding across boundaries. To avoid any alternative semantic associations of 'hybrids' and 'brokers', the term 'mediator' is preferred here to describe the bilingual and bicultural researcher's facilitating role of mediating understandings across the boundaries of national cultures in an international research team. The rest of the QUEST team were also academics with considerable research experience in comparative work in England and France; they were thus able to position themselves as insiders and outsiders as the situation demanded. Positioning occurred between researchers at all stages of research, including marking of assessments. Meetings were always held in England as QUEST was an English research study. Through negotiation, with researchers moving between insider and outsider positions, understanding about the similarities and differences in the educational and cultural systems of the two countries was developed.

Lastly, a further example of positioning took place in a small sample of cross-cultural research participants. These were the 'movers'. As the term implies, these were young children who had 'moved' – that is, taken part in a six-month exchange programme in English and French primary schools. Their discourse – not, incidentally, reported in the QUEST project – was set mostly in an outsider framework. Most of the children, most of the time, used the third-person plural, 'They', '*Ils*', to describe the rest of the class in the other country. Sometimes their discourse did tend towards a more insider positioning with the use of 'You', '*On*', but there were no examples in their accounts of the insider positioning implied by 'We', '*Nous*'. Their contributions, as outsiders, about what happens on the other side of the boundary of another country's classrooms provided illuminating data (Broadfoot et al, 2000, p. 68). An English girl reported about the class teacher's authoritarianism:

> It was really weird because even when she was telling them off and bringing them to tears, they got like upset, but they just kind of took it as her, because they really, I don't know, they had this strong bond with her, they liked her which is strange, because she wasn't a nice lady. They just kind of thought ... she's doing it for my best ... like it's fine what she's doing.

These young cross-cultural research participants were not expected, nor asked, to develop their understanding about the meaning of what they had observed, but this girl had gone some way to understand**ING** the difference between how French pupils viewed school, their motivation and their resulting relationship with a class teacher, compared with English pupils.

Study 3

The third study presented here is the ENCOMPASS project (Osborn et al, 2003), which was set up to explore secondary pupils' educational experiences, and their attitudes to schooling and learning in England, Denmark and France. This was a research project that used a multinational team made up of researchers from each of the three countries, and quantitative and qualitative methodology, to explore the role of national culture in pupils' learning. Although the study was more complex and involved a larger team of researchers, much of what has been written here about the QUEST project and its setting in the 'third space' is applicable to ENCOMPASS. Thus the whole project, from initial meetings to discuss aims and to set up the project, the design of research instruments, data gathering, interpretation of results and writing up of findings, involved a team of researchers moving across the boundaries of national cultures as both insiders and outsiders. However, there were two additions to the research design which were important for their contribution to the development of the concept of the 'third space' in international and comparative research. The first, which is referred to in Chapter 1 of this book, was the innovation of team members who were 'outsiders' in informing research questions, designing research instruments, carrying out data collection and taking part in analysis in what was essentially an inside-outsider corroborative team. Outsider researchers also supplemented observational data by contributing their perspective, specifically from another country. This brought another dimension of meaning, extra to researchers who were fluidly moving between insider and outsider positions in the countries concerned. Of course the degree to which researchers were fluid inside-outsiders varied, as did their ability to move as inside-outsiders in all three countries. Not only did outsiders have a role to play in the research, but insiders were also important in the research process as they were consulted at different stages of research to corroborate understandings. In this complex situation, the role of inside-outsiders was an important one, as it was they who mediated with researchers who were true outsiders as well as mediating with researchers who were more strongly insiders than outsiders in any given national context. Furthermore, inside-outsider positioning developed during research so that by the end of the project researchers had boosted their skills in positioning themselves as inside-outsiders in all three countries. The strange had become familiar. Another aspect of insider–outsider, which involved using findings from quantitative data to inform qualitative data collection, was built into the project. Pupils' insider perceptions, chosen from the open-ended items of a questionnaire completed by 1800 young people from the three countries, were then used as stimulus for discussion in group interviews across the three countries. For example:

> A teacher should be a kind of friend. (English)
>
> A good school is one that has a feeling of togetherness. (Danish)
>
> A good pupil is one that always does good work. (French)

While this 'spiral of understanding' approach (Lacey, 1976) was not innovative, in a multinational study it required negotiation by inside-outsider researchers in the choice of the items and their translation into the other two languages.

The second innovation in the 'third space' was the inclusion of an explicit enquiry into the boundary object of national policy discourses, as these are reifications of what is valued within a country. Working within the boundary of where the three countries' policy documents met, it became clear that despite many similarities, the focus at the time in the English policy documents was the individual child and innate abilities, the emphasis in France was a need for equity and a common experience, and in Denmark there was 'a dual focus on the personal development of individuals, linked to the need for co-operation and collaboration' (Osborn et al, 2003, p. 42). Another boundary object used in the study was documentation at the school level, including school prospectuses, policy documents and school development plans. Boundary objects were an essential part of the ENCOMPASS project as its aim was to explore how 'young people construct their identities as learners, in the light of different national policy priorities, school structures and teacher practices' (Osborn et al, 2003, p. 205).

Studies 4 and 5

The last two studies to be considered here are based on very different models of research in international and comparative education, but their contributions to understanding research work in the 'third space' are important. In the fourth study (Planel, 2009), the content of the research was essentially the same as the three other studies – looking at cultural values in English and French schools and how they frame pupils' learning. However, this study was methodologically very different. First, it was a very small qualitative study. Second, the research participants were not pupils or teachers but trainee teachers who were taking part in a joint training programme between English and French teacher training university providers. They had recently carried out classroom placements in each other's countries. Third, the role of the researcher, who led workshops with groups from the ten English and ten French primary teacher trainees, was also very different. The researcher's role was more of a teacher and mediator in small group workshops, guiding teacher trainees as they reflected on their experiences of pedagogy in the classrooms of the 'other' country. In this study it was the research participants who were working in the 'third space'. The boundary between the two value systems of each other's countries was so great that the teacher trainees were not always able to recognise those moments when the learning of new concepts, skills or facts was taking place. They expressed this mutual lack of understanding of the act of teaching in the 'other' country:

> I definitely didn't understand why they were teaching in the way they were teaching. (English trainee)

> I didn't really understand how the lessons functioned. (English trainee)

> J'ai pas eu l'impression d'avoir vraiment vu une leçon avec une trace ècrite [I don't think I really saw a lesson with any written evidence] (French trainee)

It has been suggested (Planel, 2008) that with the researcher/teacher as cultural translator, the trainees moved from an initial outsider stage of cultural shock to a second stage where they were able to cross cultural boundaries, start to understand pedagogy in the 'other' country, as well as critique that of their own country. Some trainees were entering a third stage of a deeper understanding of pedagogy in general – they were becoming inside-outsiders. An English teacher trainee in another institute commented of their own trainees:

> All of them have engaged in informal and spontaneous and comparative studies of their own, so startled were they by differences between the two educational systems.

In complete contrast, the final study to be considered here was a much larger and quantitative study comparing the teaching of reading and pupils' achievement in reading in England, France and Luxembourg (Andrieux et al, 2002). Building on the QUEST project, the aim was to explore whether there were qualitative differences in children's performance at reading which might be related to how reading was taught in the three countries. The research instruments used were: reading assessments of final-year primary school pupils; pupil questionnaires about attitudes to reading; teacher questionnaires about pedagogy and reading; and, finally, classroom observations of the teaching of reading. The positioning of researchers varied according to the stages of research. The setting up of the study, the research instruments and managing the study involved insiders from one country meeting insiders from another country, with little inside-outsider mediation. In developing research instruments, which were representative and culturally valid in the three countries, researchers had to negotiate across national boundaries. National reading assessments were explicit boundary objects which were used in the setting up of research instruments. However, the model used in carrying out the research was that of insiders working in their respective countries. Thus sampling, classroom observations, questionnaire coding and test marking were carried out by insiders. Statistical analysis was divided up between the three countries and the study was written up by the French team. Furthermore, the insider role differed from that of the other studies. The study was instigated by the European Union and involved not only universities, but also ministries of education, or, in the English case, the government agency the Qualifications and Curriculum Authority. The study was ambitious. It was exploring qualitative differences in reading and linking them to teaching practice in the classroom using quantitative methods only. Although the research was in international and comparative education, some countries had an additional agenda of exploring the teaching of reading together with pupil performance specifically in their own country.

There were some general cross-cultural conclusions: each national sample of pupils performed best at its own national tests and English pupils performed better at open-ended test items than did their peers in France and Luxembourg, which confirmed the QUEST findings; also, English pupils were more likely to prefer reading poetry than their peers; for French pupils it was magazines, and for Luxembourg pupils it was factual texts. However, the study failed to relate pedagogy to reading performance cross-culturally (Andrieux et al, 2002, p. 102), which had been the aim of the study. Nationally, the findings were beneficial to each country; both England and Luxembourg produced their own reports for their educational systems.

While methodological reasons, such as the classroom observations of how reading was taught, were put forward for the study's limitations, it is suggested here that the study would have benefited from more understanding and engagement across the boundaries of national cultural values. In conclusion, what emerged from this multinational study was a greater understanding of the teaching of reading and children's achievements within each country but not across countries. The difficulties encountered were those fundamental methodological problems (Osborn, 2004) of conceptual equivalence, equivalence of measure, linguistic equivalence and sampling, and problems associated with international and comparative research, which require negotiation in the 'third space'.

Conclusion

Several themes underlie the five studies presented here. Each study shared the broad aim of exploring the relationship between pupil learning and national contexts. In exploring differences between national contexts, researchers had to negotiate meanings in the gaps between different systems of values. The crossing of boundaries required the understanding that meaning was related to national context. Such basic terms as *teacher*, *pupil*, *teaching*, *learning*, *pupil*, *school*, *classroom*, *lesson*, *assessment* and *work*, whose meaning might be self-evident in one national context, had different meanings in another national context. These meanings related to socio-historical cultural values. The theoretical basis of the studies was socio-constructivism. Teachers taught and pupils learnt according to shared national understandings about school.

Table I shows a comparison of research and the main themes in the five studies. The maximum number of countries was three. Alexander (2001), in his in-depth work on the relationship between culture and pedagogy, included five countries. PISA's 2012 survey (OECD, 2012) covered 65 countries. It may well be that 'third space' research is more appropriate to a small number of countries as it is difficult to envisage how the initial setting up of research, design of instruments, and addressing of differences in meanings can function in studies involving large numbers of countries. Breadth takes over in priority from depth.

Name of study	Number of countries	Methodology	Research in the 'Third Space'		Positioning of researchers	Use of boundary objects
			Researchers	Participants		
PhD	2	Qualitative	Yes	No	Inside-outsider	Implicit
QUEST	2	Qualitative and Quantitative	Yes	Yes (movers)	Inside-outsiders, insiders	Implicit and explicit
ENCOMPASS	3	Qualitative and Quantitative	Yes	No	Inside-outsiders, insiders, outsiders	Implicit and explicit
Teacher Trainees	2	Qualitative	Yes	Yes	Inside-outsiders	No
Reading Assessment	3	Quantitative	Some	No	Insiders, minimal inside-outsider	Some implicit, some explicit

Table I. The main themes of the five studies.

There was variation in the emphasis the studies gave to qualitative, quantitative or mixed methodologies. Studies such as QUEST and ENCOMPASS, where work in the 'third space' occurred at all stages of the research process, showed that quantitative methods could be used to explore qualitative issues provided there had been sufficient prior engagement in the negotiation of meanings across national contexts. The reading-assessment study, despite its initial aims, was methodologically closer to large-scale quantitative studies such as PISA. In order to fully carry out its research aims it is suggested that it would have been more successful had there been more inside-outsider input at all stages of the research process.

Reflection on the studies gave rise to the concept of boundary objects and the accompanying idea of reification. Boundary objects, such as national assessments or national aims in education, and their analysis for cultural values could be either an implicit part of research (the PhD) or an explicit part of research (ENCOMPASS). A further example of a boundary object in the 'third space' which could have been used is the school textbook (Bierhoff, 1996; Howson et al, 1999); another potential boundary object is the school report.

The five studies have yielded interesting material about the positioning of researchers and research itself. First, the professional status of researchers may affect research aims and outcomes (Crossley, 2014, p. 17). It is suggested that the four studies that were led by seasoned comparativists engaged more with meanings across national contexts than the reading-assessment study which was led by ministry-funded researchers. The latter were closer to PISA researchers who are technical and statistical experts, often from large-scale economies.

Second, researchers could also be participants, as occurred in two of the studies. In the teacher trainee study, trainee positioning developed from that of outsiders whose ethnocentric assumptions about learning prevented them from understanding the pedagogy they experienced in the classrooms of the other country, to that of inside-outsiders. Their perceptions triangulated the findings of researchers about the framing of learning by national contexts. They were termed 'cross-cultural participants' to distinguish them from research participants from within only one country.

Third, positioning roles were explored. The term *inside-outsider* was preferred to *inside outsider*, as the hyphenation captures the duality of meaning. The hyphenation also suggests the concept's fluidity as it implies that there is movement between two words, 'inside', 'outside', and two worlds. The two worlds are not separate but are bound together in one individual who moves between cultural boundaries according to national context and situation. Inside-outsiders mediate between national cultures and translate cultural concepts, in the same way as an interpreter translates meaning between two languages. The positioning of researchers influences research outcomes. It is a given that research including inside-outsider positioning will be culturally more valid to the countries involved.

As well as fluidity, the inside-outsider role also includes relativity – the degree of insiderness and outsiderness can vary. Positioning is relative, depending on not only professional occupation, but also individual experience and mastery. Second, it is relative according to the perceptions of different actors. 'True' bilingualism and 'true' inside-outsider positioning are rare. While researchers may identify themselves as inside-outsiders, they may be defined as outsiders by research participants and insiders within another country. This suggests that location is a second factor. A third factor in relativity is time and change. Cross-cultural participants were seen to change from outsider positioning to inside-outsiders. Similarly, academics who build up an in-depth cultural understanding of two or more countries acquire the status of inside-outsiders, in the same way as good linguists master another language, even though they will not have equal mastery of both languages and both cultures. Inside-outsidership is thus a skill which can change over time, developing in fluency like a language. To conclude, it is suggested that the inside-outsider concept is both fluid and relative. There is variation in the degree of equitability in 'inside-outsidership' within the one researcher as well as between different researchers. There is relativity depending on the perceptions of others, location and time.

The reading-assessment study suggests that even with the inclusion of fluidity and relativity, the three positioning terms of insider, outsider and inside-outsider are not sufficient. Researchers in this study were specialist insiders who negotiated with minimal inside-outsider mediation to achieve a research aim which was not so much 'outside', or even 'inside' each country, as it was 'above'. There are some similarities with PISA surveys. PISA aims for objectivity and cultural validity by attempting to be culture free. Tests are developed which are not directly linked to school curricula and which assess the extent to which students can apply their knowledge to real-life situations. Arguably positioning is 'above'. However, actual positioning – 'above', 'outside' or 'inside-outside' – may be relative to the degree a country taking part in PISA participates as an insider, or the degree to which a country's educational and cultural values match those of insider countries.

The conclusions from this comparison of five studies are twofold. First, the studies, which had the broadly similar aim of exploring national cultural backgrounds to learning, show that the 'third space' can be pertinent to research in international and comparative education. National boundaries in education should neither be ignored nor assumed to have no existence, nor should they be viewed as barriers. On the contrary, it was seen that national boundaries have a very positive role to play in research. 'third space' research crosses national boundaries of meanings. In the five studies it was negotiation about meanings in the gaps and between the boundaries of cultural values that allowed underlying cultural understandings about learning, which could affect pupils' achievements, to rise to the surface. The role of the 'third space' needs to be explored in a greater variety of studies before an attempt is made to develop a theory of the 'third space' in international and comparative education.

Second, and to add to the ongoing debate about 'cultural borrowings' (Crossley, 2014), positioning needs to be rethought. Positioning of researchers is bound up with the positioning of research. It is argued here that positioning is an extra methodological dimension, which should be included, along with the quantitative–qualitative continuum, under the umbrella of 'big data' (Mayer-Schönberger & Cukier, 2013; Uprichard 2013), for it is not only researchers who need to take positioning into account. In evaluating a research project and its implications for national policy implementation, policy makers, whether in education or indeed international development, should consider not only whether a research project was qualitative or quantitative but also the degree to which research positioning was from the inside (the bottom-up approach from within the country), the outside (explicitly outsider research, as in ENCOMPASS), the inside-outside (research working between and across national boundaries) or 'above' (outside research from countries with large-scale economies, with some technical inside consultation). This would allow policy makers to assess the role played by context in research, and thus the cultural validity and relevance of research for their national context, before making and introducing new policies.

References

Alexander, R. (2001) *Culture and Pedagogy: international comparisons in primary education.* Malden, MA: Blackwell.

Andrieux, V., Bonnet, G., Cholet, P., et al (2002) *Enseignement et Compétences en Lecture à la Fin de la Scolarité dans Trois Pays Européens.* Paris: Réseau Europén des Responsables des Politiques d'Evaluation des Systemes Educatifs.

Banks, J. (1998) The Lives and Values of Researchers: implications for educating citizens in a multicultural society, *Educational Researcher*, 27(7), 4-17. http://dx.doi.org/10.3102/0013189X027007004

Benet-Martınez, V., Leu, J., Lee, F. & Morris, M. (2002) Negotiating Biculturalism: cultural frame-switching in biculturals with oppositional vs. compatible cultural identities, *Journal of Cross-cultural Psychology*, 33, 492-516. http://dx.doi.org/10.1177/0022022102033005005

Bhabha, Homi, K. (1994) *The Location of Culture.* London: Routledge.

Bierhoff, H. (1996) Laying Foundations of Numeracy: a comparison of primary school textbooks in Britain, Germany and Switzerland. Discussion Paper no. 90, National Institute of Economic and Social Research.

British Council (2015) Syria: third space. http://www.britishcouncil.org/arts/syria-third-space/#sthash.L6ghFH1F.dpuf

Broadfoot, P., Osborn, M., Planel, C. & Sharp, K. (2000) *Promoting Quality in Learning.* London: Cassell.

Creswell, J. (2003) *Research Design, Qualitative, Quantitative, and Mixed Methods Approaches.* London: SAGE.

Crossley, M. (2014) Global League Tables, Big Data and the International Transfer of Educational Transfer of Educational Research Modalities, *Comparative Education*, 40(1), 15-26. http://dx.doi.org/10.1080/03050068.2013.871438

Douglas, M. (1966) *Purity and Danger: an analysis of concepts of pollution and taboo.* London: Routledge. http://dx.doi.org/10.4324/9780203361832

Ganga, D. & Scott, S. (2006) Cultural 'Insiders' and the Issue of Positioning in Qualitative Migration Research: moving 'across' and moving 'along' researcher–participant divides, *FQS Forum: qualitative social research*, 7(3), Art. 7.

Gutiérrez, K.D. (2008) Developing a Sociocritical Literacy in the Third Space, *Reading Research Quarterly*, 43(2), 148-164. http://dx.doi.org/10.1598/RRQ.43.2.3

Hoogvelt, A. (1997) *Globalisation and the Postcolonial World: the new political economy of development*. Baltimore: Johns Hopkins University Press.

Howson, G., Harries, T. & Sutherland, R.J. (1999) *Primary School Mathematics Textbooks: an international study summary*. London: Qualifications & Curriculum Authority.

Hübinette, T. (2004) Adopted Koreans and the Development of Identity in the 'Third Space', *Adoption & Fostering*, 28(1) (April), 16-24.

Hulme, R., Cracknell, D. & Owens, A. (2009) Learning in Third Spaces: developing trans-professional understanding through practitioner enquiry, *Educational Action Research*, 17(4), 537-550. http://dx.doi.org/10.1080/09650790903309391

Kelly, M. (2009) A Third Space for Europe: intercultural communication in European language policy, *European Journal of Language Policy*, 1(1), 1-20. http://dx.doi.org/10.3828/ejlp.1.1.2

Lacey, C. (1976) Problems of Sociological Fieldwork: a review of methodology of Hightown Grammar, in M. Hammersley & P. Woods (Eds) *The Process of Schooling*. London: Routledge.

Leach, E. (1964) Anthropological Aspects of Language, Animal Categories and Verbal Abuse, in S. Hugh-Jones & J. Laidlaw (Eds) *The Essential Edmund Leach*, vol. I, pp. 322-343. New Haven, CT: Yale University Press.

Levy, R. (2008). 'Third Spaces' Are Interesting Places: applying 'third space theory' to nursery-aged children's constructions of themselves as readers, *Journal of Early Childhood Literacy*, 8(1), 43-66.

Mayer-Schönberger, V. & Cukier, K. (2013) *Big Data: a revolution that will transform how we live, work and think*. London: John Murray.

McNess, E., Arthur, L. & Crossley, M. (2013) 'Ethnographic Dazzle' and the Construction of the 'Other': revisiting dimensions of insider and outsider research for international and comparative education, *Compare*, 45(2), 295-316. http://dx.doi.org/10.1080/03057925.2013.854616

Mercer, J. (2007) The Challenges of Insider Research in Educational Institutions: wielding a double-edged sword and resolving delicate dilemmas, *Oxford Review of Education*, 33(1), 1-17. http://dx.doi.org/10.1080/03054980601094651

Merton, R.K. (1972) Insider and Outsiders: a chapter in the sociology of knowledge, *American Journal of Sociology*, 78(1), 9-47. http://dx.doi.org/10.1086/225294

Miles, M. & Huberman A. (1994) *Qualitative Data Analysis*, 2nd edn. London: SAGE.

Milligan, E. (2014) Insider–outsider–inbetweener? Researcher Positioning, Participative Methods and Cross-cultural Educational Research, *Compare*, published online 26 June. http://dx.doi.org/10.1080/03057925.2014.928510

Ogbu, J.U. & Matute-Bianchi, M.A. (1986) Understanding Sociocultural Factors: knowledge, identity, and social adjustment, in California State Department of Education, Bilingual Education Office, *Beyond Language: social and cultural factors in schooling*, pp. 73-142. Sacramento: California State University–Los Angeles, Evaluation, Dissemination and Assessment Center.

Organisation for Economic Co-operation and Development (OECD) (2012) PISA 2012 Technical Report. http://www.oecd.org/pisa/pisaproducts/pisa2012technicalreport.htm

Osborn, M. (2004) New Methodologies for Comparative Research? Establishing 'Constants' and 'Contexts' in Educational Experience, *Oxford Review of Education*, 30(2), 265-285.

Osborn, M., Broadfoot, P., McNess, E., Planel, C., Ravn, B., Triggs, P. (2003) *A World of Difference? Comparing Learners across Europe*, Maidenhead: Open University Press.

Planel, C. (2000a) National Assessments: underlying cultural values revealed by comparing English and French national tests, *European Journal of Education*, 35(3), 361-374. http://dx.doi.org/10.1111/1467-3435.00032

Planel, C. (2000b) Two Worlds Two Minds: an ethnographic study of primary schooling in England and France. http://www.ethos.bl.uk/.

Planel, C. (2008) The Rise and Fall of Comparative Education: should it rise again as comparative pedagogy? *Compare*, 38(4), 385-399. http://dx.doi.org/10.1080/03057920701467867

Planel, C. (2009) Les Pratiques de Classe, partie émergée de l'iceberg des valeurs culturelles, *Revue Internationale d'Education*, 50, 75-86. http://dx.doi.org/10.4000/ries.519

Poortinga, Y. (1993) Use of Tests across Cultures, in W. Lonner & J. Berry (Eds) *Field Methods in Cross Cultural Psychology*, pp 17-46. Newbury Park, CA: SAGE.

Schratz, M. (1992) *Qualitative Voices in Educational Experience*. Basingstoke: Falmer Press.

Serrant-Green, L. (2002) Black on Black: methodological issues for black researchers working in minority ethnic communities, *Nurse Researcher*, 9, 30-44. http://dx.doi.org/10.7748/nr2002.07.9.4.30.c6196

Stein, M. & Coburn, C. (2007) Architectures for Learning: a comparative analysis of two urban school districts, *American Journal of Education*, 114, 583-626. http://dx.doi.org/10.1086/589315

Thiery, C. (1978) True Bilingualism and Second-language Learning, in D. Gerver & H. Sinaiko (Eds) *Language, Interpretation and Communication*, pp. 145-153. New York: Plenum Press.

Uprichard, E. (2013) Focus: big data, little questions? http://www.discoversociety.org/focus-big-data-little-questions (accessed 1 October 2013).

Wenger, E. (1998) *Communities of Practice: learning, meaning, and identity.* Cambridge: Cambridge University Press. http://dx.doi.org/10.1017/CBO9780511803932

Williams, D. (1994) Creating Matched National Curriculum Assessment in English and Welsh: test translation and parallel development, *Curriculum Journal*, 5(1), 17-29.

CHAPTER 6

Methodological Challenges: negotiation, critical reflection and the cultural other

NICOLA SAVVIDES, JOANNA AL-YOUSSEF,
MINDY COLIN & CECILIA GARRIDO

Introduction

During every research journey the production of ethical and credible research depends on researchers reflecting critically and being transparent about the methodological issues and challenges they face, including how their background and position as insider or outsider might shape the generation and interpretation of data (Court & Abbas, 2013). In this chapter we consider influences that challenge traditional methodological dichotomies of insider/outsider and self/other (defined by characteristics such as gender, ethnicity, language and professional status) as we recognise the limitations of these dichotomies in considering both our own role as researchers and that of our participants.

Postmodern movements have led to the transformation of the qualitative researcher from an 'unreflective holder of power and knowledge to reflective participant in the co-construction of knowledge together with research subjects' (Court & Abbas, 2013, p. 486). The qualitative researcher is not, therefore, 'a "miner", digging facts out of the ground' to produce authoritative and objective research outputs, but rather 'a "traveller", meeting people and experiencing different landscapes on his or her research journeys' (Court & Abbas, 2013, p. 486). Thus, researchers and participants recognise that there is a level of instability in their relationship (Filmer et al, 1998), and their interactions can be deconstructed to better understand the underlying realities and reformulate assumptions to produce valid outcomes. The message from qualitative researchers across disciplines is that understanding the dichotomies posed by the insider/outsider debate enables them to become aware of the implications of occupying 'the space between' (Dwyer & Buckle, 2009, p. 54) insider/outsider positions and how this impacts on the research process and on the production of ethical and credible research.

In the next sections we reflect on the theoretical and methodological considerations and implications of the insider/outsider debate for qualitative research in international educational settings and illustrate this discussion with a collection of four research vignettes. We argue that although the dichotomies exist, researchers need to go beyond their rhetoric and challenge the traditional insider/outsider positioning through critical reflexivity to recognise changes in researcher positionality throughout the research. We first challenge existing discourses of self/other and insider/outsider, noting that identity and belonging do not emerge from static conceptual categories, but from fluid engagement between researchers and participants. We then develop further Dwyer and Buckle's (2009) notion of the space between insider and outsider positions in qualitative research. This leads to our examination of the role of critical reflexivity (Alvesson & Sköldberg, 2000) in analysing researcher and participant actions and identity (trans)formation (Ybema et al, 2009). This, we argue, is important for working towards ethical and credible research as it enables the researcher to consider and make transparent how changes in their positionality and identity impact on the entire research process. We then exemplify these concepts with experiences in which we negotiated our roles and positions throughout the research process in order to co-construct knowledge with participants (Hammersley, 1993; Labaree, 2002).

Self and Other

The process underlying qualitative research involves a set of social interactions between the researcher and participants as well as between these parties and the broader context in which the research takes place (Gu et al, 2010). The tensions between a researcher's agency and the norms, processes and forces that govern research structures have given rise to the notion of the 'Cultural Other' (Sanderson, 2004, p. 1), 'us' and 'them', and the interaction between both. During the research process, the researcher is also in constant dialogue with the demands of the research subject matter and the research process itself, and with the social and academic norms of the research context. The Cultural Other, embodied in research by researchers and participants, can be seen as a threat and a challenge to familiar norms and contexts, thus causing fear of the unknown and reluctance to engage with Otherness. This discourse of us and them has defined boundaries between the researchers and the researched, drawing lines and creating the polarities of insider (us and what we know about the Cultural Other) and outsider (them and what we ignore about the Cultural Other).

Initial arguments about the advantages and/or disadvantages of being on one side or the other of the us/them divide placed researchers strictly as insiders or outsiders (Merton, 1972; Surra & Ridley, 1991; Christensen & Dahl, 1997). As a result of the divide between the researcher and the researched, many of the methodologies familiar to qualitative researchers are based on the assumption that certain individuals belong to fixed groups, otherising them and treating them as outsiders. These polarised positions have generated many debates regarding the credibility of research generated from an insider or outsider perspective. Among other things, these include debates regarding access, bias, culture shock, realistic cultural interpretations, and trust or acceptance as a member of the community (Sherif, 2001; Labaree, 2002; Kusow, 2003; Hellawell, 2006; Braithwaite et al, 2007).

However, we argue that these debates are fundamentally flawed because they do not take into account individuals' multiple identities, which enable them to move fluidly between groups (McNess et al, 2012). The debates also ignore individuals' agency in relation to the structures they interact with. An added level of complexity for the researcher is introduced by the identity conflicts brought about by the researcher's dual or even triple identity as self (both as an individual and as a researcher) and societally as part of the research community. These multiple identities give rise to what Ybema et al (2009, p. 301) call identity formation, seen as the development of a negotiated outcome between the researcher's internal aspirations and value systems, external prescriptions, and the labelling that may have arisen from the interplay of these preconceptions.

Other challenges arise when researchers get caught in a power conflict resulting from perceived differences in status between the research players. Both inside knowledge and outside observations are vulnerable to perceptions of how knowledge is being represented and interpreted (Mullings, 1999; Labaree, 2002). Researchers are accountable for their representation of knowledge and realities in their research outcomes and, in their role as insiders and/or outsiders, are equally at risk of being accused of portraying inaccurate representations. Thus, the methodologies that inherently define qualitative research boundaries need to change to allow researchers to view their roles and those of participants as overlapping, multidimensional, blended together, and depending on a variety of factors including social, cultural and spatial contexts.

It is clear that the above-mentioned challenges are difficult to resolve when approached from the traditionally polarised definitions of insider or outsider. There is, therefore, a need for other perspectives (e.g. poststructuralist, postmodernist or postcolonial) that allow agency and context to blur the boundaries between insider and outsider, and consider qualitative researchers as 'multiple insiders and outsiders' (Labaree, 2002, p. 102). By being both insiders and outsiders, repeatedly involved and estranged (Hammersley, 1993), qualitative researchers operate in a fluid space somewhere between the two, stepping from one to the other with 'a new understanding of the inside' (Labaree, 2002, p. 110) and, we argue, thereby generating more credible and valid research outcomes.

The Space Between

Identity negotiation and (trans)formation, as mentioned above, is a phenomenon common to qualitative researchers because, as Dwyer and Buckle (2009, p. 61) point out, they 'cannot retreat to a distant "researcher" role. Just as our personhood affects the analysis, so, too, the analysis affects our personhood. Within this circle of impact is the space between'. There is a fluidity and amorphousness to the space between that is somewhat governed by the qualitative methodology a researcher chooses. Ethnographic and action research, for example, force the researcher to be both a researcher and a participant *at the same time* (Sherif, 2001; Braithwaite et al, 2007). However, other qualitative methodologies are comparatively less contingent on creating trusting relationships with participants, and may occupy a less complex insider/outsider space than ethnographic and action research studies.

Hellawell (2006) suggests that qualitative researchers can explore, methodologically, their own degree of insiderness or outsiderness by thinking of the space between as containing many linked continua of values, social mores, cultural tones, and other contextual elements that have proven difficult to reconcile from a structuralist approach. Many of the cultural and contextual aspects of the space between are what link these continua together and allow the researcher to negotiate many aspects of the research process as governed by their chosen methodology. Attending to these continua can help the researcher critically reflect on and account for methodological issues that arise from context, multiple identities and culture.

Merriam et al (2001) describe three of these linked continua as positionality, power and representation. 'Positionality is thus determined by where one stands in relation to "the other". More importantly, these positions can shift' (p. 411) on the basis of cultural factors that make up the positionality sub-continua, such as race, religion, gender, language, family ties, education, marital status and age. According to Kusow (2003), acknowledging these positionality factors, and their interconnectedness, can help the researcher examine their position in relation to them, their participants, and the research context. Thus, the researcher must become aware not only of the cultural norms of their participants, but also of their own norms, biases, prejudices, positions, fears and self-imposed barriers in regard to these factors as well (Sanderson, 2004).

Positionality becomes closely intertwined with power continua as local cultural norms affect the negotiation of rapport between a researcher and his/her participants, particularly in local political, economic, social and historical discourses (Merriam et al, 2001). The balance of power between the researcher and participants is also linked to how the participants are represented by the researcher. By acknowledging that they move fluidly in a space between inside and outside, researchers can manipulate their position on the sub-continua to establish common empathy. This way the research outcomes are more likely to be negotiated achievements in which both the researcher and the researched are authentically represented.

Researchers can account for positionality, power and representation issues by recognising that 'the constant shifting of boundaries between people becomes an important part of the research process' (Sherif, 2001, p. 435). These elements introduce the necessity of continual critical reflexivity regarding the researcher's decisions and how they effect changes on relevant continua in that study's space between. Stepping in and out, or fluidly inhabiting the space between, allows engagement with otherness and creates 'a necessity to dis-engage with one's own identity and self-reflect on its construction' (Sanderson 2004, p. 15).

Understanding Positionality through Critical Reflexivity

The role of reflexivity as an approach for ensuring methodological rigour (Nilan, 2002) is widely recognised, yet how and why reflexivity ought to be used during the research process, particularly within international studies whereby researchers often operate in transnational contexts, still requires theorisation and debate (Subedi, 2006; Dwyer & Buckle, 2009).

The literature on reflexivity highlights the need for qualitative researchers to be open, accountable and ethical in the research process in two key ways: (1) in terms of the researcher acknowledging how they have conducted and been involved in the research and produced knowledge (Hellawell, 2006; Subedi, 2006; Sultana, 2007); and (2) in terms of the researcher being upfront about their own identities, backgrounds and epistemological perspectives (Subedi, 2006). These help reduce some of the concerns associated with insider/outsider membership (Dwyer & Buckle, 2009). Reflexivity also enables the researcher to support their claims by demonstrating accountability and transparency regarding their analysis and interpretations according to their stated positionality (Mullings, 1999). Reflexivity also helps ensure that participatory research is built on good trusting relationships between the researcher and their participants (Sultana, 2007), and that the researcher is responding to the complex nature of ethical dilemmas during fieldwork (Subedi, 2006).

Van Heugten (2004) stresses that the researcher should also continuously challenge the above reflexive practices, particularly as they change due to interactions with participants and the broader structures and contexts within which researchers operate. Alvesson and Sköldberg (2000) define this as 'critical reflexivity, [which involves] interpreting one's own interpretations, looking at one's own perspectives from other perspectives, and turning a self-critical eye onto one's own authority as interpreter and author' (p. vii). Sultana highlights the need to also reflect on and *critically* examine 'power relations and politics' (2007, p. 376) particularly in international research where differences and inequalities are wide.

Engaging in rigorous critical reflexivity, as opposed to mere navel-gazing and introspection, means participating in 'deliberate self-scrutiny' (Hellawell, 2006, p. 483). This must occur throughout the entire research process rather than being added on at the end (Sultana, 2007). Critical reflexivity aids researchers in creating and maintaining dynamic interactions between self, participants and data, which allow them to investigate the reasoning that 'inform[ed] decisions, actions and interpretations at all stages of research' (Etherington, 2006, p. 81).

Critical reflexivity is therefore not merely a technique, but rather a 'philosophy-driven practice' that qualitative researchers need to engage with (Cunliffe, 2004, p. 408). Critical reflexivity approaches reality from a unique ontological point of view that questions the identities of researchers, how they transform their relationship with participants, and the ethicality of their actions. Therefore, as critically reflexive researchers, 'we become more aware of, and skilled in, constituting and maintaining our realities and identities' (Cunliffe, 2004, p. 410). In this sense, critical reflexivity may also lead researchers to make changes to their attitudes and future actions.

In thinking about the usefulness of critical reflexivity for extending traditional insider/outsider discourses, the crucial element is not whether the researcher is seen to be an insider or an outsider, but it is about being 'open, authentic, honest, deeply interested in the experience of one's research participants, and committed to accurately and adequately representing their experience' (Dwyer & Buckle, 2009, p. 59). Thus, the key value of critical reflexivity is to gain a better understanding of why and how a researcher negotiates their insider/outsider positionality, and of its transformational capacity as the researcher shifts from just thinking about things to pushing outside their comfort zone and developing critical self-awareness and skills that allow for the development of changed perspectives that will impact future practice (Shaw, 2013).

Reflections on Insider/Outsider Experiences

The discussion above reveals important theoretical and methodological issues regarding the insider/outsider debate. The most important of these is recognising that qualitative researchers are never fully insiders or outsiders, but instead constantly shift their position and identity, which requires them to engage in critical reflexivity throughout the research process in order to produce ethical and credible research. In the following sections, we illustrate this through four vignettes of our research experiences, drawing on many of the themes raised previously.

Vignette 1: Sliding around the space between as a returning researcher to Mauritius (Mindy Colin)

The first example illustrates some ways that researchers might use critical reflexivity to manage the (trans)formation of their identity while sliding around the space between. It refers to a qualitative case study I conducted that included participants from two very unequal levels of the education system in Mauritius: primary school teachers and programme directors at the Ministry of Education (Colin, 2015).

Though I am American, the Mauritian context was very familiar to me because I had lived in Mauritius from time to time for more than twenty years – first as a student, then later as a researcher, teacher trainer and spouse to a Mauritian national. Thus, as a returning researcher with extensive insider and outsider understanding, I had to make conscious choices about portraying myself as an insider or outsider according to Mauritian social hierarchies. For example, I knew that if I spoke English with the government officials they would interpret it as a sign that I was well educated and a professional social scientist. In contrast, with teachers I chose to be a participant observer and, as such, felt that I should act as 'local' as possible, speaking only Mauritian Creole and discussing my personal and family history.

Having not engaged with the literature on the space between insider and outsider research (Dwyer & Buckle, 2009) and identity formation (Ybema et al, 2009) prior to the study, I did not know that my multi-layered case study was designed in a way that would make me repeatedly slide around the power, positionality and representation sub-continua described by Merriam et al (2001). Thus, as I proceeded with fieldwork I ran into insider/outsider issues that I had not prepared to address. For example, I noticed that I felt uncomfortable in meetings wherein I simultaneously interacted with teachers and ministry officials. I felt that my persona changed when speaking to participants from differing levels of the education system, and I worried that those at the bottom levels would judge me harshly for it. These situations prompted me to ask myself questions such as: Was I being insincere and/or hypocritical? Was I maintaining rapport by switching personas, or disrupting it? Was I losing my identity by trying to live up to others' expectations?

These types of questions led me to engage in critical reflexivity and openly contemplate deeper questions about my own identity. As I considered the literature and discussed my questions with colleagues at the BAICE Thematic Forum that spurred this book I began to understand what switching personas meant for me as an insider–outsider. For example, I could see how I used my agency to manipulate the amorphous nature of insider/outsider spaces and negotiate interactions with participants by intentionally sliding along the various sub-continua in the space between (Merriam et al, 2001; Dwyer & Buckle, 2009).

By engaging in critical reflexivity I also realised that I have many roles in life that are highly intertwined, but independent as well. For example, my roles as wife and mother are highly intertwined, but necessarily independent. Likewise my roles as a professional researcher in Mauritius are highly intertwined, but being a genuine participant observer with teachers did not preclude me from concurrently being a professional social scientist with ministry officials. In questioning the reasoning behind my actions and reactions I found answers to my self-reflexive questions. I came to understand that I was not losing my identity, or being insincere and hypocritical when I switched roles. Instead, I was expanding and honing a distinct part of my overall identity: that of educational researcher. I also began to understand how to analyse and represent my participants' identities as more complex than just the unchanging 'other' (Sanderson, 2004). This awareness has taught me to (re)define my own identities, roles and research boundaries and more authentically represent my participants' perspectives in methodologically sound ways.

Vignette 2: Positionality and the balance of power in a multilingual and intercultural context (Cecilia Garrido)

The second experience outlines the journey from being a seemingly insider researcher to a reflective participant in the co-construction of research knowledge by considering how insider/outsider positionality can affect the balance of power between the researcher and the researched in the qualitative research process.

I carried out some research about teaching practices that can promote the development of intercultural competence among distance learning students of languages. Part of this research consisted of a series of interviews with language tutors who were from different nationalities and therefore spoke different languages. In some cases these tutors were based outside the UK and had very diverse cultural backgrounds. However, we shared a common teaching purpose and overall homogeneity that, according to Merriam et al (2001, p. 407), would foster 'a sense of community that could enhance trust and openness throughout the research process'. I assumed this common context would categorise me as 'insider' and, thus, would grant me insider research benefits, such as knowledge and access, that are traditionally implied by the insider/outsider dichotomy (Mullings, 1999; Merriam et al, 2001). I took it for granted that such status would guarantee an open, equal relationship between me and the tutors, and would promote affinity and develop a sense of rapport (Labaree, 2002).

As I interviewed the tutors about their teaching practices, I realised I needed to present myself in a researcher role to gain credibility. However, I became worried that such a presentation could create a power conflict that might prevent mutual trust and acceptance of me as a researcher of our common research community. I also worried that tutors might become concerned about the way I represented their practice and knowledge in research outcomes. Thus, I began to look at our roles in the research process as overlapping and multidimensional, not simply as being in a single camp as insider or outsider.

Reflecting about this positionality allowed me to negotiate my research status and allowed the tutors to engage in the research process on 'equal' terms. I entirely agree with Kusow's (2003) view that 'research status is something that participants continuously negotiate and locally determine' (p. 597). As Merriam et al (2001) state, 'power is something to not only be aware of, but to negotiate in the research process' (p. 413).

Through this process I also recognised that my initial assumptions were being challenged and I regularly had to question my methodology and deconstruct my interactions with the tutors as the research progressed (Savvides et al, 2014). Critical reflexivity facilitated my understanding of the limitations of my own initial reflections and assumptions (Clayton, 2013) and I became very aware of my continuous fluctuation between not quite being an insider nor an outsider. As Kusow (2003) states, when quoting Holstein & Gubrium (1995), 'the degree of "outsiderness" or "insiderness" emerges through a process that links the researcher and the participants in a collaborative process of meaning-making' (p. 598). In my case, my fluidity between the two positions and critical reflexivity facilitated the de-construction of interactions with the tutors and the co-creation of research knowledge with their full participation.

Vignette 3: Multiple identities: research on the internationalisation of higher education (Joanna Al-Youssef)

The third research example refers to qualitative, largely inductive, research carried out at a UK higher education institution (HEI) (Al-Youssef, 2010). The aim was to explore meanings of internationalisation as understood by university members who were involved in developing an internationalisation strategy at the time. Findings show that the term *internationalisation* is quantified as it is seen in relation to numbers of international staff, students and partnerships. The strategy focuses on increasing those numbers to presumably create an international ethos on campus. This view of internationalisation seems to reflect an understanding of HEIs as a structure that contains those numerable items. The findings are characterised by a discourse of 'us' (British) and 'them' (international), drawing boundaries between the two.

The data show that the dichotomy was present in the participants' views. International students as one group were seen as Cultural Others characterised by certain language, educational and social needs which required the institution to respond in certain ways (Sanderson, 2004). In addition, while the views emphasised the need to provide support to international students (them) to help them adapt to British (us) university life, participants also emphasised the importance of mutual learning taking place in the shared space on campus between 'them' and 'us'. It was not clear, however, how such a shared learning environment could be effective when those involved were adopting a position inside or outside it.

The above views presented me, the researcher – also labelled 'international' – with an opportunity to confront them and reflect on my own identity in relation to the research topic in question. I seemed to float in a space between being an outsider (which was the result of my national identity in a UK context) and being an insider as a member of the research community (reflecting my academic identity). These multiple identities and belonging required constant critical reflexivity, self-observation and inner dialogue, in order for me to understand my position, and for my professional as well as personal growth (Archer, 2007). Therefore, exploring the research topic became an exploration of my own identity, and the presence of 'self' and 'other' was manifested not only in my relationship with the participants, but also more prominently within myself as a researcher as I was constantly constructing my identity through my interactions with participants (Ybema et al, 2009) and through an inner dialogue between my self as a member of the British academic community, and my 'self' labelled as 'international other'. The divide between 'self' and 'other' during my research journey was therefore twofold. At data level, the dichotomy was most evident in the views of international students as others who, in most participants' views, were expected to make a huge effort to adapt to 'our' British way of life and to how things were done over 'here'. On the other hand, at a researcher level, my exposure to the above dichotomy led to the surfacing of a dichotomy within myself that kept unfolding as the research process progressed.

The questions raised as a result of the above-mentioned divide were related to the meanings that were being created for terms like 'international' within a specific 'national' context. It was becoming clearer to me as a researcher as I more actively engaged with critical reflexivity that a term such as 'international' created around me a bubble of imprisoning concepts that separated me from those 'outside'; I was categorised and put into a box with others with similar nationality labels. It was interesting to see how, during my interactions with the participants and the research topic, I was in several boxes at the same time, and that moving from one space to another was a consequence of the constantly changing context, time and actors around me. My critical reflections on these interactions and the labels led me to realise that the labelling and categorisations also involved an element of choice on my part that was fed by my own understanding of boundaries and groups and my past experiences. In other words, in many of these interactions, I made the subconscious decision to be either an insider or an outsider.

The way confining terms such as 'international' were beginning to unfold had an influence on my interpretations not only of the term itself but also of how it was being used, or even rejected, by HEIs (Stier, 2002). Critical reflexivity helped me as a researcher to unpack several meanings of such a term. More importantly, it enabled me to gain a form of self-knowledge and mindfulness that equipped me with the ability to be comfortable in my position in the space between.

Vignette 4: Sliding towards insider status while researching the European dimension in education at European Schools (Nicola Savvides)

In this final vignette I discuss how my positionality during the research process shifted from outsider towards insider and illustrate the concept discussed earlier that qualitative researchers occupy a space between (Dwyer & Buckle, 2009) the insider/outsider continuum that is constantly shifting as the research process unfolds. I note the key benefits, concerns and challenges experienced, commenting on the importance of critical reflexivity (Alvesson & Sköldberg, 2000) in trying to make sense of the impact of my changing positionality on the research.

My research involved a comparative multiple case study to explore how the European dimension in education was being incorporated at three of the intergovernmental European Schools, located in England, Belgium and Spain (see Savvides, 2006a,b, 2008, 2009). I used a qualitative research approach, drawing on ethnographic methods that included semi-structured and focus-group interviews, participant observation and documentary analysis.

I embarked upon my research with the view that I was largely an outsider as I had no direct experience of the European School system and had little knowledge of it, as it was a largely under-researched area. My outsider status became even more evident when several participants asked me if I had been educated in or had worked in a European School. When I answered 'no', I was questioned as to why I was interested in conducting research on the European Schools. This was a good opportunity to discuss my interest in understanding how they incorporate a European dimension in education and explain how I had come to read about the schools and learn about them through friends who had attended.

I had concerns about how my outsider status might affect the research, particularly in terms of building a relationship with participants. The fact that I was a doctoral student who was not a qualified teacher and had little experience of teaching in schools made me feel even more distanced and I wondered how I would relate to these teachers and establish rapport. Interestingly, our conversations did not revolve around local pedagogical matters but more around our common interests concerning the wider European, international and global dimensions of education. The insecurity I had felt because of my own initial perceived outsider status started to fade as we discovered shared interests, views and perceptions, enabling me to slide more towards an insider status. These conversations were an important part of getting to know one another and establishing rapport and trust.

I thought it was important that participants reveal their understandings and perceptions of the research topic without too much influence from my own input. I therefore started to conduct interviews early on during fieldwork, while I was still more of an outsider, to minimise my potential influence. Maintaining a friendly and approachable persona helped the participants feel comfortable to open up and share their knowledge and experiences, although there were a few senior teachers who remained guarded because of their suspicion towards me.

As I spent more time in the field, I came to realise that there were many insider elements to my positionality as I had much in common with my research participants. For example, we all saw ourselves as having post-national identities that encompass European, international and intercultural elements of citizenship and belonging; we shared experiences of having lived in more than one (mostly European) country, a passion for encountering and interacting with different people and speaking in different languages, and a shared idealism in tolerance and learning to live together.

As my insider status became more recognised, I felt advantages such as the building of trust and rapport, which led to very interesting and relevant conversations about my topic of investigation. I also experienced new challenges; for example, my research presence over time did inevitably draw attention to the idea of the European dimension in education in teachers' minds and I noticed through my observation of lessons that some teachers were increasingly drawing attention to a

European dimension in the classroom. Having conducted interviews early on I was able to elicit teachers' initial perceptions and understandings and through critical reflexivity I could think about these in line with the changes I was noticing both in the classroom and during staffroom and further conversations with teachers.

I found that engaging in critical reflexivity during all stages of the research was important as it enabled me to work through some of the tensions, confusions and insecurities experienced as part of my shifting outsider/insider status. It enabled me to work towards a deeper understanding and awareness of my own identity and positionality in the space between (Dwyer & Buckle, 2009) and how these interact with those of my participants and impact on the research process and the co-construction of knowledge (Sultana, 2007).

Conclusion

We have reviewed some of the key theoretical and methodological challenges and issues of negotiating insider/outsider status when engaged in qualitative research in international educational settings. By presenting a collection of reflections from our own research experiences, we support and extend the notion that qualitative researchers are not either/or insiders/outsiders. Instead, they continuously negotiate their multiple identities and aspects of the research process by moving fluidly within the space between (Dwyer & Buckle, 2009), which contains several linked social, cultural and other continua and contextual elements (De Andrade, 2000; Sherif, 2001). These include the ways that cultural positioning and representation influence the balance of power and rapport between participants and the researcher, both initially and over time. Researchers' manipulation of their positionalities in relation to contextual factors also impacts on their sense of identity, their relationship with the Cultural Other, the entire research process, and the production of knowledge.

Our examples reinforce the methodological benefits of rigorous and continuous critical reflexivity as this enables researchers to frame and problematise the impact of their subjectivities on the research environment. It also transforms the researcher by allowing them to dynamically critique and challenge their own values, be outside their comfort zone when inhabiting the space between, actively deconstruct preconceived assumptions, and develop new research theories and practices for the future. The values that critical reflexivity promotes allow for the co-creation of knowledge among researchers and the researched, and they are, therefore, more likely to generate strong, authentic and credible research outcomes.

Qualitative researchers, particularly those in the field of international education, can learn much from the historical and contemporary debates on insider/outsider dilemmas. As we have argued, an understanding of the theoretical, conceptual and methodological opportunities and dilemmas of insider/outsider positions can enable qualitative researchers to better prepare for and tackle the challenges of producing reliable and ethical research findings. Critical reflexivity is an integral part of this process as it enables researchers to be constantly aware of their position in the space between. Such awareness enables researchers to make informed decisions with regard to research methodology, data and research outcomes.

Acknowledgements

The final, definitive version of this paper has been published in *Research in Comparative and International Education*, 9(4) December 2014 by SAGE Publications Ltd.

References

Alvesson, M. & Sköldberg, K. (2000) *Reflexive Methodology: new vistas for qualitative research*. London: SAGE.

Al-Youssef, J. (2010) *The Internationalisation of Higher Education Institutions: meanings, policy and practice*. Saarbrücken: VDM Verlag Dr. Müller.

Archer, M. (2007) *Making Our Way through the World: human reflexivity and social mobility*. Cambridge: Cambridge University Press. http://dx.doi.org/10.1017/CBO9780511618932

Braithwaite, R, Cockwill, S., O'Neill, M. & Rebane, D. (2007) Insider Participatory Action Research in Disadvantaged Post-industrial Areas: the experiences of community members as they become community based action researchers, *Action Research*, 5(1), 61-74. http://dx.doi.org/10.1177/1476750307072876

Christensen, D.H. & Dahl, C.M. (1997) Rethinking Research Dichotomies, *Family and Consumer Sciences Research Journal*, 25(3), 269-285. http://dx.doi.org/10.1177/1077727X970253002

Clayton, K.A. (2013) Looking beneath the Surface: a critical reflection on ethical issues and reflexivity in a practitioner inquiry, *Reflective Practice*, 14(4), 506-518. http://dx.doi.org/10.1080/14623943.2013.808180

Colin, M. (2015) Improving the Quality of Teaching and Learning in Mauritian Primary Schools: the role of learner-centred pedagogy in current educational reform. Doctoral thesis, University of Bristol.

Court, D. & Abbas, R. (2013) Whose Interview Is It, Anyway? Methodological and Ethical Challenges of Insider–Outsider Research, Multiple Languages, and Dual-Researcher Cooperation, *Qualitative Inquiry*, 19, 480-488. http://dx.doi.org/10.1177/1077800413482102

Cunliffe, A. (2004) On Becoming a Critically Reflexive Practitioner, *Journal of Management Education*, 28(4), 407-426. http://dx.doi.org/10.1177/1052562904264440

De Andrade, L.L.D. (2000) Negotiating from the Inside: constructing racial and ethnic identity in qualitative research, *Journal of Contemporary Ethnography*, 29(3), 268-290. http://dx.doi.org/10.1177/089124100129023918

Dwyer, S.C. & Buckle, J. (2009) The Space Between: on being an insider-outsider in qualitative research, *International Journal of Qualitative Methods*, 8(1), 54-63.

Etherington, K. (2006) Reflexivity: using our 'selves' in narrative research, in Sheila Trahar (Ed.) *Narrative Research on Learning*, pp. 72-92. Bristol Papers in Education: Comparative and International Studies. Oxford: Symposium Books.

Filmer, P., Jenks, C., Seale, C. & Walsh, D. (1998) Developments in Social Theory, in C. Seale (Ed.) *Researching Society and Culture*, 23-36. London: SAGE.

Gu, Q., Schweisfurth, M. & Day, C. (2010) Learning and Growing in a 'Foreign' Context: intercultural experiences of international students, *Compare*, 40(1), 7-23. http://dx.doi.org/10.1080/03057920903115983

Hammersley, M. (1993) *Social Research: philosophy, politics and practice*. London: SAGE.

Hellawell, D. (2006) Inside-out: analysis of the insider–outsider concept as a heuristic device to develop reflexivity in students doing qualitative research, *Teaching in Higher Education*, 11(4), 483. http://dx.doi.org/10.1080/13562510600874292

Holstein, J.A. & Gubrium, J.F. (1995) *The Active Interview*, 1st edn. Thousand Oaks, CA: SAGE. http://dx.doi.org/10.4135/9781412986120

Kusow, A.M. (2003) Beyond Indigenous Authenticity: reflections on the insider/outsider debate in immigration research, *Symbolic Interaction*, 26(4), 591-599. http://dx.doi.org/10.1525/si.2003.26.4.591

Labaree, R.V. (2002) The Risk of 'Going Observationalist': negotiating the hidden dilemmas of being an insider participant observer, *Qualitative Research*, 2(1), 97-122. http://dx.doi.org/10.1177/1468794102002001641

McNess, E., Arthur, L. & Crossley, M. (2012) 'Ethnographic Dazzle' and the Construction of the 'Other': revisiting dimensions of the insider and outsider in international and comparative research. Paper presented at *Revisiting Insider/Outsider Perspectives: methodological considerations in the context of researcher mobilities and international partnerships*, BAICE Conference, University of Cambridge, Churchill College, 8-10 September.

Merriam, S.B., Johnson-Bailey, J., Lee, M., Kee, Y., Ntseane, G. & Muhamad, M. (2001) Power and Positionality: negotiating insider/outsider status within and across cultures, *International Journal of Lifelong Education*, 20(5), 405. http://dx.doi.org/10.1080/02601370120490

Merton, R.K. (1972) Insiders and Outsiders: a chapter in the sociology of knowledge, *American Journal of Sociology*, 78(1), 9-47. http://dx.doi.org/10.1086/225294

Mullings, B. (1999) Insider or Outsider, Both or Neither: some dilemmas of interviewing in a cross-cultural setting, *Geoforum*, 30(4), 337-350. http://dx.doi.org/10.1016/S0016-7185(99)00025-1

Nilan, P. (2002) 'Dangerous Fieldwork' Re-examined: the question of researcher subject position, *Qualitative Research*, 2(3), 363-386. http://dx.doi.org/10.1177/146879410200200305

Sanderson, G. (2004) Existentialism, Globalisation and the Cultural Other, *International Education Journal*, 4(4), 1-20.

Savvides, N. (2006a) Comparing the Promotion of European Identity at Three 'European Schools': an analysis of teachers' perceptions, *Research in Comparative and International Education*, 1(4), 393-402. http://dx.doi.org/10.2304/rcie.2006.1.4.393

Savvides, N. (2006b) Developing a European Identity: a case study of the European School at Culham, *Comparative Education*, 42(1), 113-129. http://dx.doi.org/10.1080/03050060500515801

Savvides, N. (2008) The European Dimension in Education: exploring pupils' perceptions at three European Schools, *Journal of Research in International Education*, 7(3), 304-326. http://dx.doi.org/10.1177/1475240908096485

Savvides, N. (2009) Exploring the European Dimension in Education: a comparative study of three European Schools in England, Belgium, and Spain. Doctoral thesis, University of Oxford.

Savvides, N., Al-Youssef, J., Colin, M. & Garrido, C. (2014) Journeys into Inner/Outer Space: reflections on the methodological challenges of negotiating insider/outsider status in international educational research, *Research in Comparative and International Education*, 9(4), 412-425. http://dx.doi.org/10.2304/rcie.2014.9.4.412

Shaw, R. (2013) A Model of the Transformative Journey into Reflexivity: an exploration into students' experiences of critical reflection, *Reflective Practice*, 14(3), 319-335. http://dx.doi.org/10.1080/14623943.2013.767229

Sherif, B. (2001) The Ambiguity of Boundaries in the Fieldwork Experience: establishing rapport and negotiating insider/outsider status, *Qualitative Inquiry*, 7(4), 436-447. http://dx.doi.org/10.1177/107780040100700403

Stier, J. (2002) *Internationalization in Higher Education: unexplored possibilities and unavoidable consequences*. Paper presented at the European Conference on Educational Research, University of Lisbon.

Subedi, B. (2006) Theorizing a 'Halfie' Researcher's Identity in Transnational Fieldwork, *International Journal of Qualitative Studies in Education*, 19(5), 573-593. http://dx.doi.org/10.1080/09518390600886353

Sultana, F. (2007) Reflexivity, Positionality and Participatory Ethics: negotiating fieldwork dilemmas in international research, *ACME: an international e-journal for critical geographies*, 6(3), 374-385.

Surra, C.A. & Ridley, C.A. (1991) Multiple Perspectives on Interaction: participants, peers, and observers, in B.M. Montgomery & S. Duck (Eds) *Studying Interpersonal Interaction*, pp. 35-55. New York: Guildford Press.

Van Heugten, K. (2004) Managing Insider Research: learning from experience, *Qualitative Social Work,* 3(2), 203-219. http://dx.doi.org/10.1177/1473325004043386

Ybema, S., Keenoy, T., Oswick, C., Beverungen, A. Ellis, N. & Sabelis, I. (2009) Articulating Identities, *Human Relations*, 62(3), 299-322.

CHAPTER 7

Insider–Outsider–Inbetweener? Researcher Positioning, Participative Methods and Cross-cultural Educational Research

LIZZI O. MILLIGAN

Introduction

Insider and outsider positionings have long been theorised in the social sciences, with their definitions differing over time and across disciplines. Steeped in the history of both anthropology and sociology, these perspectives are integral to the debates regarding what valid research is deemed to be. In the field of international and comparative education, a number of authors have recently sought to reconsider insiderness and outsiderness and argued against their fixed dichotomous entities (Arthur, 2010; Katyal & King, 2011; McNess et al, 2013). Arthur (2010) argues that a researcher's identity can shift dependent on the situation, the status of a researcher as an insider or outsider responding to the social, political and cultural values of a given context or moment. While this recent attention has highlighted theoretical developments in thinking about insider–outsider perspectives, less focus has been paid to the methodological processes that contribute to such shifting positionings while conducting cross-cultural research. This chapter seeks to address this by reflecting on the researcher experience during one such qualitative study.

The study involved four months' fieldwork in one rural community and two of its secondary schools in western Kenya. It sought to explore local perceptions of quality education through critical analysis of the perspectives and insights of a range of stakeholders across parents, teachers, management committee members and students (Milligan, 2014a). The rationale for the research had come from many years' experience as a volunteer, and more recently trustee, of a British nongovernmental organisation (NGO) which works to improve the quality of secondary education in rural Kisii. In this time, I have visited more than seventy secondary schools within the region and I have close working relationships with many school principals. Significantly, I have also developed strong friendships with many people both in Kisii town and in the village where I conducted my case studies. However, I speak very little Ekegusii, the local, and for many of the community's inhabitants, only language. I was also the only white person living in the area and I was often the only woman in male company. Therefore, while I represented many of the stereotypical outsider traits on entering the field, I was also in the rare position of having intimate knowledge and experience of, and relationships in, the community.

During the four months that I spent in the rural community, I took detailed fieldwork notes which enabled me to reflect on the research process. On reading them back on my return to the UK, I recognised that my positioning and, significantly, how others viewed me was a frequent concern that I returned to time and again. This has led me to reflect on my positioning and consider how I represented a number of different identities and what processes contributed to these. The shifting identities were often characterised by different situations, as Arthur (2010) has suggested. For example, I could be said to have been more of an insider in the school staff room than in the local market place. In the former, English was the primary language and I was mainly treated as a colleague, albeit often a 'strange' one whose experiences of living in the UK were often drawn out and discussed in detail. In the latter, I was always the *mzungu* (European), although towards the end of the four months, I was also known as the *mwalimu* (teacher) and associated with the family with whom I stayed. This already points to the multiple identities I took on and the fact that these were not static but changed over time. However, in this chapter, I put forward the notion that as much as it was situational, the shifting positioning was also reflective of a conscious effort in research design for me not to remain an outsider. This was particularly in relation to the students, whom I expected, from my experience working in schools, to be most in awe of the outsider and with whom building meaningful relationships would be most difficult.

In the light of this and as the main focus of this chapter, I reflect on the participative methods used with young people in their final year of secondary school and how using such techniques contributed to my own changing position within the field. I first consider the use of such techniques to garner a degree of authoritative insider perspective on their educational lives, both in and out of school, and to gain the ability to enter spaces that as both an adult and an outsider I would not have otherwise been able to access. The chapter then turns to a discussion of how this research process enabled some shift in many students' perceptions of myself and my positioning. In the latter parts of the chapter, I reflect on the contribution of participative methods in shifting such positioning and building relationships of trust. Conclusions argue for the development of the concept of the 'inbetweener' researcher which challenges traditional dichotomies of the insider and outsider which may be less relevant in contemporary international and comparative educational research.

The Research Project

The research project was based in one rural community in the Kisii region of western Kenya and two of its secondary schools. Owmana and Eskuru Secondary Schools are primarily day schools, with all students coming from the Inka village community (pseudonyms given throughout). They have relatively small student bodies, with less than fifty students in each class group. The village, although rural, is not remote and is connected to Kisii town by two main roads (for more detail about the research context and its rurality, please see Milligan, 2014c). Its relative rurality is important since it constitutes the context which I entered and the extent to which I was seen as an outsider. For the young people at the secondary schools in which I worked, seeing *wazungu* may not have been uncommon in the local town where some small NGOs are based. However, interacting on a daily basis was not something that most had done (when I and other British volunteers worked in the community, it had been in other local schools).

As the focus of my study was on the quality of education offered, I designed the project from an understanding that those who are most closely involved in educational practice, as well as the students for whose benefit educational policies are developed, are often left out of the debate about what constitutes quality education. I used a range of participative methods, appropriate for the different participant groups, drawing on Kendall's (2007, p. 706) argument:

> Educational quality is only shallowly intersecting with communities', parents', children's, and teachers' daily educational experiences and desires ... educational quality, as defined by various local and non-local actors, could be strengthened by good participatory approaches.

Including the young people who, as the students, were the 'consumers' of educational policy and the direct beneficiaries of education in practice was an integral part of the research design. It has been widely argued that children tend to be constructed as objects of research rather than active participants (Cox et al, 2008; Thomson, 2008). Karlsson (2001) has further highlighted that this is often exacerbated by the fact that student participation in school-based research is relatively limited. I chose to include students because, as Thomson says, they can bring unique and specific insights

> about their everyday lives at home and school and their view and hopes for their futures – which can easily slip below the horizons of older inquirers. The omission of these perspectives can easily lead to researchers making interpretations and representations that are very short-sighted and which miss the point. (Thomson, 2008, p. 1)

In addition, my experience with the NGO has shown me that students can be reluctant to share their views or may lack confidence to be able to say anything that might be useful for me. This was backed up throughout the fieldwork process as students often asked me questions such as, 'Is this the sort of thing you want me to say?', 'Can I take a photo of ...?' and, 'I'm just writing about my normal life, are you sure that is good enough?'

It is important to note that although I describe the methods as participative, I did not take a wholly participatory approach. A fully participatory approach would have involved participation of the students throughout the research process. This would include in the development of the research questions and data collection tools, and full participation in the analysis and identification of key themes of the research. Wang (1999) also highlights the importance of the emancipatory aspects of participatory research in which participants can become empowered through the process of designing, collecting and analysing data. Rather, I understand the methods I used to be participative in as much as they involved some shift in power dynamics by allowing students to guide the data collection by choosing the data they collected and the form of the interview which followed. I conducted twenty diary- and photo-linked interviews with Form IV students, aged between 17 and 22. The photo-linked technique I used drew on the data collection method of 'photovoice' which has been used predominantly in participatory community research to address issues of injustice, inequality and exploitation (Wang, 1999). In this methodology, participants are encouraged to take photos and share these and their interpretations in focus-group discussions. The choice of using diaries was based on a similar rationale.

Put simply, these techniques offered a combination of participant data collection and unstructured interviewing. At each case-study school, I worked together with the class teacher to identify ten Form IV students of mixed gender and ability who were given either disposable cameras or diaries for one week to chart what they deemed to be important to their education. Those with cameras received a sheet on which they could record why they took each photo. I showed them how the cameras worked since most had not used one before (and none had even seen a disposable version). In each diary, I asked students to reflect on what they were doing and how they were feeling. All were given limited instructions to remind them to focus on what was important to them in their education and a letter explaining the purpose of the research and various ethical issues, including the voluntary nature of taking part and the right of withdrawal. This was particularly significant considering that their mock national exams were pending, and taking part would impact on their time for revision. All students chose to participate and many clearly enjoyed the process – a point which I will return to later. After a week, I collected the cameras and diaries before developing the photos. These or the diary text were used as the basis for a narrative interview with each student which was designed to be a 'participative activity to generate knowledge, a two-way learning process, where the subjectivities of the research participants influence data collection and the process of "making meaning"' (Shah, 2004, p. 552).

Power, Privilege and Positioning in the Field

Much of the existing insider–outsider literature has tended to focus on how researchers view *themselves* in the research process. In this chapter I argue that insiderness and outsiderness can be seen as a balancing act between the positioning that the researcher actively takes and the ways in which their role is defined by how *others* involved in the project, research participants and those further afield, view the researcher. In my research journal, I often reflected on the discrepancies between the image I had of myself and how others in the community viewed me:

> Maybe I have been idealising my position as an insider because there are a small number of people who see me as (*my name*) rather than simply the mzungu. For the vast majority I'm simply from the land of plenty who they hope can sweep in and make changes they want personally and at the school ... my knowledge is seen as superior, the outsider who can change their world. (Research journal, 23 May 2011)

This quote from my research journal highlights the importance of power and privilege in how participants view a researcher coming from outside the community and more specifically from the UK. I came with a certain degree of cultural, linguistic and economic capital, whether real or perceived. This points to the importance of considering alternative perceptions of an individual's 'status set' and the potential pitfalls of the illusions of being an insider. Merton (1972) first challenged the belief that an insider researcher must mean someone who is a member of a particular ethnic or social group and put forward the idea that we all have multiple identities which take precedence at different times. His notion of 'status sets' is a useful tool for considering the different identities that I held which contributed to my insider–outsider positioning in the field. These statuses included being white, an adult, a young adult, a woman, a teacher, an unmarried woman and an English speaker. What is significant here is, first, that these status sets reflect our multiple and shifting identities – to be both 'white' and 'a woman' each bring their own statuses, and these will be different to that of 'a white woman'. Furthermore, by considering status rather than the 'shades' of positioning referred to by Hellawell (2006), it highlights the considerable power implications that accompany the statuses that the researcher embodies. This suggests the importance of a researcher reflecting on their different statuses as a part of the research process.

Power relations between researchers and participants, as McNess et al (2013) argue, can also influence the way in which knowledge is constructed and what becomes 'known'. A key part of the argument is that there is a need for researchers to consider both the ways in which participants view them in the field and how active choices in research design and positioning can contribute to shifting relationships. Here, the literature related to participatory approaches which seeks to challenge and even out power relations in the field can offer some important insights. One of the main aims of this methodological approach is to dissolve boundaries between the 'researcher' and the 'researched'; put differently, this could be the boundaries between the 'insider' and the 'outsider'. As outlined in the previous section, in this project, I drew on the participatory literature which promotes the use of photos and other visual media to include children and young people in the research process (Karlsson, 2001; Sharples et al, 2003; Mizen, 2005). The authors just cited have argued that it is important to consider the positioning of the researcher from the point of view of participants and the potential benefits of shifting researcher positioning to enable more authentic research. Here, the argument is that by prioritising participant-driven data, rather than relying on researcher assumptions in research design and data collection, the outcomes will be both more realistic and trustworthy. The promotion of the use of participatory approaches is based on their potential to challenge the power relations between researcher and researched, engage the younger and more shy research participant, and give children 'a voice' to construct new forms of knowledge (Packard, 2008).

In the following sections of this chapter, I consider the active role that I took as a researcher to develop stronger relationships with the young people in the research (and their teachers and parents) and allow for more meaningful knowledge (co)-construction.

Phase 1: 'insider' perspectives

Giving cameras and diaries to students provided access to insider views of everyday learning spaces and events. This allowed me to enter spaces both within and outside the school environment which I would not have otherwise been able to access as an outsider, a researcher, an adult, a non-speaker of the local language and a woman. Through their pictures and diary text, students provided intimate insights into their home lives and the out-of-school challenges which they perceived to be important in their education. All students took photos outside the school environment, but these photos represented the continuation of their learning. These home pictures and the subsequent interviews contributed significantly to one of the key findings of the study – that home life challenges make it difficult for students to participate in out-of-school learning. Elsewhere I have reflected on some of the intimate portrayals of home life that using this methodology allowed me to access (Milligan, 2014c). Here I want to draw on just one example from within the school context. In comparable research with students in urban schools in South Africa, Karlsson (2001, p. 24) reflected on giving students cameras to gain insights into their lives 'beyond the space-time confines of the timetable and geo-space of the school', where she interacted with them. Similarly, here, through the diaries and photos, students offered access to new insider spaces within the school context. Damaris took a photo of the girls' toilets during break time; Peter captured the event of boys moving into the newly constructed dormitory. Both of these are spaces within the school that are not easily accessible as both an adult and a female. Evelyn's photo (Figure 1) of two boys fighting during quiet study time in the lunch break was indicative for her of the wider issue of ill-discipline among students in her Form IV class. When this photo was taken, it is likely that I was sitting in the staffroom some fifty metres away, oblivious to such behaviour, despite Evelyn later telling me that this was a common occurrence in the lunch hour. This is a space where the insiders are the Form IV students. This event would not have happened if I, or another adult, had been present in the room. Having myself as an outsider present in the classroom would probably have led to a distorted or inauthentic portrayal of student behaviour.

Above I have mentioned just a few photos which illustrate the insider data that students provided by using these participative techniques. However, it is each student's narrative based on all their photos or diary entries which create a powerful representation of students' everyday educational lives. Thus, these offer personal insights at different points in their day which suggest how challenging their lives are and the many interlinking pressures that impact on their educational engagement, well-being and achievement. The data collected by the young people were significant in themselves for the insights that they offered in spaces that an outsider could not enter. However, they also gained greater context through the narrative interviews which followed.

Figure 1. Evelyn's photo.

Phase 2: knowledge co-construction

The follow-up interviews took place in a private office on the school grounds during holidays when most Form IV students were in school revising before their mock examinations. The interviews took between 30 and 45 minutes. I positioned the chairs so that we sat next to each other and looked through their photos or diaries next to each other so that they would feel less like they were in a formal interview situation. By allowing the text and photos to form the basis of the narrative interviews, this created an environment where students appeared to be relatively comfortable, and most spoke at length about the data that they had produced.

At first, most of the students appeared nervous and waited for me to ask a question, often replying with short responses which required me to follow up with probing questions. This tended to shift during the interview, with some taking control of the interview by the end, taking each photo and explaining it without waiting for a prompt from me. When reflecting back on my interview with Damaris, my notes suggest:

> To begin with, she was hesitant, awaiting questions leading me to take the first photo and lead the conversation. By the fifth photo that we were discussing, she was visibly more relaxed, taking each photo and explaining why she had taken

> it in detail and without being asked. Significantly, she also shifts from talking about 'students and their challenges' more generally to her own experiences and views suggesting that she felt more comfortable to share these with me. (Researcher's reflective notes)

It is also important to note that the photo about which Damaris spoke so animatedly was one of the 'insider photos' discussed in the previous section. It seemed that discussions of the photos in spaces that I was not able to enter as a relative outsider were particularly significant for shifting power relations between me, as the researcher, and the participants. These were examples of occasions where we were then discussing events and places that I did not know about and I could see that my lack of knowledge here changed how the young people felt with me. They showed surprise if I seemed to not know something, often laughing out loud.

Across these examples, as well as the interviews more widely, I felt that the otherwise uneven power relations were, to some degree, evened out. This allowed for some collaboration and knowledge co-construction, argued as one of the strengths of using photo- and diary-linked interviewing (Wang, 1999; Packard, 2008). However, this also supports Packard (2008) when she argues that there is a tendency among those who promote photo-linked interviewing to assume that this approach enables the power relations to be fully balanced out, and I would not wish to argue that this was the case in my research. Students continued to call me 'Miss' and some were reticent to speak at length in the interview. Through interviews with teachers and parents, it also became clear that some students had omitted important information about themselves even when prompted. This was particularly in relation to more private issues such as their relationships or parental income. Students clearly did not feel at ease to share such information with me, whether as an outsider, a woman, an adult, a teacher-figure or a combination of all of these identities.

Therefore, in the process of interviewing, my positioning shifted dependent on the young person with whom I was sharing the interview. With some, I became more of a conspirator, the sole adult in the school setting to have been shown into their personal spaces. With others, I remained very much an outsider with whom they were reluctant to share personal details and with whom they only shared brief or generalised points in interviews. However, for the majority, the process of the interview and, with it, the validation of their opinions, viewpoints and insights provided a more balanced context for data collection and arguably the construction of more valid 'knowledge'.

Phase 3: shifting researcher positioning

The use of participative techniques was only with the students at each school. However, on reflection, I can see how my positioning changed both within the school and the wider community. I would argue that the inclusion of the young people in this more participatory approach contributed to this. With the students who had been co-researchers and some of the wider student community, I was no longer either '*mwalimu*' or '*mzungu*'. By placing importance on the students' data, I had contributed to a shift in how students saw me, to where they viewed me as someone who was interested in their lives and their opinions.

My changing positioning was not only in relation to how the students saw me. It also had some influence on the students' parents and teachers and subsequent data collection with these groups. I conducted interviews with parents of twelve of the students involved in the photo- and diary-linked research. These interviews took place during vacation time in students' homes. Many showed me in person the images they had captured in their photos or what they had been explaining in their diaries. Dorothy, for example, wanted to show me the family land where she had been working when she had wanted to revise. Damaris, similarly, introduced me to her mother as 'the one who was advising my siblings', reminding me of the photo that she had taken. This allowed me to enter, in some way, spaces that would otherwise have remained hidden. It also enabled a more insider perspective as a basis for the interview with parents; some were actively surprised by how much I seemed to know about the community, the school and their child in particular. This enabled the parent interviews, despite taking place with a translator and when I had only recently met them, to be more relaxed and less like a complete outsider turning up at their home to question them. This, arguably, meant that they shared more with me than they would have otherwise.

When I wrote in my research journal that I was seen as the 'knowledgeable outsider', I presumed that this was related to my previous experience of working in secondary schools in the Kisii region. However, on reflection, and through follow-up discussions with teachers at Eskuru School, I see that much of this 'knowledge' was based on the insights that students had given me by trusting me and allowing me into their spaces. Two years after the fieldwork took place, I returned to the schools to deliver a report based on the research project. After reading it, the Eskuru principal spoke about my identity which I reflected on in my research journal:

> Returning to the schools has been just as emotional as I thought it would be. The overwhelming emotion that I have felt is pride – in one moment in particular. After Mr John [the Eskuru principal] had read the report, he shook my hand and

> said thank you. I said there was nothing to thank me for and he shook his head saying 'no, I want to say thank you for all the work you did here to find out everything about our school. These students really trusted you. This report shows you really have known. (Research journal, 5 September 2013)

Looking back on what Mr John said to me, it particularly struck me that he highlighted both trust and knowledge. While Mr John may not make the explicit link between the two, I would argue that the use of participatory methods with the students allowed me to develop both trust and, in turn, more authentic knowledge construction within the interviews. However, significantly, this also had the positive effect of enabling me to build more meaningful relationships both in the school and in the wider community.

Conclusions

This chapter has illustrated one way in which a cross-cultural researcher can actively negotiate their position in the field. I have argued that the active choices made in research design and approaches to data collection can affect the way in which a researcher is viewed and responded to. This suggests the potential for the consideration of the new term – the 'inbetweener' – in cross-cultural research, supporting Hellawell (2006), Arthur (2010) and Thomson and Gunter (2010), who have argued against the fixed and dichotomous notions of insiderness and outsiderness. However, the active term of 'inbetweener' also recognises that the researcher can be proactive in their attempts to place themselves in between. This is in contrast to the concepts of liquid identities (Thomson & Gunter, 2010) or an insider–outsider continuum (Hellawell, 2006; Arthur, 2010) which suggests a lack of agency from the researcher themselves. This is in recognition of the fact that on entering the field, much of my identity in this cross-cultural ethnographic research was given to me by the wider community who saw me as the '*mzungu*'. The active attempts made to move from being an outsider to an 'inbetweener' had significant implications for being able to develop relationships, built on trust and comradery, both with the students engaged in the participative research process and with the school and surrounding community. This is to argue not that I was perceived differently by all members of the community, but rather that, for those actively involved in the research process, there was some change in their perception of me. By gaining personal insights from students, alongside being able to build on my own previous experience of working in the Inka community and secondary schools across the Kisii region, I became a 'knowledgeable outsider' and subsequently an 'inbetweener'.

In a study that sought to understand local perspectives on quality secondary education, it was important to find ways to enable the participants to share what they thought rather than what they thought I wanted to hear. By building relationships based on trust and respect of different views, the data collected suggest more authentic portrayals of the perceptions of those in the Inka community. This is just one way in which the revisiting of insider–outsider perspectives can offer new and important understandings to the field of international and comparative education.

Acknowledgements

A more detailed version of this chapter was published in the journal *Compare: a journal of comparative and international education*; please see Milligan, 2014b below. With thanks to the publishers, Taylor & Francis Ltd (www.tandfonline.com), and the editors of *Compare*, for permission to rework this material here.

Notes

[1] All names used for the village, schools and individuals are pseudonyms.

[2] Participants have given consent for all data included in this article, including the photographs, to be used for research dissemination.

References

Arthur, L. (2010) Insider–Outsider Perspectives in Comparative Education. Seminar presented at the Research Centre for International and Comparative Studies, Graduate School of Education, University of Bristol.

Cox, S., Robinson-Pant, A., Dyer, C. & Schweisfurth, M. (Eds) (2008) *Children as Decision Makers in Education: sharing experiences across cultures*. London: Continuum.

Hellawell, D. (2006) Inside-out: analysis of the insider–outsider concept as a heuristic device to develop reflexivity in students doing qualitative research, *Teaching in Higher Education*, 11(4), 483-494. http://dx.doi.org/10.1080/13562510600874292

Karlsson, J. (2001) Doing Visual Research with School Learners in South Africa, *Visual Sociology*, 16(2), 23-37. http://dx.doi.org/10.1080/14725860108583833

Katyal, K.R. & King, M. (2011) 'Outsiderness' and 'Insiderness' in a Confucian Society: complexity of contexts, *Comparative Education*, 47(3), 327-341. http://dx.doi.org/10.1080/03050068.2011.586765

Kendall, N. (2007) Parental and Community Participation in Improving Educational Quality in Africa: current practices and future possibilities, *International Review of Education*, 53(5-6), 701-708.

McNess, E., Arthur, L. & Crossley, M. (2013) 'Ethnographic Dazzle' and the Construction of the 'Other': revisiting dimensions of insider and outsider research for international and comparative education, *Compare*, published online 12 November. http://dx.doi.org/10.1080/03057925.2013.854616

Merton, R. (1972) Insiders and Outsiders: a chapter in the sociology of knowledge, *American Journal of Sociology*, 78(1), 9-47. http://dx.doi.org/10.1086/225294

Milligan, L. (2014a) Conceptualising Educational Quality in Kenyan Secondary Education: comparing local and national perspectives. Unpublished PhD thesis, University of Bristol.

Milligan, L. (2014b) Insider–outsider–inbetweener? Researcher Positioning, Participative Methods and Cross-cultural Educational Research, *Compare*, published online 26 June. http://dx.doi.org/10.1080/03057925.2014.928510

Milligan, L. (2014c) 'They Are Not Serious Like the Boys': gender norms and contradictions for girls in rural Kenya, *Gender & Education*, 26(5), 465-476. http://dx.doi.org/10.1080/09540253.2014.927837

Mizen, P. (2005) A Little 'Light Work'? Children's Images of Their Labour, *Visual Studies*, 20(2), 124-139.

Packard, J. (2008) 'I'm Gonna Show You What It's Really Like Out Here': the power and limitation of participatory visual methods, *Visual Studies*, 23(1), 63-77. http://dx.doi.org/10.1080/14725860801908544

Shah, S. (2004) The Researcher/Interviewer in Intercultural Context: a social intruder?, *British Educational Research Journal*, 30(4), 549-575. http://dx.doi.org/10.1080/0141192042000237239

Sharples, M., Davison, L., Thomas, G.V. & Rudman, P.D. (2003) Children as Photographers: an analysis of children's photographic behavior and intentions at three age levels, *Visual Communication*, 2, 303-320. http://dx.doi.org/10.1177/14703572030023004

Thomson, P. (2008) *Doing Visual Research with Children and Young People*. Oxford: Routledge.

Thomson, P. & Gunter, H. (2010) Inside, Outside, Upside Down: the fluidity of academic researcher 'identity' in working with/in school, *International Journal of Research and Method in Education*, 34(1), 17-30. http://dx.doi.org/10.1080/1743727X.2011.552309

Wang, C. (1999) Photovoice: a participatory action research strategy applied to women's health, *Journal of Women's Health*, 8(2), 185-192. http://dx.doi.org/10.1089/jwh.1999.8.185

CHAPTER 8

Multiplicities of Insiderness and Outsiderness: enriching research perspectives in Pakistan

SUGHRA CHOUDHRY KHAN

Introduction: inside out and in between

In this chapter I reflect upon my doctoral research in which I explored the perceptions of 'feeling valued' held by primary school teachers working for an educational organisation in rural, mountainous northern Pakistan. I did this as a bicultural [1] researcher who possessed multiplicities of 'insidernesses' and 'outsidernesses' related to the research context and my previous professional experience within the organisation.

In considering the theory surrounding the concepts of 'insiderness' and 'outsiderness', I acknowledge that rather than using a dichotomy of being either an 'insider' or an 'outsider' we need to have a more detailed understanding of how various researcher positionalities interact, as well as of the possible continuum along which they might move and how they influence the research process. I draw on the deemed advantages and disadvantages of being an insider and an outsider by virtue of the numerous interrelating and interacting 'status sets' (Merton, 1972) that I held.

Merton (1972) claims that we are all insiders or outsiders in various situations, stemming from the fact that as an individual one does not hold a sole status but a set of statuses – such as being a woman, black, educated, urban, middle class and middle-aged. These would then render communication more complex when relating, for example, to young working-class white rural men. Merton argued, therefore, that we confront one another simultaneously as insiders and outsiders, each having a distinctive and interactive role (1972, p. 21).

Additionally, Hellawell refers to varying 'shades' of 'insiderism' and 'outsiderism' placed along multiple series of continuums. I moved back and forth along and across these in my research (Hellawell, 2006, p. 488). Indeed, for much of the time, I experienced a 'role dualism' (Hurworth & Argirides 2005, cited in Ritchie et al, 2009), in which I held both an insider and an outsider role at the same time. However, as my research shows, I was working within Bhabha's (1994) 'Third Space' – the 'liminal space of in-betweenness' where insiderness and outsiderness meet (McNess et al, 2013, p. 12).

Dwyer and Buckle (2009, p. 61) state that 'as researchers we can only ever occupy the space between'. I conducted my research in this third in-between space, as the 'in betweener researcher' (Milligan, 2014), who was neither a total insider nor a total outsider and at the same time both, working within my own bicultural and therefore intercultural spaces.

I raise questions as to what can be deemed 'authentic' research and maintain that the most important quality of good research is not whether one is an insider or an outsider; rather, it is the skill with which it is conducted. I conclude that having multiplicities of insider- and outsidernesses enabled richer, more nuanced perspectives to emerge while exploring what 'feeling valued' means to primary school teachers in northern Pakistan. The next section introduces my research before positioning me as the bicultural researcher.

My Research: feeling valued

My research aimed to understand primary school teachers' perceptions of 'feeling valued' and the effect these had on their work for a private educational organisation in a remote rural mountainous region of Gilgit-Baltistan, in northern Pakistan.

My motivation for the research topic came from my previous experience working for the organisation as a senior manager dealing with a general climate of low teacher morale. As the research progressed, a deeper personal connection to the topic emerged as I realised that being a British-born teacher of South Asian heritage gave me a voice, and made me significant and also independent as a woman living within the male-dominated North and South.

My concern was to understand the subjective world of the primary school teachers; 'to investigate "from the inside" through a process of *verstehen* or empathetic understanding' (Morrison, 2002, p. 19). I wanted to conceptualise the teachers as being 'insider-teachers' in the research process and myself as being both the 'outsider–insider learner', well explained by Spradley:

> I want to understand the meaning of your experience, to walk in your shoes, to feel things as you feel them, to explain things as you explain them. Will you become my teacher and help me understand? (1979, p. 34, cited in Kvale & Brinkmann, 2009)

I drew on an ethnographic enquiry approach which leant towards critical ethnography in my desire to give voice to and empower teachers (Creswell, 2003). A sample of forty-four teachers collaborated in focus groups, and ten teachers took part in participant observation and in-depth interviews in rural primary schools over a seven-week period.

Positioning the Bicultural Researcher

In approaching my research, I considered myself both a partial insider and a partial outsider in relation to my participant teachers and the context of rural northern Pakistan.

I was of Pakistani–Kashmiri ethnic heritage – my parents were originally from the North, and from a village background, like the teachers; however, they had migrated to the UK in the 1940-1950s. I considered myself British – I was English at school and Pakistani at home; but my first language was English. I learnt languages easily at school and yet was chastised for not knowing my mother tongue, a dialect of Panjabi, fluently (see Sherif, 2001 for a similar experience). As a Pakistani Muslim, I was familiar with a Muslim background and I had studied at degree level the Pakistan lingua franca of Urdu, the language in which teachers had been educated.

In trying to become educated I had to fight traditional family resistance to females being educated and resist being married at an early age. I had started my career as a teacher – having now become middle class – and still considered myself as one even when I moved into teacher education and management. As a South Asian female professional I had experienced sexism and racism in British society. Subsequently, I also tackled the challenges of working within the patriarchal society of Pakistan as a female senior educational manager. I lived in urban Karachi but frequently travelled north to the rural context of schools in Gilgit-Baltistan.

Fay tells us that 'there is no self-understanding without other-understanding' (1996, cited in Dwyer & Buckle, 2009, p. 60). A bicultural/bilingual person perhaps contains within her/himself a more internal insider–outsider understanding. There is some evidence that bicultural people have more divergent thinking, have social and cognitive flexibility and are able to see the relativity of their own cultures. They are more adaptable, bilingual, possess intercultural sensitivity and are used to cultural frame switching (Byram, 2003; Benet-Martínez et al, cited in Nguyen and Benet-Martínez, 2007). As such, I was used to moving in and out and between my 'selves' automatically, constantly switching roles, practising 'polyvocalities' (Chavez, 2008) as a feature of everyday life. I was neither an insider nor an outsider in England or Pakistan and yet an insider and outsider in both – to myself as well as to insiders. Like Sultana (2007), I was not returning 'home' when in Pakistan for fieldwork, but elements felt like coming home as I was so familiar with the context. However, ultimately I returned as the 'western researcher' from a 'western/northern' university.

Trinh Minh-ha eloquently elucidates the position of the post-colonial woman:

> Not quite the same, not quite the other, she stands in that undetermined threshold place where she constantly drifts in and out ... her intervention is necessarily that of both not quite an insider and not quite an outsider. She is, in other words, this inappropriate 'other' or 'same' who moves about with always at least two gestures: that of affirming 'I am like you' while persisting in her difference and that of reminding 'I am different' while unsettling every definition of otherness arrived at. (1997, cited in Sultana, 2007, p. 377)

Dimensions of Insider- and Outsiderness

In Tables I and II, I describe and discuss how the various dimensions of my background, or role statuses, in terms of professional and personal attributes, positioned me in relation to the teachers who took part in the study and speculate on how that might have impacted on the data collected. However, it should also be noted that what is more difficult to portray is how the boundaries between these various professional and personal attributes are not fixed but interact with each other to varying degrees, at various times. For example, as a professional woman with experience of working in a male-dominated society, I was able to relate to female teachers' experiences of discrimination. However, as an ex-senior manager I would have liked to have used the opportunity to make changes, though as a researcher I was aware that I needed to focus on my data collection.

Similarly, the tables only depict one side of the researcher–participant relationship. The teachers also brought to the research process their own sets of identities/social statuses and positioned themselves, as well as me, according to their own perceptions. For example, though I approached a focus group as a researcher, the teachers could first see the ex-senior manager and view me as an insider of the organisation and then position themselves as teachers with grievances, or teachers who needed to be extremely mindful of the hierarchical status within the traditional culture of Pakistan. Alternatively, they could have seen me as guest (an 'outsider') to be treated graciously.

This raises the question of how effectively research can be done by (ex-)senior managers within an organisation, when leaders/managers are often viewed as the 'other', not able to understand grassroots employees. Would my former position and multiplicities of insider- and outsiderness render the research less 'authentic' than if it had been undertaken by someone who was more of an 'outsider' to the teachers and their context?

The Ex-senior Manager/Teacher as Researcher: how would I be viewed?

Identity/Status	Insider←		→Outsider
Profession/ Status	Originally a teacher	Ex-manager in sister organisation in Pakistan	Ex-senior manager in the organisation in Pakistan. Teacher – UK context
	Ex-senior manager in organisation		High status in relation to low status of teachers
	Experience of working in Pakistan		Experience of working in UK.
Knowledge of institution, politics and culture	Deep recent knowledge Ex-senior manager Worked on resolving teachers' grievances		No longer with the organisation External researcher No longer involved
Significant shared experience	Discussions with teachers on concerns		No longer involved
Knowledge of the region and teachers' work	Lived and worked in Pakistan		Based in urban Karachi in the South and not in the rural North.
	Familiarity with the region through regular visits		Never worked in the region full time
	Visited schools and teachers		No prolonged time in one school

Table I. Researcher insider and outsider positionalities: professional attributes.

I was particularly concerned about how teachers would respond to me as an ex-senior manager. I was aware that teachers would be gauging whether I could be trusted, what I could offer and whether they could exploit this previous connection. A teacher's interpretation of 'feeling valued' could be one that teachers wanted me to hear, or one I myself interpreted in the light of my understanding of the past.

So did my former position and status hinder or facilitate the participation of teachers? Although all teachers in the sample schools expressed an interest in participating in my research, they may also have felt obliged because of the way the field office introduced my research along with my letter of introduction. They may have felt it was an honour, but they may also have felt that they needed to extend courtesy to an ex-senior manager.

Both Pardhan (2011) and Qureshi (2011) discuss the difficulty of getting 'true' informed consent in contexts of the South, while Katyal and King (2011) question the relevance of it in collective cultures, such as Pakistan. One teacher told me that he wanted to take the opportunity to ask me questions, and another 'to take advantage' of the situation, showing, in fact, that I was still being viewed as someone with inside knowledge and influence.

Yet the next focus group were very happy to participate and wanted me to visit each one of them in their schools. Was this because of my previous insider standing, or were they being hospitable to a guest? Dimmock (2002, p. 36) also refers to the complexity of gaining access and willing participation: 'in cultures where power, influence and status are of great importance ... participation is more likely if the researcher is perceived by respondents to have power, standing and status'.

As an ex-insider I gained easy access. However, it was also a complicating factor. I had to both build upon previous relationships but not let negative aspects get in the way of honest communication. In essence, as Crossley and Watson (2003, p. 36) state, researchers need to be aware of the influence of past baggage.

Although I did not suffer the culture shock of a complete outsider, I was more vulnerable, due to being an ex-insider bicultural researcher. I had to be conscious of not becoming defensive. This was particularly so in one focus group that started a little tensely. Questions were posed to me, showing clearly that the teachers had positioned me in my former role and thus as an 'insider' whom they had a right to question, as this extract from my field notes shows:

> Wow, that was a bit of a tough session! ... it was a bit strained – avoiding eye contact. Little talk. ... It did get better but I found myself resisting too. One latecomer x resisted ... saying that if [they] stay in grade 1 then what valuing was there? ... They wanted to ask me questions as the ex-[x]. I said after the session. I kept thinking how to tackle this and decided to persist, be gentle and open. (Focus Group 3 Memo 21/9/2011)

I agreed to respond to teachers' questions as an ex-manager at the end of the session. I had to be sensitive, firm and coaxing and address teacher scepticism about their voices being heard. A teacher-in-charge interviewee later apologised for his tone and the questions he asked under pressure from teachers for whom he was responsible, who had expected him to raise their issues in the focus group.

In contrast, teachers too could feel ill at ease. One teacher seemed nervous at the beginning of his interview: 'I feel the teacher-in-charge is a little tense or not sure how to take me...' (School 6), revealing his vulnerability. My research therefore, needed strategies to build trust, which I discuss later.

The Difficulty of Being Seen as an Outsider

It was difficult for some teachers to view me as an outsider given my ex-managerial role. This meant I had to consciously make sure I did not slip back into my former role. Teachers were sometimes a little uneasy that I wanted little extra attention paid to me. When I openly discussed how it felt to participate in my research, teachers often spoke of how deference had to be shown to me whether or not my previous managerial role was current.

Aamir was 'inspired' and surprised by my behaviour, not expecting me to teach as an equal with the other teachers:

> Whether you are the x or the x, we have to respect you ... But we are extremely happy with how friendly you are with us, with the children ... When classes have been without a teacher you did not feel that you can't go in and teach ... and as a boss won't go in ... you didn't let us notice a difference. You have been as a teacher. I have been very inspired especially in our Pakistan context. (Aamir, lines 395-406)

However, 'especially in our Pakistan context' implies that I was able to do this *because* I was an outsider and not hindered by the importance of status in society.

In contrast, Zakir, the teacher-in-charge of a school with an old building with poor facilities, stated that he thought that I would not stay:

> no one could ever imagine a x setting foot here ... You've seen the state ... you were to work here for three days; you've been in a best position, ... in good places ... I just thought that you would see the school the first day and say that you would not work here any more! ... would run away ... but I am very happy that you have spent three days with us in the extreme poverty in which the school is. (Zakir, lines 310-319)

These examples show how teachers would often first place me into the ex-insider role but take on a different perception as my positionality changed, even taking on a 'valuing' role, which I turn to next.

The Ex-insider Researcher as the Valuer

Although I had planned to value teachers and 'give back' to teachers during my research, I did not anticipate that my very presence as an ex-senior employee and researcher would in itself become such a source of value.

Barkat commented that when his school village community saw that the school was receiving attention by a 'leader' who unusually arrived early, this raised its status and expectations of school improvement. This, in turn, had ethical implications.

In addition, teachers who had been selected as research participants also felt honoured. Indeed Aliyah took it as confirmation that there was something of worth within her:

> But believe me, I consider myself lucky that you chose me, sat in my class ... face to face ... So I feel very valued .... teachers told me that madam is coming to me. So I said there and then that ... it means that *I am something.* (Aliya, lines 100-102)

Many teachers talked about having heard my name, received a letter or seen my photo and wishing to meet someday, some calling it a 'dream'. Although I (the British outsider) found the deference embarrassing, it was also a humbling reminder of the power and obligation of my roles and the need to portray teachers' perspectives as truly as possible.

The Ex-insider Researcher with Knowledge of the Region and Teachers' Context

Retaining the outsider researcher positionality became difficult when questioned by some teachers on matters that were being worked on while I was in the organisation. Addressing me as the ex-insider senior manager, some teachers wanted to have honest answers as to what exactly had been done to improve teachers' lives and how far a resolution had been reached. This was difficult to respond to as I could not reveal confidential information, even if this would have satisfied teachers. However, I did know that a significant decision was about to be revealed which would have pleased teachers. This made it easier to respond to teachers and deal with any distress and anger portrayed during the research process.

Laying Open the Insider Role: did teachers tell me the truth?

In order to 'de-mystify' my previous role as a senior manager, and assess whether interview data were 'true', I specifically discussed my ex-role and the impact of it. When I questioned whether teachers' responses would have been the same if I had still been in the organisation, most teachers said that they had responded honestly because, for example, of my nature, because it was research and/or because one needs to be honest, as the following excerpt demonstrates:

> No. No there would be no difference. ... whether you are current x or the ex; you are definitely an educationist ... linked to this organisation. We should present our problems frankly ... You have examined the economic state of our area ... What can we hide from you, what more could we say ... or fear you and say something else? I said this at the beginning – honesty – it's the one thing we should not compromise on. (Diyanat, lines 476-484)

In contrast, two teachers said that they would have emphasised the negative aspects of their work in order to try and get what they needed, such as a higher salary. Kabir, who had asked me if I was going to return to the organisation (perhaps wondering if he had been too honest), stated that he would never have admitted that he did not like teaching, as it would have been highly inappropriate. However, he said that he had been utterly truthful and that if I returned there was both fear and hope:

> There are two things here. One that you would remove me from the system or the second – that you would promote me! (laughing out loud). (Kabir, lines 409-411)

Moreover, three teachers said that there would have been some apprehension if I were still in post, and fear of retribution if, for instance, they had not taught well, offended me in some way, or had been found lacking in terms of showing respect and hospitality.

Such responses provide an insight into the highly hierarchical and status-conscious nature of the society in which the teachers live. It also showed, however, that openness and honesty can be achieved and that as an ex-employee I had an advantage of being both an insider and an outsider in my research.

The Teacher/Teacher Educator as Researcher: how could I build trust?

I drew on my insiderness as a teacher to develop trust with participants but was constantly aware of how far I could go in challenging convention and how far being identified as a teacher colleague, with the 'embodied situatedness' (Sultana, 2007) of the insider, could break down potential barriers. I sat on the floor with teachers; taught with the same lack of resources; ate food donated from the community with them, and drank tea with salt instead of sugar (as this was too expensive).

I heard a surprised teacher tell his head teacher, 'She teaches really well!', which may have meant that I was becoming a credible insider. Some teachers asked me to give feedback on their teaching and wanted to observe me teach. In addition, my training in basic counselling proved helpful in generating a safe interview environment, given that I was conscious that I may be 'revisiting of unhappy experiences' (Birch & Miller, 2000), or conducting research 'that probes the very personal, subjective truths of people's lives' (Clarke & Sharf, 2007, p. 399).

Significantly, my insider teacher and teacher-educator roles enabled me to work alongside teachers to explore the meaning of 'feeling valued' in more depth. Within the focus groups, I noticed that I used to say 'we' in trying to explore the meaning of 'feeling valued' with teachers. For instance, when teachers laughed spontaneously in an exercise that revealed that most teachers actually felt valued, I gently asked, 'Why did we all laugh just now?', positioning myself with the teachers through a shared experience.

Teachers had the opportunity to explore, learn and reflect together, sometimes surprising themselves in the content of what emerged, the depth of discussion, and the level of enjoyment that they had. I found that participants, generally, became deeply engaged in discussion and would challenge and argue with each other on, for example, whether they really felt pride or a sense of inferiority when students did well and earned more than they did. They would also question each other on, for example, the point of feeling valued when it is a cultural requirement that a student greets them in a particular way. As the facilitator/catalyst I was able to provoke a critical analysis of such teacher perceptions.

Interestingly, an unexpected result was that the innovative workshop format changed teachers' views of research. Some teachers reported that they were expecting to be bored or write a number of pages, or even wondered if they would cooperate with me. However, when the session started they found it easy and enjoyable. This may be more evidence that, rather than seeing me as an ex-manager from the urban south of the country who did not understand teachers' realities, they began to position me as a skilled teacher who could induce more meaningful participation.

One unexpected spin-off from the focus-group format was that teachers gained ideas for teaching:

> If we teach children this way, make these kinds of activities,
> our children will learn a lot. (Focus Group 2, 734)

Likewise, a spontaneous remark from a teacher in the middle of a focus group – 'this *really* is research!' – revealed that he thought the process enabled teachers' inner thoughts to emerge:

> I had some questions in my mind ... I don't know how you did
> it in such a way that things came to the fore. (Focus Group 3,
> 649)

And another teacher admitted:

> I think we disclosed some of our secrets to you! (*laughter*).
> (Focus Group 3, 635)

Such positioning allowed me to enter the teacher world as an insider and pull down barriers. Wray and Bartholomew (2010, p. 13) argue that the similarity between researcher and participants may be less important than the identifying, scrutinising and destabilising of power relations that maintain insiderness and outsiderness.

Personal Attributes and Positionalities: the female researcher

I will now turn to how my personal background might have influenced the research process. Table II identifies my personal attributes and positionalities, and shows how these rendered me both an insider and an outsider to my research participants and their context.

A Female Researcher in a Traditional Male-dominated Society

As a woman of South Asian heritage I was constantly aware of the image that I was portraying through my dress, voice and demeanour and what this could mean for developing beneficial relationships. I was acutely aware of safety concerns travelling and living as a lone female in a patriarchal society, similar to those expressed by Pardhan (2011). To be fully prepared, I undertook a fieldwork risk assessment, covering aspects such as physical and personal safety, transport, health and communications and the implications of these for me as a female researcher. The support of the organisation was crucial in this respect.

As a female living alone in a hotel, I had to ensure that I wore traditional modest dress, that my hair was tied back and that I wore a headscarf/shawl when situations demanded. I ensured that I behaved modestly, particularly in mixed-gender situations, such as when I received visitors or conversed with other hotel guests (always in public). In effect, I sought 'culturally desirable ways' of representing myself (Lim, 2012, p. 6) to be more acceptable as an insider to the research context.

However, having formerly held a senior position within the organisation, this added to the respect and care that was shown to me, which is an example of how various status positions interacted. A brother of an organisational employee worked as a gardener in the hotel and seemed to have been given the charge of 'looking after', me as he would come to visit me and give me local apples! Being female and an ex-senior manager was also an advantage when talking to both female and male participants, an aspect I turn to next.

Identity/Status	Insider ←-------------------	-------------------------------------	-------------------→Outsider
Ethnicity/ cultural knowledge	South Asian/North Pakistani. Parents from village background		British – born & educated, urban background
Gender – female	To female teachers	Honorary male due to age and former role in organisation	To male teachers
Significant shared experience	Educated woman in male-dominated society Educated woman living with 'uneducated' in-laws		Relative freedom in UK UK 2nd-generation 'immigrant' experience
Language	Urdu speaker – but with 'foreign' accent Familiarity with multilingual personal and professional environment		Fluent native speaker of English Non-speaker of local languages of research context
Religion	Muslim	Knowledge of sects present in Pakistan & experience of personal and professional relations	British Muslim
Social class	Working-class origin		Middle class through education and profession
Age	Same age as some teachers		Older than some teachers

Table II. Researcher insider and outsider positionalities: personal attributes.

The Female Researcher Talking to Female Participants

I found that female teachers wanted to talk to me about dilemmas as educated women. Living in traditional homes with uneducated in-laws, they were expected to take on the household chores when they needed to have time to prepare lessons. As a woman who has also struggled to become educated and also has 'uneducated' in-laws, I found myself empathising and feeling protective of female teachers. For example, I noted Khadima's yearning for education and frustration with family conditions and the need to talk about how difficult it was for her. Some female teachers also expressed the difficulties of working with male teachers who held sexist attitudes, and I could also identify with them. In such cases it was my female and researcher positionality that came to the fore. I also had to honour confidential information shared by females that I would have otherwise reported.

The Female Researcher Talking to Male Participants

My position as a mature female researcher gave me an advantage in relation to male participants as my age bestowed a level of seniority and respect that would not have been there for a younger female researcher. Added to this was the seniority of my former position. Put together, I feel this rendered me – for men – an 'honorary' male, which gave me access to men of all ages and led to fruitful discussions.

The Cultural Insider as Researcher

'Ruhaani Rishta': the spiritual relationship between teacher and student

As an 'insider' in terms of both my personal and my professional attributes, I felt I could relate to teachers more easily than, perhaps, someone with only northern perspectives. Nettles (2011) and Pring (2011) refer to the dilemma of how researchers from one tradition can struggle to understand people and education from very different traditions. However, my position as a bicultural person who shares both insider and outsider perspectives added to my ability to ask basic questions, while also having an understanding of the social, cultural and organisational contexts.

I was also able, as a Muslim, to probe the religious significance when teachers referred to, for example, teaching being a prophetic profession, or said that their honest work resulted in their being showered with 'blessings', such as always being given a lift home or having their meagre salary stretch a long way in meeting their basic needs.

One particular 'feeling valued' incident expressed by a teacher, as shown in the excerpt below, challenged me in terms of being a researcher. I wonder if I may have 'over-empathised', because the story brought tears to my eyes. On reflection I realised how my background enabled me to truly understand the significance of the event and how deeply this occasion must have affected the teacher.

> We had a non-Ismaili girl, a Pathan [originally from the Khyber-Pukhtunkhwa province of Pakistan (bordering Gilgit-Baltistan) and known for their strict observance of 'protecting' women] ... I was on the bus bringing my family from Gilgit ... There were two empty seats in front of us which had been reserved. After leaving Gilgit quite far behind ... a woman in a burqa [cloth covering a woman's body from head to toe, worn by women from conservative Muslim families, such as Pathans] came in with a man and sat in front. I recognised the man ... from Gupis ... We shook hands. My family was sitting with me, my small son on my lap at the time.
>
> After about 5-10 minutes the Pathan man turned around and said, 'Respected Ustaad [teacher], the woman sitting next to me was a student of yours. She said she wants to meet her teacher in the bus. She says she cannot bear sitting in front of her teacher with him sitting behind and not being able to greet him. She had left school after matriculation ...'
>
> After thinking about it I said that it did not seem right that we meet in the open in a moving bus. He said, 'No, no. She respects you'. So I said that if she didn't mind lifting her veil among so many people and considered it an honour to greet me then I had no objection.
>
> So that young lady ... held the seat and stood up in the moving bus, lifted up her veil, took my hand and kissed it ...
>
> 'Sir, you were my Ustaad, how can I be in front of you? ... I can't sit in front of you, please sit in front with my uncle and I'll sit behind with your wife.' She picked my child up and carried him to my home.
>
> So isn't this respecting me?! (Amin, pilot interview, lines 237-255)

This account is laden with values that only someone very familiar with the culture of the region can understand. The young lady wears a 'burqa' in public and is escorted by an older male relative – indicating that she belongs to a family that is very strict in the separation of women from men (other than close family). She respects her teacher so much that she feels she has to greet him – but how in a public bus when everyone would see her face?

The teacher belongs to the Ismaili sect of Shia Islam that is known for its more 'enlightened' view towards female education. However, he is well aware of the import of the situation and feels uneasy about meeting in public. But he agrees when the uncle states how much she respects her teacher. So she lifts her veil in front of everyone in the bus who now can see her (and therefore contravenes traditional cultural conventions), and gives him the traditional greeting of a kiss on the hand! To her it is an affront to sit in front of her teacher (sitting at the front is for more important people and she cannot have her back towards her teacher), so she changes seats. Moreover, she helps by carrying the child (whom he was carrying) to her teacher's home as a further mark of respect.

This account wonderfully encapsulates the meaning of the '*ruhaani rishta*' (spiritual relationship) between teacher and student. In listening to this story, I automatically suspended my more western feminist leaning which would see how bound the girl was and, indeed, how all the characters complied with socio-cultural gender roles, and felt compelled to simply appreciate the act as someone within the culture, as a Muslim woman of Pakistani origin and as a teacher.

The Bilingual Researcher in a Multilingual Environment

My personal attributes of being bilingual and familiar with a multilingual environment enabled me to embrace multiple languages and, therefore, multiple perspectives being used within my research. Although all schools were 'English medium' schools, lessons observed were in fact taught multilingually – in the local language such as Shina or Burushaski, as well as in Urdu, the national language, and English. I therefore conducted research mostly in Urdu, although younger teachers tended to use more English. I also had to speak more slowly to allow teachers to get used to my English accent. My insiderness with regard to being Urdu-speaking assisted communication and enabled me to probe the depths of concepts teachers used to try to fathom the meaning and significance of 'feeling valued'. In contrast, my outsiderness in being a native English speaker created desires in teachers to improve their English-speaking competence.

Working in Urdu posed a challenge for transcription. I used 'roman' Urdu [2] and then translated and worked on the data in English. Finding exact English equivalents was an interesting exercise in trying to capture the essence of meaning; for example, one respondent used the phrase '*ma'muli makhluuq*' (that I translated as 'a lowly creature') (Kabir, 195).

Teachers also spontaneously chatted in local languages which I sometimes asked to be translated. Although their use of local languages may have signified their being at ease and engaged with the process, it could also have meant a loss of data if some aspects were being kept hidden. Including teachers' own languages in the fieldwork and presentation of findings enabled a more nuanced understanding, was inclusive of teachers, and also recognises that readers of research may themselves be bi/multilingual.

Tensions within the Bicultural Researcher Self

However, even within my bicultural self that understood both cultures there was a tension. Despite wanting to 'democratise' relationships, I had to accept the 'blinding' respect and deference that younger teachers would give to older teachers, for instance, or the role that female students and teachers took in preparing tea in school. I also felt uncomfortable being called 'Madame' or 'Ma'am' and with the gratitude teachers expressed in meeting someone they considered of high status.

Contrary to my ethical guidelines that included not placing an unnecessary burden on teachers with regard to the demands of traditional hospitality, it was extremely difficult to refuse teachers' invitations to their homes, when this was considered an honour. While insisting that no extra trouble was taken, I (the insider) eventually visited three teachers, enabling me to also see them within their home and family contexts. Consequently, while my bicultural researcher self helped increase inclusivity, I also had to respect the limitations and stay respectful to the culture within which the research was taking place, thereby curbing any desire to change things from an 'outsider' perspective.

It is also possible for the multi-identities of the researcher self to 'get it wrong'. Within one of the focus groups a female teacher who I hoped would consent to being interviewed in school had refused. As it happened, I selected her head teacher as an interviewee and ended up in her school, only to find out that she was ashamed of the poor state of her school and facilities that she did not think worthy of a visit from a senior guest, whom she had deemed an honoured 'outsider' with high 'insider' status.

Discussion

When interpretative research requires us to step into the shoes of our participants, why are we still being challenged with respect to objectivity and the pull of positivism? When there are multiple and diverse perspectives, where 'fieldwork is personal, relational and political' (Lim, 2012, p. 10) and one can only 'partially know' (Usher, 1996), why then would research knowledge produced by the outside anthropologist who has learned to be a 'native' over time and yet remain distinct (Hockey, 1993, cited in Hellawell, 2006) be deemed more authentic than that of an insider who has learnt to stand back and attain intellectual distance?

In my research I undertook a number of roles, not all planned, including facilitator, catalyst, guide, instructor, educator and advocate, and engaged in 'continually shifting relationships' (Thomson & Gunter, 2011, p. 25). So the question arises, do the concepts of the insider or outsider disappear to reveal complex individuals with their own unique histories?

I suggest that what separates a good piece of research from another is not insider/outsiderness but the skill with which the research has been conducted and conveyed, having reflected on these concepts.

As a bicultural insider with shared cultural, religious and institutional experiences and as a teacher/educator with 'intuitive sensitivity' (Merton, 1972, p. 15), a sincere desire to change teachers' lives for the better, I was more easily accepted, had more credibility and could build on my understanding of the context. This led to a high level of teacher contribution. Would an 'outsider' have understood the cultural context, institutional history and teacher context so easily?

Moreover, as a bicultural insider, as a researcher from the North, as someone no longer formally linked to the organisation, perhaps I was able to pursue the 'dialogic encounter' (McNess et al, 2013) of cultures within myself. I was still able to ask detailed questions and practise reflexivity, to constantly question what was happening within the research relationships. This enabled me to generate contextually relevant theory and recommendations grounded in teachers' views, particularly important considering the critique of applying northern concepts and policy solutions, de-contextualised, to the South (see Crossley & Watson 2003).

Robinson-Pant (2013) argues that the notion of insider–outsiderness may be useful as a culturally essential tool that can be used as a starting point for researchers to think about their perspectives and how they affect their research. However, it has been argued that empathy, rather than closeness or distance to the research context, is a critical factor for good research. For Dwyer and Buckle (2009, p. 59), the core ingredient is 'to be open, authentic, honest, deeply interested in the experience of one's research participants, and committed to accurately and adequately representing their experience'.

How does one teach researchers to feel empathy and enter the 'secret garden of reflexivity', to explore the 'disguised hidden elements' (Hellawell, 2006, p. 492) that may have drawn them to the topic in the first place? Perhaps we need to return to the word 'research' and '*re*-search' within ourselves throughout the process of inquiry. However, questioning oneself and being vulnerable and uncertain does not come easily to most. Such teaching could develop competences such as care, sensitivity and the heightened self- and social awareness needed to plan and conduct insider/outsider, in-between research and tap into the internal reflexive dialogic process.

Hellawell (2006) uses the insider–outsider concept as a heuristic tool to develop the ability of students to become reflexive, defined as the conscious revelation of the roles of beliefs and values held by researchers in the selection of research methodology. My reflexivity as the researcher added to the rigour of the research, by checking any 'subjective' bias and creating transparency through exploring power and ethical issues (Etherington, 2004). Developing ethical guidelines and a fieldwork risk assessment was extremely beneficial in helping me think through potential challenges of insider- and outsiderness and attain a state of 'ethical mindfulness' (Etherington, 2001) before going into the field. Research by scholars such as Chavez (2008) and Sherif (2001) shows how naive thinking before entering the field can lead to challenges that could have been anticipated.

One can see that the context and the multiple perspectives in my research rendered it far from straightforward. It was indeed messy, and only some aspects of this were anticipated. However, is this 'messiness' not the very substance of reality and research that is based on developing relationships that are dependent on the participation of teachers? Do we not need to acknowledge 'the mess inherent in all collaborative enterprises conducted in the real micro-political worlds' (Jones & Stanley, 2010, p. 151)?

In the end, my biculturalness and biography full of multiplicities enabled me to research within the 'in-between space', lay open the researcher positionalities and employ the skills of being a good listener. I believe that these multiplicities allowed teachers and myself to communicate more effectively and, for them, as one respondent said, 'to express things that were hidden inside' (Focus Group 4, line 486). However, perhaps what was ultimately important was 'to carry out work respectfully, in ways that increase, rather than diminish, equity' (Dickson & Green, 2001, p. 257).

Notes

[1] I use the term 'bicultural' here to generally refer to being able to relate to both the North (UK) and the South (Pakistan) cultural contexts. However, I acknowledge that in fact there are multi-cultures within which I function (e.g. gender, class) and that cultures are not static.

[2] Urdu is written in a cursive script, from right to left, similar to Arabic and Persian. I did not have Urdu software on my computer.

References

Bhabha, H.K. (1994) *The Location of Culture*. London: Routledge.

Birch, M. & Miller, T. (2000) Inviting Intimacy: the interview as therapeutic opportunity, *International Journal of Social Research Methodology 2000*, 3(3), 189-202. http://dx.doi.org/10.1080/13645570050083689

Byram, M. (2003) On Being 'Bicultural' and 'Intercultural,' in *Intercultural Experience and Education*, chapter 4. Clevedon: Multilingual Matters.

Chavez, C. (2008) Conceptualising from the Inside: advantages, complications, and demands on insider positionality, *The Qualitative Report*, 13(3), 472-494.

Clarke, M.C. & Sharf, B.F. (2007) The Dark Side of Truth(s): ethical dilemmas in researching the personal, *Qualitative Inquiry*, 13(3), 399-416. http://dx.doi.org/10.1177/1077800406297662

Cresswell, J.W. (2003) *Research Design: qualitative, quantitative, and mixed methods approaches,* 2nd edn. London: SAGE.

Crossley, M. & Watson, K. (2003) *Comparative and International Research in Education: globalisation, context and difference.* London: RoutledgeFalmer. http://dx.doi.org/10.4324/9780203452745

Dickson, G. & Green, K. (2001) The External Researcher in Participatory Action Research, *Educational Action Research,* 9(2), 243-260. http://dx.doi.org/10.1080/09650790100200150

Dimmock, C. (2002) Cross-cultural Differences in Interpreting and Doing Research, in M. Coleman & A.R. Briggs, *Research Methods in Educational Leadership and Management*, pp. 28-42. London: Paul Chapman.

Dwyer, S. & Buckle, J. (2009) The Space Between: on being an insider–outsider in qualitative research, *International Journal of Qualitative Methods*, 8(1), 54-63.

Etherington, K. (2001) Research with Ex-clients: a celebration and extension of the therapeutic process, *British Journal of Guidance and Counselling,* 29(1), 5-19.

Etherington, K. (2004) *Becoming a Reflexive Practitioner.* PowerPoint presentation at Doctoral Programmes Conference, University of Bristol, 15-16 July. http://dx.doi.org/10.1080/03069880020019347

Hellawell, D. (2006) Inside-out: analysis of the insider–outsider concept as a heuristic device to develop reflexivity in students doing qualitative research, *Teaching in Higher Education*, 11(4), 483-494. http://dx.doi.org/10.1080/13562510600874292

Jones, M. & Stanley, G. (2010) Collaborative Action Research: a democratic undertaking or a web of collusion and compliance?, *International Journal of Research and Method in Education*, 33(2), 151-163. http://dx.doi.org/10.1080/1743727X.2010.484549

Katyal, R.K. & King, M. (2011) 'Outsiderness' and 'Insiderness' in a Confucian Society: complexity of contexts, *Comparative Education*, 47(3), 327-341. http://dx.doi.org/10.1080/03050068.2011.586765

Kvale, S. & Brinkmann, S. (2009) *Interviews: learning the craft of qualitative interviewing*. London: SAGE.

Lim, M. (2012) Being a Korean Studying Koreans in an American School: reflections on culture, power, and ideology, *The Qualitative Report*, 17(18), 1-15.

McNess, E., Arthur, L. & Crossley, M. (2013) 'Ethnographic Dazzle' and the Construction of the 'Other': revisiting dimensions of insider and outsider research for international and comparative education, *Compare*, 45(2), 295-316. http://dx.doi.org/10.1080/03057925.2013.854616

Merton, R. (1972) Insiders and Outsiders: a chapter in the sociology of knowledge, *American Journal of Sociology*, July, 9-47.

Milligan, L. (2014) Insider–Outsider–Inbetweener? Researcher Positioning, Participative Methods and Cross-cultural Educational Research, *Compare*, published online 24 June, 1-16. http://dx.doi.org/10.1080/03057925.2014.928510

Morrison, M. (2002) What Do We Mean by Educational Research?, in M. Coleman & A.R. Briggs (Eds) *Research Methods in Educational Leadership and Management*, pp. 3-27. London: Paul Chapman.

Nettles, M. (2011) Afterword, in A. Halai & D. Wiliam (Eds) *Research Methodologies in the South*. Karachi: Oxford University Press.

Nguyen, A.D. & Benet-Martínez, V. (2007) Biculturalism Unpacked: components, individual differences, and outcomes, *Social and Personality Psychology Compass*, 1(1), 101-114. http://dx.doi.org/10.1111/j.1751-9004.2007.00029.x

Pardhan, A. (2011) Ethnographic Field Methods in Research with Women: field experiences from Pakistan, in A. Halai & D. Wiliam (Eds) *Research Methodologies in the South*. Karachi: Oxford University Press.

Pring, R. (2011) Researching Very Different Societies: an impossible task?, in A. Halai & D. Wiliam (Eds) *Research Methodologies in the South*. Karachi: Oxford University Press.

Qureshi, R. (2011) Who Pays the Price? The Ethics of Vulnerability in Research, in A. Halai & D. Wiliam (Eds) *Research Methodologies in the South*. Karachi: Oxford University Press.

Ritchie, J., Zwi, A.B., Blignault, I., Bunde-Birouste, A. & Silove, D. (2009) Insider–Outsider Positions in Health-development Research: reflections for practice, 19(1), 106-112. http://dx.doi.org/10.1080/09614520802576526

Robinson-Pant, Anne (2013) Exploring the Concept of Insider/Outsider in Comparative and International Research: essentialising culture of culturally essential? Key note paper presented at the BIACE Thematic Forum Conference *Revisiting Insider/Outsider Perspectives in International and Comparative Education*, February 2014, University of Bristol.

Sherif, B. (2001) The Ambiguity of Boundaries in the Fieldwork Experience: establishing rapport and negotiating insider/outsider status, *Qualitative Inquiry*, 2001(7), 436-447. http://dx.doi.org/10.1177/107780040100700403

Sultana, F. (2007) Reflexivity, Positionality and Participatory Ethics: negotiating fieldwork dilemmas in international research, *ACME: an international e-journal for critical geographies*, 6(3), 374-385.

Thomson, P. & Gunter, H. (2011) Inside, Outside, Upside Down: the fluidity of academic researcher 'identity' in working with/in school, *International Journal of Research and Method in Education*, 34(1), 17-30. http://dx.doi.org/10.1080/1743727X.2011.552309

Usher, R. (1996) A Critique of the Neglected Epistemological Assumptions of Educational Research, in D. Scott & R. Usher (Eds) *Understanding Educational Research*, pp. 87-99. London: Routledge.

Wray, S. & Bartholomew, M. (2010) Some Reflections on Outsider and Insider Identities in Ethnic and Migrant Qualitative Research, *Migration Letters*, 7(1), 7-16.

CHAPTER 9

Outside Inside, Inside Out: challenges and complexities of research in Gypsy and Traveller communities

JULIET McCAFFERY

Introduction

This chapter examines insider–outsider experience during research on literacy among Gypsies and Travellers. It outlines the theoretical concepts underlying the approach and the ethnographic and constructivist methodologies adopted. It reflects on the process of gaining access to a marginalised community. It describes Gypsy and Traveller multiple identities, their culture and history and their suspicion of researchers. It refers to the settled or mainstream community's prejudice, lack of knowledge of Gypsies and Travellers and the ongoing tension between the two communities.

I am not a Gypsy or a Traveller and have no genealogical links to the community. I am a Gaujo, a non-Gypsy, an 'outsider'. My research carried out between 2004 and 2012 explored Gypsies' and Travellers' perceptions of, and attitudes towards, literacy, and found that, unlike most communities, many Gypsies and Travellers do not consider literacy or success in formal education contributes to their social status, their self-esteem or economic success. Other factors are considered more important.

My interest in marginalised communities began when I worked on a literacy project among the semi-nomadic Fulani in north-eastern Nigeria. My initial research design had been to compare the relevance of adult literacy provision for the Fulani in Nigeria with the provision for Gypsies and Travellers in England. But shortly after I began my research, I discovered there was no literacy provision targeted at Gypsies and Travellers in southern England, so I had to rapidly redesign my research.

I decided to focus on the attitudes of Gypsies and Travellers towards literacy and formal education.

Before starting the research, I had not realised the difficulty of accessing the Gypsy and Traveller communities, nor anticipated the degree of their distrust of outsiders. The title of this chapter reflects the journey I undertook. During the research I moved from being a complete outsider with little knowledge of the community, to someone who gradually came to be known and accepted as a supporter, someone who would speak up for Gypsies and Travellers. I was seen and trusted as a participant in what is perceived as a struggle. Though my research is completed, I am still involved in a project to increase Gypsies' and Travellers' contribution to the decision-making processes which affect their lives. As I learnt more about the community, I began to understand its strengths and boundaries and how close-knit it is. I moved from the barren outside towards a warmer inside and, though increasingly accepted, as I learnt more I became aware that while I was accepted by many in the community, I was, and always would be, an outsider. The title reflects this 'outside-inside, inside-out' journey.

I start by outlining the theoretical concepts underlying my approach and the methodology I adopted. In order to understand this particular insider–outsider situation, the reader, like the researcher, needs to have some knowledge and understanding of Gypsy and Traveller culture, the history of the community, their complex identities and the difficulties many encounter daily. I outline these and suggest reasons for their suspicion of outsiders, including researchers. I then explain how I was able to access the community through my different roles as researcher, supporter and elected councillor to explore their attitudes to literacy and education, and how moving towards an insider position enabled a co-construction of knowledge.

Theoretical Concepts and Methodological Framework

Many people have contributed to the theoretical concepts of the insider–outside debate, including Harris (1990), Crossley and Watson (2003), Kelly (2013), Robinson-Pant (2013) and McNess et al (2013). I do not repeat the debates here, but mention certain aspects such as the concept of the 'outsider' and 'third spaces' that are particularly relevant to my research with Gypsies and Travellers.

The challenge of researching marginalised communities and the impact this has on research design is well documented (Malinowski, 1922 [1961]; Evans-Pritchard, 1937; Shostak, 1981), but the research by these cited authors explored and documented communities in distant places. Much of the literature discusses these issues in depth and provides accounts of how ethnographers 'gained entry', though these accounts are inevitably one-sided (Lareau & Schultz, 1996). Gypsies and

Travellers in the south of England, on the other hand, are not distant, they are nearby and often not easily distinguishable from the mainstream community (Bhopal & Myers, 2008; McCaffery, 2012). The concept of the wanderer who 'is near and yet far', choosing to remain an outsider (Bauman, 1991), reflects the position of many Gypsies and Travellers who, since their arrival in England five hundred years ago, have largely chosen to remain outside the mainstream settled community (Levinson, 2008; McCaffery, 2012).

Gaining access to marginalised groups within the researcher's own geographical environment has also been documented (Whyte, 1955; Whitehead, 1976). Levinson (2008) gives a graphic account of his difficulties researching Gypsies and Travellers in the UK. He describes his surprise at their reluctance to participate and the length of time it took him to gain their trust. He suggests that when undertaking her research, Okely (1983) took a position as a warden on a Traveller site, as she feared she would gain little information if they knew she was a researcher. She needed to become in part an insider to gain their trust. This distrust is not exceptional; the Maori researcher Tuhiwai-Smith (1999) considers that research was one of the dirtiest words in the indigenous world's vocabulary. My own experience of being part of a women's group that was 'researched' suggests that it is not only indigenous groups who experience 'being researched' as a negative process. My trepidation and moral anxiety about researching Gypsies and Travellers in part stems from my own experience.

Shortly after I began my research, two comments made by Gypsies during a conference in Birmingham confirmed my trepidation.

> An academic makes up a myth, which is then reproduced by all the others ... They come, ask us questions and then go away and build a career on the answers. (Gypsy Traveller Law Reform Conference, Birmingham, October 2004)

Tuhiwai-Smith (1999) highlights the power dimension in post-colonial research. Though the research teams may come from both the dominant West and previously colonised countries, the power is usually held by western academics. Though English Gypsies and Irish Travellers are in a different category and strongly object to any suggestion that they need to be 'developed', research into their communities has largely, though not exclusively, been undertaken by outsiders, Gaujos (non-Gypsies).

There are few written records. In part this is because education was rarely available to Gypsies and Travellers before the 1980s and recording events was not part of their culture. The lack of records may also have been deliberate in order to preserve and protect the culture from Gaujos (Levinson, 2008). More information about research issues is therefore not easily accessible to researchers (Okely, 1983; Levinson, 2008; McCaffery, 2014).

As stated earlier, there is a perception among Gypsies and Travellers that researchers are self-seekers who will use their knowledge to build careers and who may represent the community inaccurately with damaging effect. This fear of revealing information is also fuelled by memories of the 'Porajamos', the Holocaust, in which nearly a million Gypsies died. However, the situation is slowly changing and Gaujo academic research is now being challenged by 'the emergence of a Gypsy/Roma/Traveller academic community' itself (Hancock, 2010, p. 4).

In discussing insider–outsider research, Robinson-Pant (2013), quoting Holy (1984, p. 32), stresses the ethnographic approach. She points to the relationship between the researcher and the subject as having the status of a research method, as 'not just getting to know each other, but about the dialectical construction of knowledge'. As McNess et al (2013) state, outsiders need to understand the underlying meaning of historically and culturally embedded discourse. They also suggest a 'third space' which arises when insiders and outsiders meet and through discussion and dialogue develop new understandings. Shortly after I began my research, as opposed to becoming familiar to the community, I was fortunate to meet Martin, an Irish Traveller, with whom I formed a positive relationship and from our different insider–outsider perspectives we constructed joint understandings.

The practical challenges and the recognition of the multiple experiences, multiple perceptions and multiple realities which sometimes conflict suggested a constructivist methodology in which the researcher and the researched jointly construct partial and contestable interpretations of the situation, as emic insider and etic outsider perspectives. Gypsies and Travellers have acted, and are acting on the world, in particular ways, and the outside researcher's understanding and knowledge of these is dependent on their own knowledge, cultural and political perspectives and experience. I adopted an ethnographic approach using ethnographic tools, 'collecting whatever data are available' (Hammersley & Atkinson, 1995, p. 1) in a variety of situations as described below. Initially the research progressed slowly and it took four years of interacting with the community before I felt that a Gypsy or Traveller would trust me sufficiently to agree to be interviewed.

Culturalism, Constructivism and Identity

It would seem to be stating the obvious that researchers should have a good understanding of the community with which they wish to engage. But I have to admit that despite having taught two English Gypsies many years ago, I had minimal knowledge of the communities, their history or their culture.

Gypsy and Traveller identity is currently the subject of much discussion. Some of the debates demonstrate the gap in mainstream society's understanding of the community and are worth signalling here. For instance, a recent report of a local authority meeting in March 2013 [1] described an English Romani Gypsy, who had had a permanent residence for thirty years, as representing 'travelling communities'. This accords with the popular view of Gypsies and Travellers as a single homogeneous group who constantly travel, establish unauthorised encampments and disrupt the settled community. Few people realise that within this generic description of 'Travellers' or 'Travelling communities' are different ethnic and linguistic communities with different cultures, customs and religions.

Estimates of the population of English Gypsies and Irish Travellers in England and Wales vary enormously and are contested. Current estimates are between 300,000 and 400,000, of whom approximately two-thirds live in houses (Office of the Deputy Prime Minister, 2006), but the census (ONS, 2011) recorded only 57,680 in the category 'white Gypsy or Irish Traveller', and these were not separately identified. While some Gypsies and Travellers recognise the need for an accurate record of the Gypsy and Traveller population, their history of persecution, the death of nearly a million Gypsies in the 'Porajamos', and the levels of prejudice and hostility they still experience frame their attitude and militate against revealing their ethnic identity.

Whatever the exact origins as propounded by different writers, there is general agreement that over a thousand years ago Romanies travelled out of northern India and moved westwards in family groups, or possibly as a military entourage (Hancock 2008:42). Common characteristics of the Romanies are a shared culture and a dialect of north Indian origin (Okely, 1983; Acton, 1997; Kenrick, 1998; Hancock, 2002, 2008; Clark & Greenfields, 2006; Bhopal & Myers, 2008). The history of the Roma people is fascinating, depressing and complex (Okely, 1983; Acton, 1997; Kenrick, 1998; Hancock, 2002, 2008; UNESCO, 2005, 2010). In brief, it is largely one of persecution and enslavement in many countries in Europe. After they were initially accepted in England, hostility increased to the extent that in the Elizabethan era people identified as Gypsies were hanged.

There are five distinct groups of Gypsies and Travellers in the British Isles – English Gypsies, Welsh Gypsies, Scottish Gypsies, Irish Travellers and Roma. Four of these, are of Romani origin; the origins of Irish Travellers are more obscure (Worrall, 1979; Okely, 1983; Ni Shuinear, 1994; Kenrick; 1998; Binchy, 2000; Clark & Greenfields, 2006; Bhopal & Myers, 2008). English Gypsies speak Angloromani, which uses English syntax and Romani words (Matras et al, 2000), while Irish Travellers speak Gammon or Cant, which has no connection to Romanes. Today Roma are the largest minority in Europe, but the hostility towards them is considerable and is reflected in political statements and the clearance of encampments in Romania, France and Italy (Mason, 2013; Ruff, 2013).

Individuals describe themselves as, and identify as, members of one of the above groups, but 'identity' and the formation of identity are complex constructions in the theoretical literature. For instance, Holland et al (1998, p. 66) state:

> 'Identity' is a concept that invokes and relates theories from various streams of psychology, social psychology, anthropology, sociology and ... intercultural studies.

Hall (1990) posits a twofold construction of belonging, marking the place of origin and becoming – the process of transition to a new situation. Vertovec (2007) links the prejudice English Gypsies experience to current immigration debates, though their circumstances and the length of time they have been in England are not comparable as they arrived five hundred years ago. Though they recognise their origins, Said's (1978) process of 'transition', though difficult, took place for them centuries ago. English Gypsies identify with England and different communities have long historical roots in different parts of the country; they talk about coming from distinct localities.

Holland et al (1998) suggest that two key concepts addressed by those concerned with identity are culturalism and constructivism. Culturalists they describe as emphasising the impact of cultural influences such as artefacts, art, stories, literature, genealogical links, social history and shared memories, all of which contribute to the formation of identity, whatever their living circumstances. Constructivists, on the other hand, argue that identity is developed within a social and historical context in relation to dominant discourses and power structures, which the growing child imbibes and so develops 'a way of being', or 'habitus' in Bourdieu's (1991) terminology. Holland et al (1998) argue that in different ways both theories impact on identity formation and 'habitus'. While a shared culture is an important signifier of Gypsy identity, so is the impact of dominant discourses and structures of power, both local and national. I adopt Holland's perspective.

Berni, a Romani Gypsy, demonstrates the relevance of both theories. He was clear about his identity:

> I mean I feel ... I'm just normal. I know who I am ... a Gypsy, what I do ... at least it comes naturally. It is the same as Gaujos ... what they do, comes naturally. (Berni, interview, August 2008)

Yet the structures of power deeply affected Berni and his family, as they were among the English Gypsies forcibly evicted from the New Forest and resettled in 1947.[2]

Researchers should also recognise that Gypsy and Traveller identity is not a

> one dimensional social or ethnic type ... but complex and ever changing ... as ideas and people themselves adapt to, develop and incorporate their environment over time. (Belton, 2010, p. 39)

During my research, I gradually realised that many Gypsies and Travellers do not travel and they cannot be identified solely by a travelling status as 75% live in 'bricks and mortar'. Nevertheless, for many Gypsies and Travellers the concept of travelling is deeply embedded and for some it is a way a way of life – that is, an emotional, psychological and cultural imperative (OPM, 2010). There are a variety of different patterns of living – bricks and mortar, mobile homes on private sites with or without planning permission, mobile homes or large caravans on council sites, short- and longer-term transit sites or recourse to unauthorised sites for those who travel or who have not obtained a pitch on a permanent site. Many of those on authorised pitches park up in the winter months and travel in the summer, though many never travel.

Many, but not all, who move into housing maintain their distinctive cultural beliefs and practices and continue to identify as Gypsies or Travellers. During my research I came to realise that, as mentioned earlier, Gypsies and Travellers have long-standing links to particular geographical areas and in terms of identity they refer to their families as coming from particular counties.

However, some academics consider Gypsies and Travellers as much a social construction as a genetic and biological identity. Hancock, a Romani professor, asserts:

> If groups of individuals identify themselves as Romanies and assert their ethnicity, to ally themselves with other such groups similarly motivated, then this is entirely their own business. (Hancock, 2008, p. 43)

However, ethnicity and identity confer legal status and this, like their history, is contested. After forty years of contestation, they are recognised in law as an ethnic group and are covered by the Race Relations Act 1976 and Human Rights Act 1998.

The question of identity has not only social and psychological importance but has daily consequences. In 2004, a family living in Kent was evicted after losing their appeal for retrospective planning permission on land they had bought. They lost on the grounds that they no longer travelled and were therefore not Gypsies and not entitled to special consideration under the planning laws.[3]

In 2006, Circular 1/2006, 'Planning for Gypsy and Caravan Sites', issued by the Office of the Deputy Prime Minister (ODPM), widened the legal definition of Gypsies and Travellers to include former nomads:

> Persons of nomadic habit of life whatever their race or origin, including such persons who on grounds only of their own or their family's or dependents' educational or health needs or old age have ceased to travel temporarily or permanently, but excluding members of an organised group of travelling show people or circus people travelling together as such. (Circular 1/2006, para.15, p. 4)

In 2006, in response to high-profile community tensions over unauthorised encampments in England, the government placed a duty on councils to identify land for sites. This has again raised the question of identity – for whom has land to be found? The definition above implies the inclusion of 'New Age Travellers' who travel for economic reasons (Johnson & Willers, 2004, p. 16).

In 2014, the government proposed to withdraw the ethnic definition from Gypsies and Travellers who have settled in housing. If the proposal is successful, those in housing would no longer be able to apply for a place on a permanent or transit site and the number of pitches required would be reduced. The police have formally objected to any change along the lines proposed.[4]

These complexities of description, ascription and legal definition are problematic and researchers need to be cognisant of which legal definitions are used under which circumstances. They also need to know which terms are acceptable to the particular individuals and groups with whom they engage. Identities shift and the use of the wrong word can cause hostility and can end the interaction.

Another key issue in addressing identity is nomenclature, also a sensitive and complex issue. When used alone, the term 'Gypsies' tends to refer to English Gypsies/Romani Gypsies or Romanichals, and 'Travellers' refers to Irish Travellers. The term Gypsy/Traveller seems to me a misnomer as it implies travelling and, as stated above, many English Gypsies and Irish Travellers no longer travel.

The terminology they prefer shifts and changes. Some Gypsies prefer to be called 'Travellers', viewing the term 'Gypsy' as insulting; others wish to emphasise their Romani heritage to disassociate themselves from New Travellers. Some English Gypsies refer to themselves as Romani Travellers. In Europe the term 'Gypsy' is considered derogatory. In England the term 'Gypsy, Roma, Traveller' or 'GRT' is increasingly common. The descriptors used in the English education system in 2011 were 'Gypsy/Roma' or 'Traveller of Irish heritage'. The fact that English Romani Gypsies speak English as a first language, whereas the European Roma do not, and therefore have very different educational needs, appears to have been considered unimportant. The term 'Pikey', often used to describe Irish Travellers, is considered an insult. The choice of nomenclature is difficult for the researcher. I prefer the term 'English Romanies', but it is not in common use, so I resort to Gypsies and Travellers.

Researchers who are not members of the community should familiarise themselves with various aspects of the culture, particularly those that are less visible and take longer to learn. These include the importance of cleanliness; a gendered division of labour, with few married women working outside the home; intergenerational living arrangements; and a tradition of self-employment, including house-to-house calling, tree cutting and tarmacking. Weddings [5] and funerals provide important social occasions, as do both local and national horse fairs. Communication, whether personal or for business, is usually conducted orally, though Facebook is increasingly being used for personal communication. This limited use of written text makes questionnaires an inappropriate research tool.

An example of the impact of constructivism and ways in which dominant power structures impact on individuals is the availability of stopping places, somewhere to park caravans or mobile homes, either temporarily or permanently. Nearly 10 years after the 1959 Act, when hawking or stopping on the roadside were made illegal, the 1968 Caravan Sites Act directed Local Authorities to provide sites for Gypsies and Travellers, but many local authorities simply ignored the directive. In 1994 the Caravan Sites Act of 1968 was repealed and replaced by the Criminal Justice and Public Order Act (CJPOA), which made unauthorised encampments illegal. Gypsies and Travellers were recommended to make their own provision, and many bought land. However, ninety per cent of Gypsy and Traveller planning applications were initially rejected (ACERT, 1997). In March 2005, a leading Gypsy campaigner and his extended family were evicted after losing an eight-year legal battle to remain on land they owned [6], and in July 2010 a family lost their appeal to stay on their land in East Sussex (McCaffery, 2012) and were forced to return to travelling with nowhere legal to stop. The eviction of the encampment at Dale Farm in Essex in August 2011 highlighted the situation. While the number of successful planning applications by Gypsies and Travellers for private sites has increased, the number of successful appeals is still much lower than it is for the settled community. This may change, as in January 2015 the High Court ruled that Eric Pickles, Secretary of State for Communities and Local Government, had discriminated unlawfully against a racial group by subjecting planning applications from Gypsies and Travellers to special scrutiny.[7]

Nationally, evictions from unauthorised sites have been estimated to cost around £18 million a year. In 2006 the government undertook an accommodation needs survey in order to determine the needs of the Gypsies and Travellers. The survey identified the need for 225 additional pitches in Sussex, more than double the number provided at the time of the survey (South East Regional Assembly March, 2009). The land required to provide a legal pitch for the 25,000 Gypsies and Travellers in England who have no legal stopping place is estimated to be equivalent to two football pitches.

Public Discourse and Identity

The tension and misunderstanding between the settled or mainstream community on the one hand, and travelling communities on the other, caused by centuries of living apart, coupled with the difficulties of travelling or securing a site, are difficult for the outside researcher to overcome. The mainstream community knows little about English Romani Gypsies and Irish Travellers apart from unauthorised encampments and hostile press reports in local papers. As stated previously, self-ascribed identities change due to living circumstances and changing perceptions, but Gypsy and Traveller identity is also determined by mainstream perceptions constructed through public discourse and the media. Critical reports are frequent in local papers such as the *Bristol Evening Post* (1998), and national papers include inflammatory headlines such as the now infamous 'Stamp on the Camps' (*Sun*, 2004) and the reports of the blonde girl taken from a Gypsy family in Ireland (*Mirror, 2013).*[8]

Comments such as 'They steal babies' or 'They are spongers, as they don't pay anything' are common.[9] Even highly respected community leaders, such as elected councillors, show considerable prejudice:

> I agree with you about equalities, except where it concerns Gypsies and Travellers. (Council leader, 2006)[10]

And an MP described them as:

> People who think it's perfectly OK for them to cause mayhem, burgling, thieving, breaking into vehicles including defecating in doorways of firms. (Jack Straw, 22 July 1999)[11]

Much of the literature on Gypsies and Travellers is concerned with the boundaries between Gypsies, Travellers and 'others' which are 'always in flux ... because of changes within society and its relationship to Gypsy culture' (Bhopal & Myers, 2008, p. 14). Belton (2010, p. 23) states that 'the identification of the other [which when] seen in a positive light marks out uniqueness and difference ... can easily be interpreted as strange and/or alien'. At a conference on Romaphobia in January 2014, Le Bas, an English Romani, gave a presentation entitled 'Tax-dodging Millionaire Scumbag Beggars: the tenacity of oxymoronic anti-Gypsy stereotypes', demonstrating the conflicting negative stereotyping (Le Bas, 2014).

Bhopal and Myers (2008, pp. 98-103) state that belonging requires an opposite – a not-belonging or an 'other', an 'outsider'. They argue that Gypsies and Travellers are constructed by society to fulfil this role. They draw on Bauman's (1991) concept of the 'stranger', who is near and yet far, who comes from nowhere, but is a strong physical and presence in the neighbourhood. Morley (2000) equates this space with the concept of home which extends into the immediate neighbourhood as a place of safety and security. Thus a group of Travellers encamped in the park disrupts the use of the park bench [12], the outdoor 'private' space. The concept of occupying space has been developed by Kendall (1997), who argues that unauthorised sites can be seen by both Gypsies and Travellers and by the sedentary community as a direct challenge to authority.

Researchers may be asked to assist in different ways. Hammersley and Atkinson (1995) suggest they can provide medical or legal advice if this is requested, as there is a reluctance to approach official institutions. Lee (1993) suggests political advocacy, with which Whitehead (1976) concurs. I wrote letters, supported planning applications and, when requested, spoke to officials and advocated at both political and personal levels. This was time consuming and unrelated to the subject of my research, but it developed a level of reciprocity and trust between myself and members of the Gypsy and Traveller community. Where possible, I shared my understanding of the interviews and informal conversations with those involved and with them co-constructed an interpretation of events.

Gaining Access

Gaining access is not just an initial entry into the research setting, but an iterative process in which my insider–outsider roles interacted with their multiple and shifting identities in an ongoing process in which my presence was continually negotiated (Lee, 1993; Hammersley & Atkinson, 1995). Over the period of the research I interviewed fifteen women and seventeen men. Fourteen lived on permanent council sites, four had their own private sites, five lived in houses and two in flats; seven were on unauthorised sites when I spoke to them. Half of those I interviewed had very limited literacy skills and nine could not read at all. The better readers lived in secure accommodation and three, who lived in housing, had university degrees.

As a researcher I was inside and outside different groupings, sliding through different perspectives as the situation required. A key entry point was the Sussex Traveller Action Group (STAG), a small support organisation that I and a colleague started in 2003 after querying the recommendations in a Draft Local Authority Plan. We gained funding to survey statutory and voluntary service delivery to the Gypsies and Travellers who lived on local authority–managed sites (Forrest & McCaffery, 2006). This assisted my access to the residents when I began the research into literacy. As a representative of STAG, I was able to attend Traveller forums and the county police's Gypsy and Traveller Advisory Group (GTAG). Gypsies, Travellers and settled people attended these meetings which sometimes, though not always, provided opportunities for genuine dialogue. The various meetings can perhaps be described as 'Third Spaces' or 'in-between spaces' (Bhabha, 1994; Kelly, 2013).

Other 'in-between spaces' or 'third spaces' I attended were large conferences, local and regional forums, and various formal, semi-formal and informal meetings. Though attending as a member of STAG, I found myself on the edge of the different groups, sometimes inside and sometimes outside, and sometimes partially inside and partially outside.

My third point of access was as an elected local councillor in one of the local authorities. My position as an insider on various council committees enabled me to raise issues relevant to Gypsies and Travellers and to ask for information and request reports for committees, though these were often only produced reluctantly. It took me ten years to get a report on Gypsies and Travellers to an education committee, and when I asked about the impact of evictions on school attendance, I was told not to be political.[13]

My fourth point of entry was more traditional in terms of research. In much ethnographic research, 'gate keepers' provide an entry point to the community. As mentioned previously, I was fortunate to meet Martin, a settled Irish Traveller, who to some extent played this role. He had a very difficult childhood and then spent many years travelling round the world; he crossed boundaries and had other non-Traveller friends and good relations with his local settled community. Our relationship was very different to my relationship with those I interviewed. Over a period of two years we met and conversed many times and, in accordance with the constructivist approach, jointly constructed our knowledge and understanding. Bhabha (1994) argues that this 'Third Space' goes beyond the concepts of insider or outside to produce new meanings, and Simmel (1908 [1958]) suggests that insiders may talk to outsiders about issues they would not discuss with those on the inside. My relationship with Martin reflected both concepts as he shared his ideas with me, someone outside his community, and between us we arrived at new meanings and interpretations of the situations we witnessed (McNess et al, 2013).

Martin helped me understand the communities, how they organised and where their sensitivities lay. From him I learned of the community's pride, of their frustration, of their preference to 'keep themselves to themselves'. He also reinforced my instinct to approach Gypsies and Travellers slowly and sensitively, and I noticed he did this himself. His sensitivity and perception were a factor in our relationship and he seemed in many ways to understand me. Between us, we perhaps had what Bakhtin (1986) describes as cognitive empathy. Bakhtin refers to this as 'stranger knowledge', while McNess et al (2013, p. 307) cite Sennet (2012), who argues that

> this is a new awareness, not necessarily vocalised but involving hearing what has not been said and which requires a curiosity and openness to new understandings and a dialogic form of communication that is subjective and tentative, rather than declarative.

In case this sounds too perfect a picture, Martin controlled the situation. If he wanted support or assistance I always agreed. Contact was when he wanted to contact me, rather than the other way round. Though I formed good relationships with other Gypsies and Travellers who opened different doors, without Martin many of the gates which opened would have remained closed.

My different roles gradually enabled me to become known and seen in spaces where dialogue and discourse took place, virtual as well as real, and enabled 'people in the field to place and locate me within their experience' (Hammersley & Atkinson, 1995, p. 83). It was known that I was doing research into education, but I was primarily known as a supporter, someone who would speak up for Gypsies and Travellers. As stated above, I was seen as a participant in a struggle. I was sometimes asked to assist – to help complete a questionnaire, to help with an email, to write a letter, to contact officials over a site difficulty, to give a lift to a meeting, to advise on the purchase of a piece of land and to support a planning application. These requests did not occur until I was known and trusted. Providing support took a considerable amount of time and carried responsibilities.

I have now developed good relations with many local Gypsies and Travellers – predominantly, though not exclusively, with English Romanies resident in the area – and I continue to work with them to increase their influence on the decision-making processes which affect their lives. I like to think some have become good friends. One incident highlights my insider–outsider status. In December 2014, I was roundly castigated for being unhygienic when I put my cup of tea on the floor of a Gypsy's mobile home. A year earlier a small table would have been discreetly brought and my cup placed on a coaster on the table, but by this visit I was sufficiently 'inside' to be roundly told off. Conversely, the incident made me realise that I will never completely know the culture and ways of behaving. I may be accepted by many in the community but I can never be completely inside.

Conclusion

When writing up my research and looking back on my notes, I feel privileged to have engaged with this community and honoured that not only Martin, but all those I interviewed entrusted me with personal information. It took time to gain this trust and I hope I have not abused it. I was able to form relationships with community members because I was involved in practical issues. Though I never concealed the fact that I was doing research, this was secondary to my other involvements.

Although, as I have stated, I had little previous knowledge of the Gypsy and Traveller community, I was surprised most settled or mainstream people were almost unaware of their existence – except as the group of caravan dwellers on the edge of cities. I also noted that those who were sympathetic had much greater knowledge of the community. Several of the strongest supporters, both locally and nationally, are ex-police officers who came to know the community through their work.

I have used an ethnographic and constructivist approach to describe my journey from the outside to the inside and out again. My journey illustrates the complexities of relationships that are involved when research is undertaken in marginalised communities and the length of time required for trust to develop sufficiently to engage in co-construction of knowledge.

However much researchers desire to share their research and strive to become at least partial insiders, my reservations about researching marginalised communities remain. Yet I believe that appropriate research can improve the situation of Gypsies and Travellers.

The lack of knowledge of Gypsies and Travellers among the settled community impacts adversely on the ability to resolve conflict over public and private sites and unauthorised encampments. Outside researchers who develop good relations with, and are trusted by, the community can assist. But for real understanding to develop, more insider research is required. As an outsider I can begin to understand the present, but I can never really share the history and the past. While I can sympathise with the damaging impact of prejudice, I cannot experience it as they do.

The challenges are significant, but if more Gypsies and Travellers gain the ability to undertake research on their own communities (Hancock, 2010), a combination of inside-out and outside-in research might assist in creating a third shared space and begin to bridge the gap in understanding and knowledge, and thus reduce the tension between Gypsies and Travellers and the settled community, a situation which would be of benefit to both communities.

Notes

[1] Minutes of a health and wellbeing meeting in East Sussex, March 2013.

[2] Gypsies lived freely in the New Forest for centuries but a process of forcibly moving them into dedicated areas and later compounds started in 1926 and ended with their eviction and resettlement in 1947.

[3] In 2004 the ODPM advised that the Human Rights Act should be carefully considered in relation to parity between settled and travelling communities.

[4] Gypsy and Traveller Advisory Group, 4 December 2014.

[5] The series *My Big Fat Gypsy Wedding* (Channel 4, 2012) offended many who considered it a misrepresentation of their culture. http://www.channel4.com/programmes/my-big-fat-gypsy-wedding (accessed 7 February 2014).

[6] Kilroy-Silke, *A Week with the Gypsies*, ITV, 4 April 2005.

[7] See article in the *Independent* (Green, 2015).

[8] *Bristol Evening Post*, 28 March 1998; *Sun*, 9 April 2004; *Mirror*, 23 October 2013.

[9] Personal communications.

[10] Personal communication.

[11] Jack Straw, 22 July 1999. Interview with Annie Oathen, Radio West Midlands, quoted by Monbiot, 2004.

[12] Personal communication.

[13] Brighton and Hove Council: Children, Schools and Families Scrutiny Committee, 28 January 2009.

References

Acton, T. (Ed.) (1997) *Gypsy Politics and Traveller Identity*. Hertford: University of Hertfordshire Press.

Bakhtin, M.M. (1986) *Speech Genres and Other Late Essays*, ed. C. Emerson & M. Holquist, trans. V.W. McGee. Austin: University of Texas Press.

Bauman, Z. (1991) *Modernity and Ambivalence*. Cambridge: Polity Press.

Belton, B. (2010) Knowing Gypsies. in D. Le Bas & T. Action (Eds) *All Change: Romani studies through Romani eyes*, pp. 39-49. Hertford: University of Hertfordshire Press.

Bhabha, H.K. (1994) *The Location of Culture*. London: Routledge.

Bhopal, K. & Myers, M. (2008) *Insiders, Outsiders and Others*. Hertford: University of Hertfordshire Press.

Binchy, A. (2000) Shelta/Gammon in Dublin Societies, in T. Acton & M. Dalphinis (Eds) *Language, Blacks and Gypsies*, pp. 128-132. London: Whiting & Birch.

Bourdieu, Pierre (1977) *Outline of a Theory of Practice*. Cambridge: Cambridge University Press. http://dx.doi.org/10.1017/CBO9780511812507

Clark, C. & Greenfields, M. (Eds) (2006) *Here to Stay*. Hertford: Hertfordshire University Press.

Crossley, M. & Watson, K. (2003) *Comparative and International Education: globalisation, context and differences.* London: Routledge. http://dx.doi.org/10.4324/9780203452745

Evans-Pritchard, E. (1937) *Witchcraft, Oracles and Magic among the Azande.* Oxford: Clarendon Press.

Forrest, S. & McCaffery, J. (2006) A Report on the Survey of Travellers in West Sussex. Sussex Travellers Action Group. Brighton: Change Up (unpublished).

Green, C. (2015) http://www.independent.co.uk/news/uk/politics/eric-pickles-illegally-discriminating-against-gypsies-and-travellers-the-high-court (accessed 3 February 2015).

Hall, S. (1990) Cultural Identity and Diaspora, in J. Rutherford (Ed.) *Identity, Community, Culture, Difference.* London: Lawrence & Wishart.

Hammersley, M. & Atkinson, P. (1995) *Ethnography: principles in practice.* London: Routledge.

Hancock, I. (2002) *We Are the Romani People.* Hertford: University of Hertfordshire Press.

Hancock, I. (2008) Romani Origins and Romani Identity: a reassessment of the arguments, in *Roma Memorial Issue*, pp. 39-45. Chandigarh: Roma Publications.

Hancock, I. (2010) *Danger! Educated Gypsy: selected essays.* Hertford: University of Hertfordshire Press.

Harris, M. (1990) Emics and Etics Revisited, in T. Headland, K. Pike & M. Harris (Eds) *Emics and Etics: the insider/outsider debate. Frontiers of Anthropology*, vol. 7. London: SAGE.

Holland, D., Lachicotte Jr., W., Skinner, D. & Cain, C. (1998) *Identity and Agency in Cultural Worlds.* Cambridge, MA: Harvard University Press.

Holy, L. (1984) Theory, Methodology and the Research Process, in R. Ellen (Ed.) *Ethnographic Research: a guide to general conduct.* London: Academic Press.

Johnson, C. & Willers, M. (2004) *Gypsy and Traveller Law.* London: Legal Action Group.

Kelly, P. (2013) Researcher Positionality in Comparative Pedagogy: a relational account. Paper prepared for BAICE Insider/Outsider Forum, Cambridge, September 2012.

Kendall, S. (1997) Sites of Resistance: places on the margins – the Traveller 'homeplace', in T. Acton & G. Mundy (Eds) *Romani Culture and Gypsy Identity.* Hertford: University of Hertfordshire Press.

Kenrick, D. (1998) The Travellers of Ireland, *Patron Web Journal.* http://www.geocities.com/~Patrin/ (accessed 2 January 2008).

Lareau, A. & Schultz, J. (1996) *Journeys through Ethnography: realistic accounts of fieldwork.* Boulder, CO: Westview Press.

Le Bas, D. (2014) Tax-dodging Millionaire Scumbag Beggars: the tenacity of oxymoronic anti-Gypsy stereotypes. Presentation at Conference on Romaphobia and the Media, 20 January, King's College London.

Lee, R. (1993) *Doing Research on Sensitive Topics*. London: SAGE.

Levinson, M. (2008) Researching Groups that are Hidden and/or Marginalised, *Research Intelligence, Comment, British Educational Research Association*, 2(4), 16-18.

Malinowski, B. (1922 [1961]) *Argonauts of the Western Pacific*. New York: E.P. Dutton.

Matras, Y., Bakker, P., Hibschmannova, M., Kalinin, V., Kenrick, D., Kyuchukov, H. & Soravia, G. (Eds) (2000) *What is the Romani Language?* Hertford: University of Hertfordshire Press.

McCaffery, J. (2012) *Access, Agency, Assimilation: literacy among Gypsies and Travellers in southern England*. Stuttgart: Lambert Academic Publishers and University of Sussex. http://sro.sussex.ac.uk/38614/

McCaffery, J. (2014) Education as Cultural Conflict: Gypsies and Travellers in southern England, in R. Griffin (Ed.) *Education in Indigenous, Nomadic and Travelling Communities*. London: Bloomsbury.

McNess, E., Arthur, L. & Crossley, M. (2013) 'Ethnographic Dazzle' and the Construction of the Other: revisiting the dimensions of insider and outsider research for international and comparative education, *Compare*, 45(2), 295-317. http://dx.doi.org/10.1080/03057925.2013.854616

Monbiot, G. (2004) Jack Straw, Interview with Annie Oathen (1999), 22 July. Radio West Midlands.

Morley, D. (2000) *Home Territories: media, mobility and identity*. London: Routledge. http://dx.doi.org/10.4324/9780203444177

National Lottery Heritage Fund (n.d.) Remembering Our Family. http://www.newforestromanygypsytraveller.co.uk/history1.html (accessed 8 February 2014).

Ni Shuinear, S. (1994) Irish Travellers, Ethnicity and the Origins Question, in M. McCann, S. O' Siochain & J. Ruane (Eds) *Irish Travellers, Culture and Ethnicity*, pp. 54-77. Belfast: Queen's University, Institute of Irish Studies.

Office for Public Management (OPM) (2010) Health and Social Care Needs of Gypsies and Travellers in West Sussex. Report to NHS West Sussex County Council. London: Office for Public Management. http://rcn.org/development/practice/socialinclusion/gypsy_and_traveller_communities (accessed 5 December 2007).

Office of National Statistics (ONS) (2011) Table KS201EW. http://www.ons.gov.uk/ons/rel/census/2011-census/key-statistics-for-local-authorities-in-england-and-wales/rpt-ethnicity.html (accessed 13 April 2013).

Office of the Deputy Prime Minister (2006) Planning for Gypsy and Caravan Sites. Circular 1/2006, para. 15, p. 4. http://www.communities.gov.uk/publications/planningandbuilding/circulargypsytraveller (accessed 4 May 2008).

Okely, J. (1983) *The Traveller Gypsies*. Cambridge: Cambridge University Press. http://dx.doi.org/10.1017/CBO9780511621789

Robinson-Pant, A. (2013) Exploring the Concept of Insider/Outsider in Comparative and International Research: essentialising culture or culturally essential? Paper presented at the BAICE Thematic Forum Workshop, University of Bristol.

Said, E. (1978) *Orientalism*. London: Penguin.

Sennet, R. (2012) *Together: the rituals, pleasures and politics of cooperation*. London: Penguin.

Shostak, M. (1981) *Nisa: the life and words of a !Kung woman*. Cambridge, MA: Harvard University Press.

Simmel, G. (1908 [1958]) *Soziologie, Untersuchungen über Formen Der Vergesellschaftung* [Sociology, Studies of Forms of Socialization], 4th edn. Berlin: Duncker & Humboldt.

South East Regional Assembly March (2009) Partial Review of the Regional Spatial Strategy for the South East: provision for Gypsies, Travellers and travelling show people. Guildford: England Regional Partnership Board.

Tuhiwai-Smith, L. (1999) *Decolonising Methodologies: research and indigenous peoples*. London: Zed Books.

UNESCO EFA Global Monitoring Report (2006) *Literacy for Life 2006*. Paris: UNESCO.

UNESCO EFA Global Monitoring Report (2010) *Reaching the Marginalised*. Oxford: Oxford University Press.

Vertovec, S. (2007) *New Complexities of Cohesion in Britain: super-diversity, transnationalism and civil integration*. Commission on Integration and Cohesion. Wetherby: Communities and Local Government Publications.

Whitehead, A. (1976) Sexual Antagonism in Herefordshire, in D. Barker & S. Allen (Eds) *Dependence and Exploitation in Work and Marriage*, pp. 169-203. London: Longman.

Whyte, W.F. (1955) *Street Corner Society: the social structure of an Italian slum*. Chicago: Chicago University Press.

Worrall, D. (1979) *Gypsy Education: a study of provision in England and Wales*. Walsall: Walsall Council for Community Relations.

CHAPTER 10

(Re)constructing Identities beyond Boundaries: revisiting insider–outsider perspectives in research on international students

QING GU

Introduction

This chapter discusses the nature of international students' transnational experiences and their impact on the (re)construction of their identities within and beyond national and cultural boundaries. The discussion is located in the theoretical framework of transnationalism and explores in detail the ways in which the students negotiate *meaning* as an insider and outsider, both in the host country of their study and also on their return to work in their home countries.

Empirical evidence in the chapter is drawn from a synthesis of the findings from three studies, led by the author, which have investigated the pedagogical, sociocultural and emotional challenges that international students have encountered when studying at British universities and the perceived impact of their overseas studies on their lives and careers in their home countries. The research findings suggest that there are distinctive patterns of challenges, struggles, adjustment, change and achievement over time – all of which are embedded in the processes of socialisation, enculturation and professionalisation. Such experiences are both transitional and transformational and, most profoundly, they necessitate identity change at and across different layers of boundaries. At the heart of this identity change is a constant, emotional search for a reflexive sense of self as an embodied individual, a member of a professional group and a member of an organisation. The chapter concludes with methodological and conceptual implications for future research.

International Student Mobility: the context

Historical accounts of student mobility and intercultural education can be traced back to 272-222 BC (Ward et al, 2001). However, the forms, volume and speed of international students' mobility have undergone profound changes over time. In modern times and the last two decades especially, international student mobility has become a qualitatively and quantitatively distinct phenomenon. First, the global population of international mobile students has proliferated in recent decades and is predicted to continue to surge. In the mid-1970s, there were only 800,000 international mobile students worldwide (British Council, 2012). According to the statistics from UNESCO (2013), the number of students enrolled in educational institutions outside their country of origin increased from 1.3 million in 1999 to 4.3 million in 2011, representing an increase of almost 70%. Such exponential increase survived the most recent global economic recession and has been forecast to grow by 21 million between 2011 and 2020 (British Council, 2012).

Second, the landscape of global student mobility has become more diversified. Although the United States of America and the United Kingdom remain 'strong magnets' for students seeking quality education, enjoying 18% and 11% of the total population of mobile students, respectively (UNESCO, 2014), they have seen a decline in their favourable shares of the revenue and the intellectual capital of international mobile students (from 55% in 2000 to 47% in 2012) as regional hubs became popular destinations for students within regions (UNESCO, 2009, 2014; OECD, 2014). For example, in East Asia and the Pacific, China, Malaysia, the Republic of Korea, Singapore and New Zealand have emerged as new hot-spot destination countries, which hosted 6% of the global share of mobile students in 2012 (UNESCO, 2014).

Third, the migration of international students is not a recent repeat of a historical phenomenon of skills and knowledge mobility and exchange across borders. Rather, it brings into the foreground *current* interaction, dynamics and tensions between local, regional and global politics, cultures, and economic and social processes. The movement of global mobile students is itself deeply unequal. At the individual level, studying-abroad activities remain reserved for a select few (International Association of Universities, 2010). In the case of China, although Chinese students are the largest single international student group in the UK, only less than 2% of tertiary students from China study abroad (UNESCO, 2009). They represent two groups of elite in the society: the socio-economic elite (i.e. mostly self-funded students), and the educated elite (i.e. students funded by scholarships) (Wang & Miao, 2013).

At national levels, there are well-established associations between gross domestic product (GDP) and labour migration, skills and student mobility (ADBI, 2014; OECD, 2014). It is perhaps, then, not surprising that the predominant pattern of student movement continues to be from lower-income to higher-income countries (Seddoh, 2001; OECD, 2007, 2014; Uvalić-Trumbić et al, 2007; UNESCO, 2009, 2013, 2014), and such East–West and South–North student mobility has major implications for the generation of economic, social and intellectual capital in the host nations. It is estimated that Asian migrants alone accounted for more than 70% of skilled workers under the US H-1B specialty occupations programme (ADBI, 2014). In OECD countries, recent immigrants are found to be more highly educated than the resident population and previous cohorts of immigrants (Widmaier & Dumont, 2011).

Taken together, analyses of the current contexts of international student mobility show that international students have become, increasingly and significantly, a prominent border-crossing population in the global migration movements. They carry with them, beyond graduation, the attitudes, skills and contacts that they develop during their studies outside their usual countries of residence. The complex and heterogeneous composition of this group and the diverse and dynamic nature of their experiences have attracted scholars from different disciplines, driven by their distinct theoretical, methodological and ideological concerns, to unravel this relatively nascent field.

Psychologists and socio-psychologists have contributed by far the richest empirical evidence on the experiences of international students. Their work tends to be primarily concerned with the deterministic role of culture in international students' experiences, their subsequent stress levels and coping strategies, and the quality of the support mechanisms that are available to promote (or inhibit) students' intercultural adaptation, intra- and interpersonal interactions and psychological wellbeing (Ward & Kennedy, 1993; Cushner & Karim, 2004; Smith & Khawaja, 2011; Zhang & Goodson, 2011; Suspitsyna, 2012; Glass & Westmont, 2013). However, the limitations of their 'objectivistic' methodology (Gudykunst, 2005, p. 25) and deficit approach (Gu & Schweisfurth, 2015a) mean that they often fail to consider the role of human agency in international students' management of their overseas learning experiences or to elaborate on the complexity of international students' identity negotiations and sense-making in the cultural, social and educational worlds that they are exposed to.

In contrast, geographers are newcomers to the field. However, over the last decade, their research on mobile students has provided important evidence of the way in which biographical, sociocultural and socio-economic factors influence the geographical (im)mobility of students (e.g. Findlay & King, 2010; Carlson, 2013; Geddie, 2013; Waters & Leung, 2013), and of how mobile students' access to transnational education – whether it was through family migration (e.g. Waters, 2007) or through studying on off-shore programmes in their home country (e.g. Sin, 2013; Waters & Leung, 2013) – can be converted to social and cultural capital that fosters their social and economic advantage, class reproduction, and employment and social mobility (e.g. Brooks et al, 2012). This body of migration research tends to be qualitative and, in many cases, small scale in nature, and is primarily grounded in theories of migration, sociology and/or socio-economics.

However, despite the growing literature, well-grounded empirical research that depicts the transnational experiences of international students is still in its infancy. This is especially the case if we also include the experiences of graduate returnees in the continuum of mobility experiences. Drawing upon empirical evidence from a number studies undertaken by the author and her colleagues over the last decade, this chapter focuses on the ways in which international students' transnational experiences impact on the (re)construction of their identities within and beyond national and cultural boundaries. Concepts from theories of transnationalism are used as research lenses to explore the ways in which international students negotiate *meaning* as an insider and outsider both in the host country of their study and also on their return to work in their home countries.

Being and Becoming Transnational: identity across time and space

The theory of transnationalism has attracted a growing interest in social science in recent years – primarily as a positive response to an increasingly 'flat' world (Friedman, 2005), where a transnational life, either physically or virtually, has become a norm for many individuals across nation states. In contrast to the 'old' long-distance connections maintained by migrants 100 years ago, today's 'new' global interconnectedness, facilitated by improved technology and transformed telecommunications, is substantively different in its scale, intensity and velocity (Held et al., 1999; Portes, 2003; Smith, 2003; Vertovec, 2009). Transnationalism is essentially concerned with 'linkages between people, places and institutions crossing nation-state borders' (Vertovec, 2009, p. 1), which lead to 'sustained cross-border relationships, patterns of exchange, affiliations and social formation' (Vertovec, 2009, p. 2):

> Transnationalism describes a condition in which, despite great distances and notwithstanding the presence of international borders (and all the laws, regulations and national narratives they represent), certain kinds of relationships have been globally intensified and now take place paradoxically in a planet-spanning yet common – however virtual – arena of activity. (Vertovec, 2009, p. 3)

Using the transnational lens to delineate the lived worlds of international students during and after their studies is highly relevant in at least three respects. First, it is not a coincidence that international students have been widely regarded – by politicians as well as researchers – as a distinct migrant group. Many 'live dual lives' (Portes, 1997, p. 812) in which they move between their place of origin and the host country, maintain cultural connections and social ties in both places, and through these networks, pursue their educational and career interests across borders. As illustrated by the study on the wider benefits of international higher education in the UK (BIS, 2013), although the effects of such transnational activities of a single student on the culture of the host society may be limited, when they are multiplied across hundreds of thousands of mobile students, the value can add up to 'a social process of significant economic and social impact for communities' of which they are part (Portes, 2003, p. 877).

Related to the above is the second point in that international mobile students create their 'transnational social spaces' (Pries, 1999) in which they encounter, transfer and (re)produce meanings, attitudes and skills that embrace 'here' and 'there'. As Gu and Schweisfurth argue:

> Of particular relevance is the nature of the locality in which they live during their period abroad. Our previous research has demonstrated the importance of receiving universities typically as a particular type of community, which is intentionally, self-consciously and de facto international in its outlook and composition (Schweisfurth & Gu, 2009; Gu et al, 2010): a kind of transnational 'bubble' within a wider local and national context. (Gu & Schweisfurth, 2015a, p. 4)

It is within this transnational 'bubble' that many international students experience, especially initially, emotional loss, loneliness, isolation and detachment. However, they soon learn to use *familiar* social networks both 'here' and 'elsewhere' to engage with new places and new cultures in ways that enable them to develop *transnational* or *diasporic consciousness* that is marked by 'dual or multiple identifications' (Vertovec, 2009, p. 6). These bilateral social and cultural connections serve a dual purpose. On the one hand, social and cultural ties at home (or elsewhere) consolidate mobile students' sense of being different in the host culture and society. On the other hand, they also stimulate a desire in students to connect themselves with those who share the same 'routes' and 'roots' (Gilroy, 1987, 1993) in their transnational bubbles. As the experiences of students in our research show, such desire to connect is deeply associated with a search to belong in the locality. Gu and Schweisfurth (2015a) argue that the awareness of their need for emotional and soial connections in the transmigrant student-self facilitates a range of bonds that they build and maintain with others who have similar experiences, or whose identity or identities overlap in any number of ways with their own. In doing so, their attachments are 'de-centred', marked by a sense of being at 'home' in more than one place (or, potentially, no particular place). In this sense, transnational consciousness, which is essentially composed of an awareness of multi-locality and an abstract awareness of one's self and de-centred attachments (Collins, 2010; Ghosh and Wang, 2003; Vertovec, 2009), can ultimately lead to an enhanced sense of double or multiple belonging (Salih, 2002, 2003; Vertovec, 2004, 2009).

Last but not least, the literature on migrant transnationalism suggests that such dual or multiple orientations of 'cross-cutting belongingness' (Vertovec, 2001, p. 580) are developed in transnational social spaces that are characterised by '*triadic relationships* between groups and institutions in the host state, the sending state (sometimes viewed as an external homeland) and the minority group – migrants and/or refugee groups, or ethnic minorities' (Faist, 1998p. 213, italics in original). For many international students, the triadic relationships are the cross-border social worlds or spaces in which they negotiate their individual identities and 'an enhanced "bi-focality" of outlooks' (Vertovec, 2004, p. 970) which may continue to influence their perceptions of transnationalised self, the makeup of their social and professional networks, and their transnational practices upon return to their home countries.

In Search of the Insider and Outsider Self Across and beyond Boundaries: the research on international students

The Studies

The empirical evidence for this chapter consists of findings of three studies over the last decade, led by the author and her colleagues, investigating different aspects of international students' study and living experiences in UK higher education, and how such experience may contribute to their work and lives upon return to their home countries for work. A distinctive strength of the studies is the holistic and developmental perspective that has enabled the author and her colleagues to probe into a learning and change process that is itself holistic and developmental in nature.

Study 1. This small-scale study functioned as a pilot for Study 2 (Gu & Schweisfurth, 2006). It involved the collection of both qualitative interview data and quantitative questionnaire survey data. The study investigated the challenges that Chinese students had faced in their adaptation to the UK higher education environment. A total of 163 questionnaires were collected from Chinese students on undergraduate and postgraduate courses in four universities in England. Interview subjects included 13 undergraduate and postgraduate students in 10 universities and 2 focus groups from the questionnaire sample. Further triangulation was provided by semi-structured interviews with 10 British lecturers, probing their personal impressions and experiences of the Chinese students they had taught.

The research sample size, particularly the quantitative data, would not enable the author to arrive at generalised conclusions, but there were indicative patterns emerging from early analysis. These patterns complement findings from the other two studies, revealing a process of change in the learners, affected by a range of inter-related personal, cultural, social, psychological and contextual factors.

Study 2. This two-year ESRC-funded mixed-method research was designed to provide an investigation of the experiences of first-year international students during their undergraduate study at four UK universities (Schweisfurth & Gu, 2009; Gu et al, 2010).

The first stage was a four-page 70-item questionnaire to 1288 first-year undergraduates at four UK universities – two 'old' universities (institutions which pre-date 1992) and two 'new' ones (former polytechnics) – aimed at exploring the nature of the initial challenges and needs that international students encountered shortly after their arrival in the UK. The survey resulted in a 19% rate of return. In the second stage, ten case-study students were chosen from among those who volunteered. A series of individual interviews and one group meeting to explore their experiences were carried out over a fifteen-month period, with special attention paid to critical incidents, changes over time, and respondents' explanations for how their experiences were unfolding. The qualitative data gathering also used narrative interviews with the assistance of an instrument adapted from the Variations in Teachers' Work, Lives and Effectiveness (VITAE) study (Day et al, 2006). This instrument required students to recall peaks and troughs during their stay in the UK and to identify 'turning points' (Strauss, 1959) – that is, key moments and experiences that had had a significantly positive or negative impact on their perceptions of their effective management of their study, lives and communication with others. They related how these were managed (or not managed) over time. The final data gathering took the form of a second survey to the same set of undergraduates as in the first stage. This explored changes over time, and tested the qualitative findings from the case studies, to examine whether they had wider validity.

Study 3. The third study, funded by the British Academy, investigated the impact of study-abroad experiences on the lives and careers of Chinese returnees (Gu & Schweisfurth, 2015a). This 20-month two-stage research project also combined quantitative and qualitative methodologies.

The first stage was an online questionnaire survey which explored the Chinese returnees' perceived professional and personal change resulting from their UK educational experiences. The questionnaire was distributed by the British Council, and a total of 652 completed questionnaires were returned. Although the response rate of 8% was low and we cannot claim the representativeness of the profiles of the sample, the size of the response still enabled us to conduct robust analyses and through these, identify common patterns of the transnational experiences of this distinctive group of travellers and settlers in the current context of internationalisation. The results of the survey informed the design of the second stage of the research, whereby fourteen returnees were chosen for face-to-face semi-structured interviews. The purpose of the interviews was to investigate in greater depth the nature of returnees' transnational experiences and the ways in which such experiences continue (or do not continue) to influence them as individuals at work and in their personal lives.

For the purpose of this chapter, results related to students' transnationalised identities will be selected from the general findings for discussion. By bringing together patterns and themes identified in all three studies, it becomes clear that irrespective of their differing demographic and economic backgrounds, for many international students, study abroad is a transitional and transformational life-changing experience – in which they are engaged in a constant search for *who they are* and *whom they want to be* as they move across national borders and, also, cultural, social and structural boundaries.

In Search of the Insider and Outsider Self across and beyond Boundaries

In search of belonging: 'enjoying loneliness'. 'Enjoy' and 'loneliness' do not logically collocate well together. However, when they were put together by a postgraduate student to summarise his social life while studying in the UK, the term conveyed a powerful and profound psychological frustration that he had to cope with. The following example shows that feelings of being lonely and 'not belonging *here*' contributed to students' *sense of alienation* in the host society.

> I was just wondering why I didn't feel lonely at all when I first came here. Because I didn't know what was going to happen every day. ... So every day was a new day ... But this time I came back to England [after the Easter break], I know routinely what happens every day. I know that I will have a presentation to prepare and lots of course work to deal with ... Every day follows the same routine and feels 'normal'. To be honest, I don't like my personal life here. I enjoy my study but my personal and social life is kind of boring. ... Everybody has got their own stuff to do. ... I just feel that I don't belong here. This

> is not my place. I'm the guest and they are the host; and the guest is always less powerful. (Jiayi, China)

Jiayi is not alone. In Study 2, close to half of surveyed international students indicated that they were *unhappy with their social life*. In addition, almost a third reported that they *often felt lonely* when studying in the UK. Similar to Jiayi, the following student from Cameroon expressed similar emotional frustrations and detachment from the environment to which she was exposed:

> Back home I had a career and a future. I was in control of my own life, but I've lost track of that now. Because I had authority [as a hotel manager]. Here I'm virtually powerless ... Sometimes I miss 'home'. Sometimes I miss my parents. Sometimes I miss my mum. Sometimes I just miss being a manager in the hotel. I miss my workplace. (Doris, Cameroon)

The above accounts of international students' experiences support Furnham's (2004, p. 17) observation that 'foreign students face several difficulties, some exclusive to them (as opposed to native students)'. In our studies, these particular difficulties were shown to be caused by challenges to students' professional identities (as in the case of Doris, who had a professional career in her home country) and unfamiliarity with societal values, structures and systems, and, ultimately, feelings of 'being rejected by, or rejecting, members of the new culture' and the new environment (Oberg, 1960, cited in Furnham, 2004, p. 17) (as in the case of Jiayi). Lewthwaite (1986) concluded in his study that 'the differences in values, attitudes and beliefs between home and host cultures were seen as great and coupled with the sense of loss of the familiar (including food) put considerable pressure on the student'. An important point is that twenty years on, his observation continues, it seems, to apply to the experiences of many of today's students.

In search of a new self: 'I was made more aware of my cultural roots.' All three studies found that an unexpected but powerful outcome of international mobile students' reflexive evaluation of their past in China and present everyday experiences in the UK was a transnational perspective which enabled them to be more appreciative of their own cultural traditions and values. As Heusinkvelt pointed out, 'indeed the greatest shock may not be in the encounter with a different culture but in the recognition of how our own culture has shaped us and what we do' (1997, p. 489).

Over half of the second survey respondents in Study 2 reported that their *understanding of the host (UK) culture* had improved. In addition, 93% indicated that they had *become more appreciative of their home culture values*. Upon returning home, a 'double consciousness' (Golbert, 2001, p. 717) of the home culture and that of the hosting country garnered from attempts to connect meaningfully across national and cultural borders was perceived by the majority of the interviewed participants in Study 3 as having contributed to their heightened transnational conception of culture, values and self. The survey results also supported this observation which showed that more than 73% of Chinese returnees believed that they possessed better knowledge of the home (Chinese) culture than those who have not stayed abroad for a lengthy period of time.

Most of the interview participants in Study 3 reported that life in England was quite a lonely one. However, being alone provided them with the space and time to reflect on the unfamiliar cultural values and behaviour that they had encountered and re-evaluate their own values and the ways in which they used to deal with people in the past 'at home'. As a result, they learned more about themselves and their cultural roots. Such deep-seated self-awareness was found to continue to influence their work and lives after they had returned home for work. For example:

> The understanding of different cultures is of the greatest help to me, which can never be learned in universities at home. ... Without the study-abroad experience, maybe I would never get such a clear awareness. It made me look at things from different perspectives and thus enabled me to reflect on problems at a much deeper level. So the overseas experience is highly valuable to me and to my work. Naturally, we all hope that China will develop quickly, but we also know that we still have a lot to do to improve the country. This awareness comes from the comparison with other foreign countries ... I'm a patriot and I have become even more patriotic after being abroad, because in another country, I was made more aware of my roots in China. (Ze, China)

This sense of being closer to their cultural roots in their mind was found to have led to deeper understandings of *what being an outsider means* when living and studying in a foreign country.

Upon returning home, there was no returning to their old self either because such embodied identification of self and the experience of managing the challenge of different ways of thinking, working and living enabled them to learn to accept the diversity of the world and that of the people who live in it. As well as a general openness to diversity, this extended to a sense of pride that, compared with their peers and colleagues, they were able to 'approach problems at a different level and from a different aspect' (Wen, China). Close to half (44%) of the survey respondents felt that their colleagues treated them differently, and this was especially the case among those in their twenties. For them, it is not necessarily the achievements in their academic studies but, as Wen put it, 'the change in the world view and ways of thinking [that] is more important and fundamental'. Such profound change in mindset and values has, perhaps not surprisingly, led many to identify themselves as being different from those around them (i.e. self-identification) and also, at the same time, to feel that they are positioned by others as different 'outsiders' (i.e. group categorisation) (see below for more details on this).

Building identity in between: 'Torn between being yourself and what they want you to do.'

> It's [studying in England] opened up my thinking processes. ... When you are born and brought up in a restrictive environment, everything is about family and you only have a very limited view on things. But when you go to another country and study and you meet people from other countries, then it opens up your perspective and you realise that everything in the world is not the same. ... You are so torn between being yourself and what they want you to do – what others want you to do. (Raveena, India)

As with many other international students in our Studies 2 and 3, Reveena's study-abroad experience 'takes on the shape of a personal expansion' (Murphy-Lejeune, 2003, p. 113). The attendant exposure to new and different ways of life and of living 'makes the familiar strange' and can serve as a platform for a reflexive process – which helps to nurture the self-transforming individual and which often results in a sense of being distinctly and permanently different from others around them in the workplace and in their local networks (Gu & Schweisfurth, 2015a, b). As Reveena's example shows, what makes this process most emotionally frustrating is the realisation that 'the internalised parental voice' (Berne, 1968, pp. 23-32) in her selfhood was also challenged and that, as a result, she was 'torn' between her loyalty and a sense of attachment to her cultural and family roots and her enjoyment of the new cultures and the new worlds and constant attempts to break away from the lives and traditions that once shaped who she was.

Almost four decades ago, in his seminal work *Beyond Culture*, Hall wrote about the 'hidden controls' of human behaviour patterns and habitual responses which, although 'usually experienced as though they were innate' (1976, p. 42), are learned and acquired. When crossing cultural boundaries, these 'hidden controls' are challenged by different (and sometimes contrasting) norms, values and behavioural expectations and, subsequently, brought to the surface to be questioned, examined and evaluated. Jenkins' social identity theory suggests that 'identity is constructed in transactions at and across the boundary' in this very process of change (2004, p. 22). Jenkins argues that during these transactions, 'a balance is struck between (internal) group identification and (external) categorisation by others' (2004, p. 22). To achieve such balance, the social actor is constantly engaged in a process of identity negotiation in terms of how they perceive themselves and how they would like to be perceived by others each time they cross the boundary. 'I've got two sets of values: one is for here and one is for China,' Yijia, the undergraduate in Study 2, reported, because 'I don't want to be treated as a foreigner in either context'.

Many of the above self-awareness of transnational transformations in identities and the concomitant emotional tensions of wanting to be seen as *insiders* at and across boundaries can be summed up in this quotation from Wen, on his feelings upon returning to China after a year and a half in the UK:

> In a year and a half [of study abroad], the friendship between my friends and I was very firm ... On the one hand, I felt lost, feeling I was leaving everything behind there, including friendship, that pure life style. On the other, I felt afraid, afraid of what awaited me in Beijing, whether everything would be all right here as I expected. What's more, I had hopes, hoping to lead a different life with changes. This change was a change in role.

In search of social bonds: 'I now have a much bigger friend circle.' The transnational experiences of international mobile students encouraged and enabled them to establish embedded social networks and friendship circles within, and cross-border connections which support their transnational engagement socially, culturally, economically or politically (Vertovec, 2009). These networks spanned connections to home, affiliations with groups in the UK, and an increasing integration into supranational networks, including religious groups and subject-specific academic communities (Gu & Schweisfurth, 2015a).

Social and emotional bonds with co-nationals and people who are culturally similar to themselves were found to have played an important role in helping international mobile students to settle down in the new living environments in Study 2 (Gu, 2009). This is often in addition to their concerted (but sometimes unsuccessful) efforts to integrate with native and other international students. As the example of the following German student shows, building and maintaining monocultural (or co-national) bonds and connections *here* (i.e. in the host country) and *there* (i.e. in the home country) is of vital importance to international students because, at least in part, they help to satisfy a strong desire to be understood and supported at a level that people from 'Other' cultures may not be able to offer. Again, such desire is closely associated with a sense of deep-seated need to be attached to individuals or groups of people who share and can understand their values in depth and who are seen as 'insiders' to their past and present lives.

> I think what I miss most is not actually my parents. It's more likely to be my best friends. People who I knew for years and years and who you know how to talk to and you can tell them everything. Yes, basically just that. …
>
> I actually do feel lonely quite often. One of the things that impacted on me positively was that after Easter I met another guy from Germany on the bus from the airport to Nottingham and I made friends with him … Normally I didn't speak to the people like the Germans I meet because I just don't like the idea of staying together in your own little circle or culture. But … it was nice to get to know him because somehow I saw much more of Nottingham and I had much more time to get to know the cultural and musical scene and things. … I was surprised that it happened because, as I say, I would normally not have spoken to him. … It gave me some of the things that I am missing. One of the main things that I am missing here is just discussions about general things – life or the future or how we feel – but not just about what we did last night or about our work.

In Study 3, it was also found that relationships with other Chinese residents during their period of study and embeddedness in this network of support were sources of comfort to many. This is because, at least in part, when being exposed to an alien environment, mutual support and understanding from co-nationals provide a 'social setting for the rehearsal and affirmation of cultural identity' (Bochner, 1977, p. 290). As 25-year-old Liang noted, regarding the challenges of adaptation in the UK to a new 'system of life':

> with the mutual help of the warm-hearted local Chinese, who collected and offered a lot of useful information, I was soon fitting in … The newcomers, classmates and those who met on the plane were communicating with each other, helping each other, and exploring a new life together.

Shortly after his return to China, like the majority of his peers in this study, Liang also noticed the difference between his friends and himself. In search of a sense of attachment and belonging 'at home', he managed to not only retain his old friendship circles, but also to take advantage of his study-abroad experience to extend and broaden his social networks and ties:

> In the first three months [on my return], I could clearly feel the difference between my friends and me. It might be because we had not been in frequent contact for more than a year. So at that time, I remained in a circle of friends who had been abroad. But I am pleased that I am back in touch with my old

friends now, although we tend to have different topics from those who share study-abroad experiences. Anyway, *I am happy that I now have a much bigger friendship circle.* (emphasis added)

Concluding Reflections: researching international students in an interconnected world

Indeed, as research on international mobile students suggests, studying abroad and returning home are perceived by many students as dynamic and interconnected transnational experiences (e.g. Gu & Schweisfurth, 2015a, b). Such experiences are typically characterised by their constant negotiation, reproduction and expansion of their social, cultural and professional identities in an attempt to enact meanings 'in the course of their everyday lives within and across each of their places of attachment or localities of perceived belonging' (Vertovec, 2009, p. 77). In search of this sense of belonging, of wanting to understand and to be understood and accepted as part of the host institution and society that sometimes feel not only 'foreign' but also 'alien', they learn to be engaged in a continuous and sustained dialogue with themselves in the mind and with others in their transnational ties about the roots of their identities and social behaviour, about how the exposure to the 'Other' has helped them to know more about their roots and themselves, and about how their values, identities and capability transform as a result of the struggles to position themselves as insiders as well as outsiders as they move across borders and between boundaries. Upon returning 'home', such struggles to become and to be seen as insiders continue, and they are embedded in their effort to reconnect with their roles in the society and social networks. As time goes by, the identification of self as an outsider often becomes a quiet, internalised conversation in the mind that is mixed with nostalgia for their past international mobility experience and/or a sense of pride of being *different* from others.

Most importantly, when individual students and graduates move across boundaries and settle in, they attempt to (re)connect with the cultural and linguistic traditions in the place of origin and the host society. The outcome is not necessarily an integrated collective identity that is a synthesis of elements of 'home' and 'host' national identities. As Faist has written in his work on the experiences of transnational migrants, it can also be 'an un-integrated existence' of both identities next to each other (1998, p. 242) – that is, he is referring to being and becoming an insider as well as an outsider in the home and host societies, simultaneously. Such deep-seated self-awareness of and reflexivity in identity is perhaps best summarised in Eva Hoffman's description of her self in *Lost in Translation*. She concludes that her Polish insights could not be regained in their purity because 'there is something I know in English too' (1989, p. 273). The Polish and English languages and cultures have been blended into her sense of self in the creation of the 'new woman':

> No, there's no returning to the point of origin, no regaining of childhood unity. Experience creates styles, and style, in turn, creates a new woman. ... Polish insights cannot be regained in their purity; there is something I know in English too. ... When I speak Polish now, it is infiltrated, permeated, and inflected by the English in my head. Each language modified the other, crossbreeds with it, fertilizes it. (Hoffman, 1989, p. 273)

Implications for Comparative and International Research

Throughout this chapter, I have tried to unfold the paradoxical insider and outsider perspectives that many international students in our research have experienced. Although the mobility of international students and scholars is nothing new, the proliferation and diversification of their movement in the last two decades and the collective and cumulative impact of their movement on both the host and the sending societies have meant that understanding, researching and theorising their experiences matters – to global societies at large and to research and researchers in comparative and international education.

Our research on international students invites us to revisit some long-standing debates in comparative research. It lends support to the power, privilege and benefits of conducting research that is essentially concerned with comparing systems, activities, lives and experiences, and associated with these, traditions and values (e.g. Crossley & Watson, 2003; Crossley, 2012). As Phillips wrote more than a decade ago, 'comparing is a fundamental part of the thought processes which enable us to make sense of the world and our experience of it' (1999, p. 15). Our research experience points to the importance of the shape of the research team and the extent to which its composition would stimulate intellectually and culturally meaningful judgement. This seemingly simple point, however, profoundly determines the rigour and trustworthiness of any comparative research activity. In our research the team members were 'living' products of the university internationalisation (having studied at UK universities and then remained to become senior academics in the UK) and were therefore both insiders and outsiders to our researched students. Our complementary research expertise, different personal, cultural and professional backgrounds and, equally importantly, trusting work relationships enabled us to challenge our judgements and prejudices, question the ways in which we would make sense of the experiences of our students, and learn to use different lenses to minimise our subjective position on questions of importance. As a result, one of the most profound outcomes of our research is probably the enhanced clarity of our own values as educationalists and comparative researchers, and an understanding of the need for a more nuanced, systemic approach to studying individual experiences.

I have established at the outset that the mobility and movement of international students is, and has been, driven by dynamic and competing political, economic and cultural forces. Our research has shown that exposure to different cultures, different pedagogies and different worlds challenged emotionally, psychologically and intellectually international students' 'hidden' cultural and habitual values and behaviours. As a result, most experienced transformational changes – especially in terms of their broadened interests and worldviews, and transnationalised new competences, skills and connections (see Gu & Schweisfurth, 2015a, b) for more details). The depth of insight that they have gained to view and evaluate themselves and to view and connect with the world is perceived by students as a 'treasure' in life.

The interconnectedness of their experience calls for nuanced and systemic new approaches to researching their journeys of change and transformation in societies that are themselves experiencing various forms of far-reaching 'transformation' (Held et al, 1999; Castles, 2001). Bray (1999, p. 212) argues that 'patterns at lower levels in education systems are shaped by patterns at higher levels, and vice versa'. However, despite a resurgence of interest in research on the mobility of international students in recent years, research on international students remains narrow in focus, driven by a deficit perspective and lacking theorisation (Gu & Schweisfurth, 2015a). Moreover, it is hardly connected with the broader but closely connected debates on human, social and cultural development. Evidence from this chapter and the wider migration literature shows that dynamic and shifting social, cultural and economic structures and systems influence, and can also be influenced by, the experiences and movement of international students. The various 'brain circulation' concepts such as 'brain drain', 'brain gain' and 'the brain train' (Knight, 2015) are perhaps some of the best examples which show that international student mobility has influenced, and will continue to influence, increasingly and significantly, the mobility of skills, knowledge and talent in today's increasingly globalised, but at the same time diversified and unequal, world.

References

Asian Development Bank Institute (ADBI) (2014) *Labour Migration, Skills and Student Mobility in Asia*. Tokyo: ADB.

Berne, E. (1968) *Games People Play: the psychology of human relationships*. Harmondsworth: Penguin.

Bochner, S. (1977) Friendship Patterns of Overseas Students: a functional model, *International Journal of Psychology*, 12(4), 277-294. http://dx.doi.org/10.1080/00207597708247396

Bray, M. (1999) Methodology and Focus in Comparative Education, in M. Bray & R. Koo (Eds) *Education and Society in Hong Kong and Macau: comparative perspectives on continuity and change*. Hong Kong: University of Hong Kong Comparative Education Research Centre.

British Council (2012) *The Shape of Things to Come: higher education global trends and emerging opportunities to 2020*. London: British Council.

Brooks, R., Waters, J. & Pimlott-Wilson, H. (2012) International Education and the Employability of UK Students, *British Educational Research Journal*, 38(2), 281-298. http://dx.doi.org/10.1080/01411926.2010.544710

Carlson, S. (2013) Becoming a Mobile Student – a Processual Perspective on German Degree Student Mobility, *Population, Space and Place*, 19(2), 168-180. http://dx.doi.org/10.1002/psp.1749

Castles, S. (2001) Studying Social Transformation, *International Political Science Review*, 22(1), 13-32. http://dx.doi.org/10.1177/0192512101221002

Collins, F.L. (2010) Negotiating Un/familiar Embodiments: investigating the corporeal dimensions of South Korean international student mobilities in Auckland, New Zealand, *Population, Space and Place*, 16(1), 51-62.

Crossley, M. (2012) Comparative Education and Research Capacity Building: reflections on international transfer and the significance of context, *Journal of International and Comparative Education*, 1(1), 4-12.

Crossley, M. & Watson, K. (2003) *Comparative and International Research in Education: globalisation, context and difference*. London: RoutledgeFalmer. http://dx.doi.org/10.4324/9780203452745

Cushner, K. & Karim, A. (2004) Study Abroad at the University Level, in D. Landis, J. Bennett & M. Bennett (Eds) *Handbook of Intercultural Training*, 3rd edn, pp. 289-308. Thousand Oaks, CA: SAGE.

Day, C. W., Stobart, G., Sammons, P., Kington, A., Gu, Q., Smees, R. & Mujtaba, T. (2006) Variations in Teachers' Work, Lives and Effectiveness. Final report for the VITAE Project. London: Department for Education and Skills.

Department for Business, Innovation and Skills (BIS) (2013) *International Education: global growth and prosperity*. London: Department for Business, Innovation and Skills.

Faist, T. (1998) Transnational Social Spaces out of International Migration: evolution, significance and future prospects, *Archives Européennes de Sociologie*, 39(2), 213-247. http://dx.doi.org/10.1017/S0003975600007621

Findlay, A. & King, R. (2010) Motivations and Experiences of UK Students Studying Abroad. BIS Research Paper No. 8. London: Department for Business, Innovation and Skills.

Friedman, T.L. (2005) *The World is Flat*. London: Penguin.

Furnham, A. (2004) Foreign Students' Education and Culture Shock, *The Psychologist*, 17(1), 16-19.

Geddie, K. (2013) The Transnational Ties that Bind, *Population, Space and Place*, 19(2), 196-208. http://dx.doi.org/10.1002/psp.1751

Ghosh, S. & Wang, L. (2003) Transnationalism and Identity: a tale of two faces and multiple lives, *Canadian Geographer*, 47(3), 269-282. http://dx.doi.org/10.1111/1541-0064.00022

Gilroy, P. (1987) *There Ain't No Black in the Union Jack*. London: Hutchinson.

Gilroy, P. (1993) *The Black Atlantic: modernity and double consciousness*. London: Verso.

Glass, C. & Westmont, C. (2013) Comparative Effects of Belongingness on the Academic Success and Cross-cultural Interactions of Domestic and International Students, *International Journal of Intercultural Relations*, 38(1), 116-119.

Golbert, R. (2001) Transnational Orientation from Home: constructions of Israel and transnational space among Ukrainian Jewish youth, *Journal of Ethnic and Migration Studies*, 27(4), 713-731. http://dx.doi.org/10.1080/13691830120090467

Gu, Q. (2009) Maturity and Interculturality: Chinese students' experiences in UK higher education, *European Journal of Education*, 44(1), 37-52. http://dx.doi.org/10.1111/j.1465-3435.2008.01369.x

Gu, Q. & Schweisfurth, M. (2006) Who Adapts? Beyond Cultural Models of 'The' Chinese Learner, *Language, Culture and Curriculum*, 19(1), 74-89. http://dx.doi.org/10.1080/07908310608668755

Gu, Q. & Schweisfurth, M. (2015a) Transnational Connections, Competences and Identities: experiences of Chinese international students after their return 'home', *British Educational Research Journal*, published online 30 March. http://dx.doi.org/10.1002/berj.3175

Gu, Q. & Schweisfurth, M. (2015b) Transnational Flows of Students: in whose interest? For Whose Benefits? In S. McGrath & Q. Gu (Eds) *Routledge Handbook of International Education and Development*, pp. 359-372. London: Routledge.

Gu, Q., Schweisfurth, M. & Day, C. (2010) Learning and Growing in a 'Foreign' Context: intercultural experiences of international students, *Compare*, 40(1), 7-23. http://dx.doi.org/10.1080/03057920903115983

Gudykunst, W. (Ed.) (2005) *Theorizing about Intercultural Communication*. Thousand Oaks, CA: SAGE.

Hall, E. (1976) *Beyond Culture*. New York: Anchor Books.

Held, D., McGrew, A., Goldblatt, D. & Perraton, J. (1999) *Global Transformations: politics, economics and culture*. Cambridge: Polity Press.

Heusinkvelt, P. (Ed.) (1997) *Pathways to Culture: readings in teaching culture in the foreign language class*. Yarmouth, ME: Intercultural Press.

Hoffman, E. (1989) *Lost in Translation*. London: Heinemann.

International Association of Universities (IAU) (2010) *Internationalisation of Higher Education: global trends, regional perspectives*. Paris: IAU.

Jenkins, R. (2004) *Social Identity*, 2nd edn. Abingdon: Routledge. http://dx.doi.org/10.4324/9780203463352

Knight, J. (2015) Meaning, Rationales and Tensions in the Internationalisation of Higher Education, in S. McGrath & Q. Gu (Eds) *Routledge Handbook of International Education and Development*, pp. 325-339. London: Routledge.

Lewthwaite, M. (1986) A Study on International Students' Perspectives on Cross-cultural Adaptation, *International Journal for the Advancement of Counselling*, 19(2), 167-185. http://dx.doi.org/10.1007/BF00114787

Murphy-Lejeune, E. (2003) An Experience of Interculturality: student travellers abroad, in G. Alred, M. Byram & M. Fleming (Eds) *Intercultural Experience and Education*, pp. 101-113. Clevedon: Multilingual Matters.

Oberg, K. (1960) Culture Shock: adjustment to new cultural environment, *Practical Anthropology*, 7, 177-182.

Organisation for Economic Co-operation and Development (OECD) (2007) *Globalisation and Higher Education*. Paris: OECD Publishing.

Organisation for Economic Co-operation and Development (OECD) (2014) *Matching Economic Migration with Labour Market Needs*. Paris: OECD Publishing.

Phillips, D. (1999) On Comparing, in R. Alexander, P. Broadfoot & D. Phillips (Eds) *Learning from Comparing: new directions in comparative educational research. Vol. 1: Contexts, Classrooms and Outcomes*, pp. 15-20. Oxford: Symposium Books.

Portes, A. (1997) *Globalisation from Below: the rise of transnational communities*. Oxford: Transnational Communities Programme, Economic and Social Research Council.

Portes A. (2003) Conclusion: theoretical convergences and empirical evidence in the study of immigrant transnationalism, *International Migration Review*, 37(3), 874-892. http://dx.doi.org/10.1111/j.1747-7379.2003.tb00161.x

Pries, L. (Ed.) (1999) *Migration and Transnational Social Spaces*. Aldershot: Ashgate.

Salih, R. (2002) Shifting Meanings of 'Home': consumption and identity in Moroccan women's transnational practices between Italy and Morocco, in N. Al-Ali & K. Koser (Eds) *New Approaches to Migration?*, pp. 51-67. London: Routledge.

Salih, R. (2003) *Gender in Transnationalism: home, longing and belonging among Moroccan migrant women*. London: Routledge.

Schweisfurth, M. & Gu, Q. (2009) Exploring the Experiences of International Students in UK Higher Education: possibilities and limits of interculturality in university life, *Special Issue of Intercultural Education*, 20(5), 463-473. http://dx.doi.org/10.1080/14675980903371332

Seddoh, F.K. (2001) Internationalisation of Higher Education: what for, how and at what cost?, *International Association of Universities Newsletter*, 7(3), 1, 3.

Sin, L.I. (2013) Cultural Capital and Distinction: aspiration of the 'other' foreign student, *British Journal of Sociology of Education*, 34(5-6), 848-867. http://dx.doi.org/10.1080/01425692.2013.816030

Smith, R. (2003) Diasporic Memberships in Historical Perspective: comparative insights from the Mexican and Italian cases, *International Migration Review*, 37(3), 724-759. http://dx.doi.org/10.1111/j.1747-7379.2003.tb00156.x

Smith, R. & Khawaja, N. (2011) A Review of the Acculturation Experiences of International Students, *International Journal of Intercultural Relations*, 35(6), 699-713. http://dx.doi.org/10.1016/j.ijintrel.2011.08.004

Strauss, A. (1959) *Mirrors and Masks: the search for identity*. San Francisco: Sociology Press.

Suspitsyna, T. (2012) Socialisation as Sensemaking: a semiotic analysis of international graduate students' narratives in the USA, *Studies in Higher Education*, 39(9), 1351-1364. http://dx.doi.org/10.1080/03075079.2011.629343

UNESCO (2009) *Global Education Digest 2009*. Paris: UNESCO.

UNESCO (2013) *The International Mobility of Students in Asia and the Pacific*. Paris and UNESCO Bangkok: UNESCO.

UNESCO (2014) Global Flow of Tertiary-level Students (5 May). http://www.uis.unesco.org/Education/Pages/international-student-flow-viz.aspx (accessed 20 January 2015).

Uvalić-Trumbić, S., Daniel, J. & West, P. (2007) The Role of International Online Courses in the Worldwide Provision of Education. Paper presented at European Association of Distance Teaching Universities 20th Anniversary Conference, 8-9 September, Lisbon, Portugal.

Vertovec, S. (2001) Transnationalism and Identity, *Journal of Ethnic and Migration Studies*, 27(4), 573-582. http://dx.doi.org/10.1080/13691830120090386

Vertovec, S. (2004) Migrant Transnationalism and Models of Transformation, *International Migration Review*, 38(3), 970-1001. http://dx.doi.org/10.1111/j.1747-7379.2004.tb00226.x

Vertovec, S. (2009) *Transnationalism*. Abingdon: Routledge.

Wang, H.Y. & Miao, L. (2013) *Annual Report on the Development of Chinese Students Studying Abroad*. Beijing: Social Sciences Academic Press (China).

Ward, C., Bochner, S. & Furnham, A. (2001) *The Psychology of Culture Shock*, 2nd edn. Hove: Routledge.

Ward, C. & Kennedy, A. (1993) Where's the 'Culture' in Cross-cultural Transition: comparative studies of sojourner adjustment, *Journal of Cross-cultural Psychology*, 24(2), 221-249. http://dx.doi.org/10.1177/0022022193242006

Waters, J.L. (2007) Roundabout Routes and Sanctuary Schools: the role of situated educational practices and habitus in the creation of transnational professionals, *Global Networks*, 7(4), 477-497. http://dx.doi.org/10.1111/j.1471-0374.2007.00180.x

Waters, J. & Leung, M. (2013) A Colourful University Life? *Population, Space and Place*, 19(2), 155-167. http://dx.doi.org/10.1002/psp.1748

Widmaier, S. & Dumont, J.C. (2011) Are Recent Immigrants Different? A New Profile of Immigrants in the OECD (DIOC 2005/2006). OECD Social, Employment and Migration Working Papers, No. 126. Paris: OECD.

Zhang, J. & Goodson, P. (2011) Acculturation and Psychosocial Adjustment of Chinese Students: examining mediation and moderation effects, *International Journal of Intercultural Relations*, 35, 614-627. http://dx.doi.org/10.1016/j.ijintrel.2010.11.004

CHAPTER 11

Investigating Processes Underlying Identity Formation of Second Language Master's Students in UK Higher Education: insiders or outsiders?

HANIA SALTER-DVORAK

Introduction

As higher education becomes increasingly internationalised, a growing body of literature discusses the experiences of both home students (Ivanic, 1998; Lea & Street, 2000) and international students (Robinson-Pant, 2005; Ryan & Viete, 2009). One way of conceptualising such experience is through the insider/outsider metaphor, which can be applied to researchers and those researched. However, as McNess et al (2013) and Robinson-Pant (2014) stress, the dichotomisation implicit here can be seen as essentialising; a constructivist view of identities as multiple and fluid suggests that people can be insiders and outsiders at the same time, and in different ways. McNess et al argue that, as researchers, we are rarely entirely on one side or the other, and in practice, we are often somewhere in between (2013). A more nuanced perspective is needed, which privileges the role of context in learning and research through multiple data sets.

In this chapter I deploy the outsider/insider concept as a heuristic for investigating the processes underlying the identity formation of two second language master's (MA) students on different courses in anglophone academia. To this end, I adopt Goffman's (1959) dramaturgical 'frontstage, backstage' metaphor as an analytical lens. Viewing each course as a 'community of practice' (Lave & Wenger, 1991), in which practices, underpinned by discourses, reflect values and interests of participants, I present data extracted from a 13-month ethnographic study which focused on the experience of second language students in their social learning spaces both 'frontstage' and 'backstage'. In line with Pavlenko and Blackledge's (2004) poststructuralist view of identities, I apply a socio-historical perspective to examine how the participants' experiences contribute to the formation of both insider and outsider identities during the course of their master's programmes.

Theoretical Framework

There is a substantial literature which examines the experience of second language students in anglophone academia from the inside through participant ethnography, often undertaken by English for Academic Purposes (EAP) teachers (Swales, 1990; Casanave, 1995; Spack, 1997; Prior, 1998; Morita, 2000; Benesch, 2001, Leki, 2006; Krase, 2007; Kiely, 2009; Salter-Dvorak, 2011, 2014; Cheng, 2013). These researchers employ a 'discourse community' (Swales, 1990) or 'community of practice' (Lave & Wenger, 1991) framework to investigate their own students' socialisation into epistemological and cultural norms of their new learning communities. The socio-historic longitudinal approach used, combining what Street refers to as 'proximity and distance held in tension simultaneously' (quoted by Robinson-Pant, 2014, p. 5), reveals a number of interesting findings. First, it is clear that the huge and diverse constituency of second language students is often assumed to be homogeneous by the academy, and viewed through the 'deficit discourses' which continue to dominate the educational literature (Robinson-Pant, 2005; Ryan & Viete, 2009; Salter-Dvorak, 2014). Second, from the students' perspective, the linguistic challenges presented by writing (Spack, 1997; Kiely, 2009) and spoken interaction (Morita, 2000; Benesch, 2001; Krase, 2007; Cheng, 2013; Salter-Dvorak, 2014) intersect with the cultural, often creating a feeling of 'outsiderness' to their learning communities. Cheng (2013), for example, describes how her research participant needed to take on extra tasks in order to be accepted by the group she was assigned to on her MA course, while Benesch (2001) recounts how her students struggled to have their questions heard in lectures. What emerges here, then, is a complex picture comprising linguistic, socio-cultural, cognitive and affective factors, at the nexus of which lies identity formation; for second language students, crossing borders into anglophone academia involves not only a geopolitical move but also 'restructuring the self' to adapt to their new learning context (Pavlenko & Lantolf, quoted in Ryan & Viete, 2009, p. 307). It is particularly, as Pavlenko and Blackledge (2004) argue, when individuals find themselves in a new context that identities are in flux.

According to sociocultural theory, identities are 'an educational resource' (Lave & Wenger, 1991, p. 71); as learners build up new competences, new identities are created, which in turn enable further learning and participation in the 'community of practice'. For poststructuralists, however, this process is contingent on power relations rather than predictable; Blommaert sees identities as 'forms of semiotic potential organised in a repertoire' (2005, p. 207), while Pavlenko and Blackledge (2004, p. 14) argue that they are conceptualised as products of unique socio-historical circumstances 'constructed, validated and offered through discourses available to individuals at a particular place and time' and thus legitimised or devalued in the global or local political context. Further, a tension exists between agency and structure; as Joseph (2004, p. 162, citing Hecht) points out, the personal 'who-I-am' identity does not necessarily correspond with the enacted 'who-I-am' for others. Similarly, Pavlenko and Blackledge (2004) see that identities formed reflexively (when the individual positions her/himself) are negotiable, and can be contested interactively, or imposed by others. As Joseph (2004) argues, it is these processes, rather than the reifications of the identities themselves, that a constructivist perspective of identities privileges.

In a multidimensional view of communication and cognition, the pluralised, dynamic model of identities above is viewed as a resource for 'affordances' defined as 'signs, semiotic or otherwise, which can be taken up by learners in order to develop the learning process' (Kramsch, 2002, p. 11). In order to make available affordances for students in a heterogeneous context, then, teachers have responsibility for creating 'cohesive learning communities' (Duff, 2002). However, while teachers may assume that 'drawing learners into the community is indeed a good thing' (McNess et al, 2013, p. 301), evidence shows this to be a complex process; identities reflexively formed by the learner may not always be in line with teachers' and colleagues' interactive positionings (Duff, 2002). The question, then, is encapsulated by Ryan and Viete's (2009, p. 304) words: 'how can students build positive identities in their new learning spaces and how can teachers help them in doing so?'

For the student, the specific culture of the new learning space is thus of critical importance. However, as is now well documented in the literature, considerable variation exists in practices both between and within disciplines and departments. Lea and Street (2000), for example, illustrate how history and anthropology lecturers differ in their conceptions of clarity and argument when giving feedback on academic writing.

This chapter, premised on Foucault's notion of discourses as 'regimes of truth' (1972, p. 19), which shape institutional behaviour, draws on the body of participant ethnography discussed above to view courses as 'communities of practice' (Lave & Wenger, 1991). While not assuming these to be static, I suggest that their ideologies and discourses, founded on 'accumulated experience and socialisation' (Blommaert, 2005, p. 162), are realised through specific practices, creating learning spaces which are intrinsically social, within which identities are shaped. In order to interpret identity formation in these spaces, I have found Goffman's 'frontstage' and 'backstage' metaphor (1959) to be a useful lens. Goffman posits that institutional behaviour is highly ritualised; he likens those working in social institutions to actors whose actions differ between the frontstage (face-to-face interactions with clients) and the backstage, when they 'drop their front' (1959, p. 115). I see that this metaphor can be adapted to view the learning experiences of students: frontstage is a physical space where formal interactions (lectures, seminars, tutorials) act as literacy events whose purpose is knowledge transfer; backstage is a space, physical or virtual (corridor, email, student residence, Skype, telephone), where informal interactions may or may not provide opportunity for clarification, guidance and reflection. Interactions here may also contribute to the formation of identities and relations which could be beneficial frontstage. What I am particularly interested in is whether there is fluidity between these two social learning spaces. Deploying the insider/outsider metaphor as a heuristic, I present data extracted from a longitudinal study to discuss two second language students' experiences in the social learning spaces of their courses, and examine how the identities they arrived with were re-shaped, negotiated or replaced by others during the year.

The Study

The study was a small-scale longitudinal ethnography of communication in a UK university (Salter-Dvorak, 2011), grounded in the interpretive epistemological tradition of participant practitioner observation (Hammersley & Atkinson, 2007). Its central purpose was to provide a contrastive analysis of the dynamic between dominant discourses and language, power relations, agency, identities and affordances on two master's courses. An instrumental case-study approach was employed (Stake, 2005): two case studies of MA students within two case studies of their course communities enabled situated investigation of the students' learning experiences from start to finish (13 months). My insider position as a lecturer in EAP afforded access to multiple data sets from diverse social learning spaces, enabling 'thick descriptions' (Geertz, 1973) of the cases, which were then contrasted.

Eight master's students consented to participate by responding to a letter distributed during the second week of their ten-week EAP module (which I ran in semester one). They were asked to send me fortnightly journals as emails or voice messages on any aspect of their studies, which I followed up with interviews. I then emailed letters inviting their lecturers to participate in the study. After six weeks, I chose two students on different courses whose lecturers had also agreed to participate as a 'purposive sample' (Stake, 2005, p. 511).

The methodology was guided by Lillis' (2008) notion of 'cyclical talk' around student texts, with particular focus on what participants considered salient. Semi-structured monthly interviews (average 1.5 hours each) on texts in progress, lecturer feedback and experiences in class were triangulated with the texts, marks and feedback, interviews with lecturers and classroom observation; themes were followed up by email if necessary. The findings were filtered through my perspective of applied linguist, language educator and course designer.

Researcher Positioning: insider or outsider?

My positioning as a researcher was complex and hybridised; it reflected McNess et al's (2013) and Hammersley and Atkinson's (2007) description of 'multiple identities' often taken on by the researcher. Carrying out research in a university where I had worked for some years, I was an insider to the research context, with access to its cultural resources and experience of the 'pre-existing social realities and routines' (Hammersley & Atkinson, 2007, p. 94) which shaped its values and practices. As the English for Academic Purposes course I taught was non-credit bearing, students viewed me as an academic guide, rather than an assessor. Over the course of the year, I also became a confidante and counsellor, sympathising in the case of a failed essay or an unsatisfactory experience. These were identities of an insider to the university. When I asked the students about their courses, however, I became a researcher looking in from the outside at the values and practices described.

My interviews with lecturers presented a different scenario. While I recognised some university discourses in their representations (e.g. independent learning), I was an outsider to their courses, a stance which arguably enabled me to acquire 'a certain objectivity not normally available to culture members' (Shutz, quoted in Hammersley & Atkinson, 2007, p. 9). Neither full participant observer (insider) nor stranger (outsider), this 'liminal space of in-betweeness' (McNess et al, 2013, p. 306) created affordances as well as hindrances.

Analysis

Employing an inductive approach, the study adopted the analytic lens of identities in order to track the two students' experience over time. Following Pavlenko and Blackledge's view that identities are 'located not only within particular discourses and ideologies but also within narratives' (2004, p. 18), I see that, while identities are negotiated through interaction, it is by reflecting on experiences that individuals position themselves. The analysis stage was guided by Richards' distinction between 'in vivo' and 'in vitro' perspectives of data (2003, p. 17), which led to development of analytical categories: listening to participants' narratives 'in vivo', followed by recursive reading of the data sets 'in vitro', enabled me to identify identities which reflected both how they positioned themselves as second language learners and how they were positioned by others; I coded the identities, ascribed them to the students, and tracked them over time (e.g. references to inadequate linguistic proficiency were coded under 'defective communicator'). However, following Joseph (2004, p. 162), rather than viewing these identities as fixed products, my analysis sought to explore the processes and experiences underlying these. Due to the sensitive nature of the data, respondent validation was not sought for ethical reasons; I felt that reading the analysis could have a negative effect on participants' self-esteem. In what follows I present a contrastive socio-historic analysis of the students' experiences, from which significant differences emerge (quotations from the data are presented verbatim).

Data

To begin with, I introduce Autumn and Shahrzad, the two research participants; Table I summarises relevant background information.

Pseudonym	Age	Country of origin	BA (in home country)	MA	IELTS on entry	Composite mark on MA	Long-term ambition
Autumn	23	China	Media	Professional media	6.5	61	Work as print journalist in China
Shahrzad	23	Iran	English language and literature	English literature	7.0	54	Study for PhD in UK

Table I. Research participants.

Autumn on the Professional Media MA

The Professional Media course which Autumn enrolled on was developed specifically for international students; it centres around a theoretical framework which is applied to real-life scenarios from the media industry through problem-solving tasks and assignments. There is a clear learning trajectory with three phases, moving from 'contextual understanding of media organisations' to implementing 'strategies and plans' (course handbook, p. 14). Unusually for a UK master's degree, all six modules are compulsory and are taken by one student cohort, which comprises students from China (fourteen), India (eleven), the European Union (EU; six), Ghana and Palestine (two each), Japan, Korea and Russia (one each). As the course leader explained (interview 1, month 5), there is also diversity relating to students' previous experience, which creates two equally sized cohorts: the 'managerial' (with considerable experience in the industry), and the 'less experienced' (with an academic background in the field, but only two years' work experience).

From a constructivist analysis of all the data sets, I suggest that the ideology of the Professional Media course, founded on 'accumulated experience and socialisation' (Blommaert, 2005, p. 162), rests on the core discourses outlined in Table II.

Discourse	Description
Interaction	The strong emphasis on collaborative learning is realised through interactive problem-solving tasks, which often lead to formative presentations, followed by class discussion.
Multicultural Collaboration	Students are expected to work on assignments in multicultural groups comprising the two cohorts, thereby reflecting practices in the globalised media industry.
Media experience	Students' prior professional experience provides a key learning resource which shapes the curriculum.

Table II. Discourses on the Professional Media MA.

Autumn's Story

Autumn enrolled on the Professional Media MA immediately after graduation. My impression from initial interviews and journal entries was that she arrived with experiences and identities which were congruent with the course discourses. The only child of two print media professionals, she was already socialised into the Chinese media community through holiday internships, and projected herself as a 'media practitioner'. She was also familiar with the Interaction discourse through the pedagogical approach on her BA, and expected to be an 'active participant'. These identities framed her as an insider to the course community. As she engaged in academic and campus life, options for new identities, positioning her as outsider and insider, became available; some were imposed by the course discourses 'frontstage', while others emerged from different socio-historical factors 'backstage'. In the narrative which follows, I summarise how the insider/outsider identities above interacted between 'frontstage' and 'backstage', sometimes vying with each other, creating tensions and contradictions.

How the 'media practitioner' and 'active participant' identities were threatened by those of 'defective communicator' and 'little sister'. Autumn had already met some course mates through Facebook before the course began. The day before registration, they organised an unofficial meeting in town. She was appalled to find that she could hardly follow the speech of her Indian and African colleagues, and decided then that she was a 'defective communicator'. This negative identity, which positioned her as an outsider to the anglophone course community, was later reinforced in class, as shown by the following journal entry:

> On Thursday, we had a seminar, six person a group. In our group, there were three Chinese including me, *but each of us couldn't catch up with the other members* who came from EU, Brazil and India. *We even couldn't have no chance to say our opinions after we finally understood the topic's meaning.* (Autumn, journal entry 2, month 2, emphasis added)

Here I suggest that the problem is not language alone, but rather that her 'media practitioner' identity is being contested by her older, more experienced colleagues from the 'managerial' cohort, who are drawing on the Media Experience discourse. This she articulates in a subsequent interview, in which, unusually, she identifies the 'little sister' role imposed on her by colleagues:

> They are all 10 years older
> Their English is much better
> They all have much work experience in the media
> They have worked in electronic media, and I have worked only in print media ... so they see me as their 'little sister'.
> (Autumn, interview 7, month 4)

This interactive positioning as an outsider in the fronststage space of the seminar led to Autumn's frustration at not being able to play out her assumed 'media practitioner' and 'active participant' identities on the course.

How insider recreational identities counteracted outsider imposed identities. Autumn's recreational activities backstage on campus engendered identities which enabled her to counteract the above-mentioned outsider ones. First, the informal, organically formed 'South East Asian solidarity group' (with members from both the 'managerial' and the 'less experienced' cohorts) provided advice and encouragement on academic matters, as well as in daily life. They commiserated with each other over missing their partners, and nursed each other when ill; the italicised words in the following extract testify to Autumn's experience of the warmth of friendship:

> Dear Hania,
> Hello! This week, unluckily, I had a fever, and I felt so bad for nearly three days. But now, I've recovered because *most of my friends took good care of me*, they cooked the porridge for me, and brought me hot coco and hot cola with ginger (this is a very useful folk prescription). *How lucky I am that I have a lot*

> *good friends here!* (Autumn, Journal Entry 8, month 3, emphasis added)

Second, Autumn's accounts testify to the fact that she was an 'engaged campus resident'; she shared a flat on campus with students from Germany, India and England, with whom she often watched TV in the evenings and organised parties. She joined the gym, where she enjoyed chatting to students on other courses, and jogged at night with friends. She also ventured outside the campus to explore restaurants and markets with friends from the 'solidarity group', and with colleagues from both cohorts, 'managerial' and 'less experienced' on her course, as well as travelling around the UK with friends during vacations. These recreational identities had two positive effects: first, they enabled her to be an insider with respect to the campus; second, they created a space in which tensions built up frontstage with more experienced colleagues could be eased, arguably contributing to a sense of cohesion in the course community.

How recreational identities vied with academic identities. While the recreational identities had a positive impact on Autumn's academic life during the taught component of the course, when teaching finished in March, and students were left to focus on dissertations, these same identities threatened to pull her away from study, as shown by this extract from my field journal:

> When I met Autumn on 29 May she seemed to have lost her sense of direction: in the midst of a season of all day parties for friends returning home for data collection, she claimed she had been waiting for a month to hear from her dissertation supervisor. Were her recreational identities taking over? After our conversation, she went to see her supervisor, and sent me an email saying she had decided to cancel her planned trip to Europe with her father and return to China immediately for her data collection. (Extract from field journal, month 8)

Reflecting on the above, I suggest that the clear surprise in my facial expression during this interview led to Autumn's change of plan, exemplifying how the 'liminal space of in-betweeness' (McNess at al, 2013, p. 306) can enable the researcher/outsider to wield influence as an insider.

How course practices of accommodation supported insider identities. The biggest adaptation required of Autumn related to reading and writing. However, the practices suggested by faculty to support this adaptation were constitutive of her 'persevering writer' identity, which enabled her to express herself as a 'media practitioner' with increasing competence. The course team offered extensive formative feedback and clear advice relating to proofreading of assignments. Although she expected difficulty, she had the means to improve; her accounts over the year show no difficulty with accessing lecturers or communicating with them; rather, there is a strong sense of confidence, inspired by faculty, in her ability to do well. Autumn received a merit for her master's, and finished the year on a very positive note. She returned to the UK for the graduation ceremony, which was attended by all but three students, and followed by a series of parties and meals in restaurants.

As can be seen from the above account, Autumn's identities create a complex picture exemplifying 'perpetual tension between self-chosen identities and others' attempts to position them differently' (Pavlenko & Blackledge, 2004, p. 20). This I elaborate on through comparison with Shahrzad at the end of this chapter.

Shahrzad on the English Literature MA

Shahrzad, an Iranian student, also joined the English Literature MA immediately after graduating from Teheran University. Originally created for home students, the MA was subsequently opened to international students, both L1 and L2. The orientation is academic rather than vocational, involving familiarisation with a number of theoretical frameworks which are applied to reading literature through 'analytical, argumentative, sceptical questioning', as the course leader explains:

> The MA is a gateway, an important transition where you are moving to being part of the academic community ... from essentially learners to active participants in the discipline. (Course leader, interview 1, month 5)

In contrast to Autumn's course, the linear learning trajectory offered here is limited. There are two core modules, leaving students to choose two electives from nine. The student population is characterised by heterogeneity in terms of nationality, language profiles, educational background and study modes. Of the 20 students, six were from the UK and two from the USA. The rest were from EU countries (three), India (two) and Turkey, Iran, Nepal and Palestine (one each). This created three distinct profiles: the eight native speaker students had all graduated in English literature from UK and US universities. Of the twelve second language students, ten had graduated from their home countries, and only two from anglophone universities. There are also four study modes, creating four cohorts, which the course leader admits does not facilitate a strong structural progression on the degree.

The course discourses identified from the data are outlined in Table III.

Discourse	Description
Independent Research	Independent learning is more highly valued than collaboration; students are expected to 'produce substantial independent research' (handbook, p. 8).
Theoretical Perspectives on Literature	Knowledge of literary and cultural theory is required for the 'advanced, wide-ranging study of English Literature' (handbook, p. 2).
Critical Analysis	The course aims to develop 'critical skills in reading and analysis of texts' and 'critical reasoning' (handbook, p. 3).

Table III. Discourses on the English Literature MA.

Shahrzad's Story

Like Autumn, Shahrzad's trajectory over the year was characterised by tensions between self-chosen and imposed identities. Although her excellent school-leaving marks had qualified her to study science at Iran's top university, she had resisted this channelling, as she explains in our initial interview:

> I responded to my heart and decided to achieve my lifelong ambition which was studying English Literature. (Shahrzad, interview 1, month 1)

My initial impression was that Shahrzad reflexively positioned herself as a 'high achiever', 'literature lover' and 'confident communicator', identities which all seemed to legitimise her as an insider to the course community. She had graduated in seven semesters instead of eight, with top marks, and enrolled immediately on the MA, with the intention of studying for a doctorate in English literature. Shahrzad's family are regular visitors to the UK, as testified by her high level of spoken fluency and her International English Language Testing System (IELTS) score (see Table I). During these visits, she built up friendships with British-born Iranians, who formed what she refers to as a 'liberal Muslim Iranian community', celebrating Islamic feasts and socialising together. In what follows, I demonstrate how, during the course of the year, Shahrzad's positioning by the course ideology and its discourses, combined with other factors, led to the gradual erosion of her positive insider identities, and their replacement by imposed outsider ones.

How family illness limited options for recreational identities. Shahrzad's year was fragmented both academically and socially. She had barely started her MA when her sister was diagnosed with a serious illness, which caused her to suspend her studies at the end of October and restart the following January. This, added to the fact that she studied alongside students from four different cohorts, meant that she was never part of a cohesive group like Autumn; she did not bond with course mates, meeting them only in classes (six hours per week). In addition, her opportunities for forming friendships with colleagues were restricted by the fact that she was caring for her sister, and that her recreational identities revolved around the Iranian community in the city, which limited her social engagement in the university backstage, creating a feeling of outsiderness with respect to both the course and the campus.

How course expectations and norms were constitutive of the 'victim of unrealistic expectations' and 'silent participant' identities. From the start, Shahrzad's accounts show awareness of the high expectations, in terms of both knowledge and language, which the course placed on her. She felt at a serious disadvantage in comparison with colleagues who had taken their BAs at anglophone universities, as expressed in her first interview in October:

> I think that maybe I shouldn't take this course so soon because I've never studied here but when *they* are going to accept *us* they can see we have different educational backgrounds but when *they* ask *us* the demands they ask us as if we are equal. (Shahrzad, interview 1, month 1)

Here, her use of 'they' and 'us' in italics suggests an outsider identity, which prevented her from asking for clarification in class:

> I don't know sometimes because I think it's my own fault because I haven't done enough research around it then I feel shy if some students know then why am I asking questions I … I really feel very shy asking questions and I find it very uncomfortable. (Shahrzad, interview 3, month 2)

She also repeatedly stressed lack of guidelines provided to second language students from different educational cultures, and gradually positioned herself as a 'victim of unrealistic expectations', as the italicised words below show:

> since I came here *I had some sort of panic*, if I can say that because the method is quite different, and you know everybody says 'come and ask for help' but *there is no-one real guide for students* like us who come from different countries to say 'you should do this'. (Shahrzad, interview 2, month 1, emphasis added)

This was especially apparent in the run-up to the dissertation, during which Shahrzad's lack of familiarity with norms relating to contacting tutors caused considerable anxiety (for a full account, see Salter-Dvorak,

2014). All in all, this uncertainty, combined with the fact that she lacked the warmth of friendship and the support which recreational identities within the university could have offered, caused Shahrzad to disaffiliate herself from colleagues both frontstage and backstage; in spite of her high level of fluency, she contributed minimally to discussions or group work. In this way, the 'confident communicator' became a 'silent participant' on the English MA.

How lack of practices to support adaptation positioned the 'literature lover' and 'high achiever' as 'defective communicator'. The most challenging adaptation required of Shahrzad related to writing, which seemed to be shrouded in mystery and disappointment. Motivated by her 'literature lover' identity, she deployed her spoken communication skills to negotiate the title of her first essay, but was disappointed with her mark of 53%. The second marker's comments regarding 'awkwardness of language' (essay 1 month 5) imposed on her an identity of 'defective communicator'; expectations regarding linguistic accuracy were high, yet, in line with the Independent Learning discourse, there were no practices in place to support improvement of language, and no advice was offered relating to having assignments proofread by faculty. Shahrzad worked hard at this; like Autumn, she became a 'persevering writer', creating multiple drafts of essays on which she worked alone to correct. However, as her marks and feedback did not improve over the year, the 'defective communicator' identity came to eclipse those of 'competent communicator' and 'high achiever'. By the end of the year, she was mourning the loss of these identities:

> I used to be the top student, but since I came here I'm just thinking about passing. (Shahrzad, interview 10, month 8)

She therefore finished on an unhappy note; failing to achieve the merit grade required for PhD study, she avoided the degree ceremony. When, for our last interview, I suggested (unusually) meeting in the building where her classes had been held, Shahrzad shuddered and said, 'Oh I hate that building.'

Discussion

The accounts above of Autumn and Shahrzad's experiences and identities present two very different pictures, one positive, the other less so, reflecting two different 'communities of practice', each with its own ideology, discourses and practices. Autumn's experience clearly involved a number of challenges; she was positioned reflexively as an outsider in terms of language, and interactively as an outsider in terms of experience by the Media Experience discourse. However, she appeared comfortable and settled in the social learning space of the university, confident that she was growing in competence. Often smiling, she seemed to view me as an 'auntie' figure and to find our meetings enjoyable, while not depending on them. I suggest that this was due to two reasons. First, the design and ethos of the Professional Media MA appears to encourage a cohesive multicultural community in which all nationalities and participants are valued, and heterogeneity of the student body is harnessed by the clear learning trajectory: the fact that there was only one full-time cohort meant that students met regularly frontstage, where the privileging of multicultural collaboration led to interaction which engendered exchange of ideas for experienced students and exposure to ideas for those less experienced, like Autumn. In addition, second language students were provided with clear guidelines on how to improve their work backstage. From a Wengerian perspective, then, despite feeling an outsider at times, Autumn was enabled to move closer to the centre of her course community. Second, the integration between her academic identities (which were formed mainly frontstage) and her recreational identities (which were formed mainly backstage) created a dialectic which I suggest supported learning: sitting in restaurants with the experienced 'managerial' cohort made her feel more at ease with them in class, while socialising backstage with her solidarity group enabled her to discuss her academic concerns. However, the fact that these same recreational identities later created a drift away from academic work exemplifies the fluid and ephemeral nature of identities, as emphasised by Joseph (2004), Pavlenko and Blackledge (2004), and Salter-Dvorak (2011).

Shahrzad was also positioned as an outsider, especially in terms of prior knowledge. Her challenges, on the other hand, seemed to be intractable, rendering her frustrated and unhappy. Our meetings were intense events, often lasting over an hour, the discussion continuing long after the recorder had been switched off. She seemed dependent on these and on the advice I could offer. I suggest that this was only partly due to her sister's unpredictable illness, which led to her interrupting her studies. First, in contrast to Autumn's course, these data reveal the four-cohort English literature course as a fragmented community, in which the diverse needs of the heterogeneous student body are not accommodated. Here, the ideology rests on the premise that students are already insiders to the learning culture and the theoretical perspectives employed for studying literature in anglophone academia. However, half of the course cohort had graduated from non-anglophone universities, and were therefore outsiders to both the learning culture and the theoretical perspectives in their new context. As a result, Shahrzad experienced serious challenges of adaptation, which were not sufficiently addressed by the course, and were constitutive of her outsider identities; while criticism of her writing was harsher than on Autumn's course, due to the high standards of writing required, support (especially formative feedback) was limited. The course leader's statement that students on the MA become 'part of the academic community', then, is not borne out here. Second, for Shahrzad, whose recreational identities centred around family ties and religion, there was minimal integration between front and backstage. Had there been liberal Muslims like herself on her course, her experience may well have been different. As it was, her brief sojourns on campus meant that she lacked the opportunities not only for friendship but also for academic exchange which Autumn benefited from. All in all, the factors above seemed to form a vicious cycle, leaving Shahrzad with a growing sense of outsiderness.

Conclusion

This chapter has investigated two students' experiences as insiders/outsiders through the lens of Goffman's 'frontstage/backstage' metaphor. Autumn and Shahrzad's case reports demonstrate that these two notions are distinct and complementary: it is possible to be an insider and outsider in different ways (McNess et al, 2013) either frontstage or backstage. However, while identities may be shaped, relationships created and affordances provided by formal and informal events both frontstage and backstage, it is not possible to map identities relating to learning neatly onto one or the other space, or to disentangle those relating to learning from those relating to friendship, family and religion. This corroborates a poststructuralist view of identities as fluid, fragile and ephemeral phenomena, which can enable people to draw on different positionings in different contexts for different purposes. The findings also bring into relief the tension between structure and agency, showing that identities are dependent on options available to the individual in any context (Pavlenko & Blackledge, 2004; Blommaert, 2005); while both Autumn and Shahrzad attempted to resist discourses and maintain their self-chosen identities, this was not always successful. The crucial factor was the discourses adopted by their courses, whose designs and practices are epistemologically determined, evidencing the heterogeneous nature of anglophone academia (Lea & Street, 2000; Robinson-Pant, 2005).

For Autumn and Shahrzad, then, it seems that the feeling of belonging to the course community is directly related to a positive learning experience; at the same time, inclusion in recreational groups, especially those which include course colleagues, can be constitutive of success. While it is not possible to build an action programme on the basis of a neat mapping, I suggest that there are clear implications for educators arising from this small-scale study. First, the expectations of prior knowledge and the extent to which a specific course design allows for students' knowledge and experience to be drawn on has an impact on their inclusion and hence their feeling of insiderness; while the design of Autumn's course creates a 'cohesive learning community' (Duff, 2002), the extent to which Shahrzad's does this can be questioned. Second, accommodation of second language students (e.g. providing support for improving written work) is a significant factor which enables students to 'build positive identities', as Ryan and Viete (2009) put it; for Shahrzad, absence of such accommodation led to loss of positive identities, disempowering her and stripping her of confidence. Third, community building on courses (e.g. organising reading groups and research seminars) could contribute to building positive identities and feelings of insiderness; it is notable that neither of the courses above attempted this.

Finally, while research on second language students traditionally tends to focus on either the frontstage (formal learning) or the backstage (informal learning), the fluidity between these spaces identified above suggests a phenomenon which merits further research in a richer contextual landscape.

References

Benesch, S. (2001) Critical *English for Academic Purposes: theory, politics and practice*. Mahwah, NJ: Lawrence Erlbaum Associates.

Blommaert, J. (2005) *Discourse*. Cambridge: Cambridge University Press. http://dx.doi.org/10.1017/CBO9780511610295

Casanave, C.P. (1995) Local Interactions: constructing contexts for composing in a graduate sociology program, in D. Belcher & G. Braine (Eds) *Academic Writing in a Second Language: essays on research and pedagogy*, pp. 83-110. Norwood, NJ: Ablex.

Cheng, R. (2013) A Non-native Student's Experience on Collaborating with Native Peers in Academic Literacy Development: a socio-political perspective, *Journal of English for Academic Purposes*, 12, 12-22. http://dx.doi.org/10.1016/j.jeap.2012.10.003

Duff, P. (2002) The Discursive Co-construction of Knowledge, Identity and Difference: an ethnography of communication in the high school mainstream, *Applied Linguistics*, 23(3), 289-322. http://dx.doi.org/10.1093/applin/23.3.289

Foucault, M. (1972) *The Archaeology of Knowledge*. London: Tavistock.

Geertz, C. (1973) *The Interpretation of Cultures*. New York: Basic Books.

Goffman, E. (1959) *The Presentation of Self in Everyday Life*. Edinburgh: University of Edinburgh Social Sciences Research Centre, Anchor Books edn.

Hammersley, M. & Atkinson, P. (2007) *Ethnography: principles in practice*. London: Routledge.

Ivanic, R. (1998) *Writing and Identity: the discoursal construction of identity in academic writing*. Amsterdam: John Benjamins. http://dx.doi.org/10.1075/swll.5

Joseph, J.E. (2004) *Language and Identity: national, ethnic, religious*. Basingstoke: Palgrave Macmillan. http://dx.doi.org/10.1057/9780230503427

Kiely, R. (2009) Observing, Noticing, and Understanding: two case studies in language awareness in the development of academic literacy, *Language Awareness*, 18(3-4), 329-344.

Kramsch, C. (Ed.) (2002) *Language Acquisition and Language Socialisation: ecological perspectives*. London: Continuum.

Krase, E. (2007) 'Maybe the Communication between Us was not Enough': inside a dysfunctional advisor/L2 advisee relationship, *Journal of English for Academic Purposes*, 6, 55-70. http://dx.doi.org/10.1016/j.jeap.2006.12.001

Lave, J. & Wenger, E. (1991) *Situated Learning: legitimate peripheral participation*. Cambridge: Cambridge University Press. http://dx.doi.org/10.1017/CBO9780511815355

Lea, M.R. & Street, B. (2000) Student Writing and Staff Feedback in Higher Education: an academic literacies approach, in M.R. Lea and B. Stierer (Eds) *Student Writing in Higher Education: new contexts*, pp. 32-46. Buckingham: SRHE & Open University Press.

Leki, I. (2006) Negotiating Socioacademic Relations: English learners' reception by and reaction to college faculty, *Journal of English for Academic Purposes*, 5, 136-152. http://dx.doi.org/10.1016/j.jeap.2006.03.003

Lillis, T. (2008) Ethnography as Method, Methodology, and 'Deep Theorising': closing the gap between text and context in academic writing research, *Written Communication*, 12(3), 353-388. http://dx.doi.org/10.1177/0741088308319229

McNess, E., Arthur, L. & Crossley, M. (2013) 'Ethnographic Dazzle' and the Construction of the 'Other': revisiting dimensions of insider outsider research for international and comparative education, *Compare*, 45(2), 295-316. http://dx.doi.org/10.1080/03057925.2013.854616

Morita, N. (2000) Discourse Socialisation through Oral Classroom Activities in a TESOL Graduate Program, *TESOL Quarterly*, 34(2), 279-310. http://dx.doi.org/10.2307/3587953

Pavlenko, A. & Blackledge, A. (Eds) (2004) *Negotiation of Identities in Multilingual Settings*. Clevedon: Multilingual Matters.

Prior, P. (1998) *Writing/Disciplinarity: a sociohistoric account of literate activity in the academy*. Mahwah, NJ: Lawrence Erlbaum Associates.

Richards K. (2003) *Qualitative Inquiry in TESOL*. Basingstoke: Palgrave Macmillan. http://dx.doi.org/10.1057/9780230505056

Robinson-Pant, A.P. (2005) *Cross-cultural Perspectives on Educational Research*. Buckingham: Open University Press.

Robinson-Pant, A.P. (2014) Exploring the Concept of Insider–Outsider in Comparative and International Research: essentialising culture or culturally essential? Paper presented at BAICE Forum, 24 February, University of Bristol.

Ryan, J. & Viete, R. (2009) Respectful Interactions: learning with international students in the English speaking academy, *Teaching in Higher Education*, 14(3), 303-314. http://dx.doi.org/10.1080/13562510902898866

Salter-Dvorak, H. (2011) Capturing the Ephemeral: participation, identity and language in the experience of second language masters students in anglophone academia. Unpublished doctoral dissertation, University of Bristol.

Salter-Dvorak, H. (2014) 'I've Never Done a Dissertation Before, Please Help Me': how course design can accommodate L2 students into anglophone academia, *Teaching in Higher Education*, 19(8), 847-859. http://dx.doi.org/10.1080/13562517.2014.934344

Spack, R. (1997) The Acquisition of Academic Literacy in a Second Language, *Written Communication*, 14(1), 3-62. http://dx.doi.org/10.1177/0741088397014001001

Stake, R.E. (2005) Qualitative Case Studies, in N.K. Denzin & Y.S. Lincoln (Eds) *The Sage Handbook of Qualitative Research*, 3rd edn, pp. 443-466. Thousand Oaks, CA: SAGE.

Swales, J. (1990) *Genre Analysis: English in academic and research settings*. Cambridge: Cambridge University Press.

CHAPTER 12

Coming Alongside in the Co-construction of Professional Knowledge: a fluid approach to researcher positioning on the insider–outsider continuum

ED WICKINS & MICHAEL CROSSLEY

Introduction

This chapter reflects upon how the methodological positioning of one researcher shifted during a study about head teacher leadership challenges in international schools in Hong Kong. Although the initial research position was one of the neutral 'outsider', when data were collected and organised, the researcher moved alongside the participants to facilitate the co-construction of professional knowledge. The conclusions reflected the insider view of the lead researcher, who is working in a similar head teacher leadership role and school context as the core research participants. However, collaboration with the second author generated engagement with the broader international and methodological literature and, in the light of this, we argue that the fluidity offered by what became an 'alongsider' approach better reflected the complexity of the research process and supported the emergence of more nuanced and effectively contextualised conclusions about educational leadership in this sector of education in Hong Kong. In concluding, key findings from the Hong Kong study are identified along with a consideration of the potential of the alongsider approach for other practitioner researchers working in related fields.

Both during the research process and later, when reflecting on the research journey, neither the word 'insider' nor the word 'outsider' seemed to capture the emerging relationship between researcher and researched. A new word, 'alongsider', was needed to describe and explain this relationship – a word that referenced the insider–outsider continuum but sought an alternative fluid, active and proximal research position. A shipping metaphor seemed appropriate: a research vessel observing the data ship from afar through a shaky telescope across a choppy sea and moving carefully towards the ship for a better look. As the research vessel comes alongside, it is influenced by the same elements, shares the same context, but retains a separate identity and perspective. To further develop understanding perhaps the researcher climbs on board and joins the crew, better to appreciate the subtleties of the navigation and the peculiar challenges of sailing that particular vessel. The researcher also brings an alternative perspective, one that has been influenced by other contexts that have been witnessed on the journey. The distant disinterested outsider has become a proximal participant insider through coming alongside. Let's see if the metaphor can be sustained and what an alongsider methodology can contribute to research.

The Research Questions and Design Rationale

'Alongsider' research emerged from a particular set of research questions which generated their own dilemmas and methodological design. The focus of the research was on the narratives, the perspectives, of serving principals. What can we learn from their diverse tales about the dynamic leadership challenges that exist in international secondary schools in Hong Kong? The research explored how generic leadership challenges are shaped by Hong Kong and the international school context. How do school leaders respond to their challenges? What strategies do they use to meet them? How situational are their responses and how do their personal backgrounds shape what they do? The principals of the 23 International Baccalaureate Diploma (IBD)–authorised schools in Hong Kong were the participants in this qualitative study, and the researcher, who is also an international secondary school principal, came alongside them in developing meaning from the interview data through two participants' workshops. The discussions between researcher and participants contributed to conclusions about generic leadership issues and the Hong Kong international secondary school sector.

Hong Kong education seems to be of particular international interest as it is perceived to be very successful in global comparisons based on PISA tests (Sellar & Lingard, 2013). The academic results of international schools in Hong Kong are the envy of many schools in other parts of the world, but the aim of the research was not to suggest uncritical transfer of these strategies but to explore contextual issues (Crossley, 2010) around leadership in these schools. The developing nuanced alongsider methodology highlighted the importance of 'critical attention' when exploring cross-cultural educational policy transfer

(Phillips & Ochs, 2003; Crossley & Watson, 2009; Crossley, 2014; Forestier & Crossley 2014). This is certainly not to avoid cross-cultural transfer or seek a 'bland consensus' (Crossley, 2008, p. 331) but rather to see contextual differences as a creative stimulus for original work to improve our understanding of cross-cultural educational issues.

The research paradigm chosen reflected the bringing together of a series of epistemological, theoretical and methodological pathways. The research had a qualitative epistemology which allowed it to be intentionally personal, subjective, naturalistic and descriptive (Bogdan & Biklen, 1998, p. 3). It was also constructionist in that it involved the joint interpretation and construction of meaning by the participants (Crotty, 1998, p. 58). It adopted an interpretivist, hermeneutic theoretical perspective as it attempted to develop an understanding of a complex situational set of data that is 'culturally derived and historically situated' (Crotty, 1998, p. 67). It was also phenomenological in its concentration on describing the 'essence of the lived experience' (Lichtman, 2011, p. 244) of the participants through a focus on the challenges they face, and postmodernist in its absence of a pre-determined theoretical outcome and its focus on questioning, dilemma and doubt (Crotty, 1998, p. 185).

This theoretical background was supported by a series of methodological techniques that in turn led to choices about data collection and analysis methods. The research involved the practitioners by engaging them in the process of developing meaning from the leadership challenges they face and the strategies they use. Most of the data were collected through in-depth interviews, and the emerging analysis was shared with participants in two workshop conferences. The discussion was analysed and interpreted alongside the researcher's own analytical work in an iterative process. The distance of the practitioners from the research process decreased as the ships came alongside and they became intentionally involved in the co-construction of professional knowledge. At the same time, the researcher's perspective, which had originally been neutral, also shifted. To explain this we need to understand better the theoretical continuum along which the perspective moved.

The Insider–Outsider Continuum

An objectivist and scientific approach to research requires the researcher to take an external perspective, an outsider viewpoint. There are ethical and practical advantages to adopting this position; it reduces bias and is more likely to convince others that it is fair, reliable, triangulated and accurate. However, when research takes a qualitative, subjective, post-modernist, constructivist, phenomenological stance, as this particular research did, the outsider viewpoint itself becomes problematic as the *reflexivity* of insider perspectives are foregrounded. In such perspectives critical self-reflection and the co-construction of research findings which reflect the diverse voices of both the participants and the researcher are fundamental to the outcomes. We will first explore the debate about 'insider – outsider' research with reference to the continuum between these two theoretical positions (see Hellawell, 2006; Brannick & Coghlan, 2007; Mercer, 2007).

At one end of the continuum is insider research. In simple terms, the insider researcher is researching his or her own institution, and the practical advantages stemming from this perspective have been widely acknowledged. For example, Hockey (1993) argues that as an insider the researcher does not have to deal with 'culture shock'; Dimmock (2012) recognises the 'tacit knowledge' they already possess; and Brannick and Coghlan (2007) write in defence of being 'native', of being an insider in the research process, and researching 'in and on their own organisations'.

Brannick and Coghlan (2007) go on to argue that the insider could even be useful in different research paradigms. As an insider, access to quantitative and qualitative data is often easier and there is a pre-understanding of the subject organisation, although there are dualities to be resolved between adopting two very different roles (within the organisation, and as a researcher) and in managing organisational politics. For Mercer (2007) this makes it a 'double-edged sword', as the challenge of insider research is to resolve 'delicate dilemmas' across multiple dimensions. Mercer points out the complexities around, for example, power relationships, different perceptions of the researcher, and interview reciprocity, and she lingers on ethical concerns.

At heart these are all issues of reflexivity. The qualitative insider researcher must consciously reveal their beliefs and values as they co-construct their research findings. Such a researcher also needs to be aware that their position along the insider–outsider continuum can 'shift' (Hellawell, 2006) and that this can be helpful in entering the 'secret garden' of reflexivity (Hellawell, 2006, p. 492). In the research on international school leadership in Hong Kong this shift was from an intentionally neutral recipient of words in the semi-structured interviews, to an engaged and personal interpreter of data, and finally to a collaborative provocateur for the participants as the researcher came alongside them.

Le Gallais (2008) articulates some of the advantages for the reflexivity of the researcher of being an insider and supports our argument that the viewpoint is often fluid along the continuum. This fluidity provides an opportunity for 'richness of insight' (Le Gallais, 2008, p. 153) and therefore should be embraced. For Roland and Wicks (2009), the points along the research journey when there are significant changes in the research dynamics and where the lead changes between researcher and participant are described as 'map points'. They also argue that a team approach minimises 'potential concerns about bias' (Roland & Wicks, 2009, p. 10), and although they were describing a team of researchers, we would argue that a similar effect can be achieved through the alongsider phase of this research when co-construction of conclusions becomes the aim. Many minds being applied collaboratively to data through a fluid process maximises 'academic integrity' (Roland & Wicks, 2009, p. 10).

It is worth reflecting on a common concern with the insider approach. Drake (2009) shows that sometimes an insider researcher can be too close and argues that reflexivity can be enhanced with distance. Whereas, for Drake, this distance emerged from a period away from the research and a refreshed return, for this alongsider research the alternative perspectives are derived both from the neutral outsider initial perspective and from the active engagement of a range of diverse voices in the conclusions. Drake's worries about the isolation of the insider researcher are addressed by the diversity fundamental to this alongsider approach.

Kemmis (2012) uses the terms 'spectator' and 'practitioner' in his consideration of the insider–outsider continuum. He shows that, from a critical perspective, we can characterise an 'ecology of practice' (Kemmis, 2012, p. 889) which is complex and fluid. Participants and spectators are key elements of this ecology and have fundamental roles to play in its development. For him, the perspective of participants who live and breathe their practice contributes to our understanding of 'the experience of practice' (Kemmis, 2012, p. 891), particularly through the use of action research methodologies. He also argues that spectator and participant views are complementary. So alongsider research that emphasises the complexity of practice, that concentrates on listening to the voice of participants and that includes a complementary spectator view at the start to help interpret their experiences reflects arguments emerging from a different methodological perspective.

At the other extreme on the continuum is outsider research which seeks to establish a static, objective, neutral viewpoint and has little room for reflexivity. This is often associated with the positivist, quantitative tradition, but Dimmock and Lam (2012) show how grounded theory, within the qualitative research tradition, can adopt a similar position. It is not the only qualitative research approach seeking an outsider stance but it is worth lingering on because the three designs for grounded theory Dimmock and Lam explore span the insider–outsider continuum. Both the systematic design associated with Strauss and Corbin (1990) and the emerging design associated with Glaser (1992) insulate theorising from the research process. The aim of both designs is to keep the researcher's viewpoint neutral, or outside. Only in the constructivist design (Charmaz 2006) is the researcher encouraged to be proactive and interpretative; to permit an insider viewpoint. So the different approaches to qualitative grounded theory exemplify the continuum we have explored here.

Conceptualising the Alongsider Approach

As we reflected on the fluidity of this researcher's position in relation to the insider–outsider continuum described above it became clear that there were three distinct phases reflecting different positions along the continuum, and we will explain these now. These phases are similar to those introduced by Milligan (2014) in her research into school students in a rural community in Kenya, and although the context of this research was very different, we support her argument that there can be changing roles through the research process and that on occasion the researcher is 'neither fully inside nor outside' (Milligan, 2014, p. 5). Our notion of alongsider research builds on and develops what Milligan calls the 'inbetweener' phase.

This conceptualisation also reflects McNess et al (2013), who question the strict, fixed categorisation of research as insider or outsider, preferring to show how 'individual and group identities can be multiple, flexible and changing such that the boundary between the inside and the outside is permeable, less stable and less easy to draw' (McNess et al, 2013, p. 1). In their terms, our alongsider perspective is the 'third space' which 'pivots across the difference of being outside and inside' (McNess et al, 2013, p. 11) and can 'generate new insights' (p. 15). In developing understanding of research findings it is advisable to be nuanced in interpreting data, and such a beneficial sensitivity is enhanced by adopting different appropriate research positions.

Phase 1: Neutral Perspective

The intention at the start of the research was to minimise preconceptions and to approach the interviews neutrally, as an observer from afar. The focus was on listening to the stories of leadership. Difficulties with qualitative interviews have been well described elsewhere (e.g. Walford, 2001; Gerson & Horowitz, 2002; Silverman, 2006), and the researcher was determined to enter the interview space with an open and flexible mind. The questions were semi structured and allowed the participants the space to develop their own responses. They were asked, first, to describe their institutional and personal context; second, to identify and describe their specific contextual challenges; and finally, to explain how they strategised to meet the challenges. Inevitably each interview took a different course, but the researcher remained external to the data-collection process and didn't intervene to shape the direction of the answers. All possible precautions were taken to retain an outsider position. The interviews were recorded and transcribed independently by a third party. So during this first phase the researcher was acting as an attentive outsider gathering data neutrally and seeking to be as objective as is possible in a human research environment. He watched and listened as though from a distance.

Phase 2: Coming Alongside

When the data had been collected and the process of collation began, core themes began to emerge through the adoption of a coding technique which had been adapted from constructivist grounded theory as outlined by Charmaz (2006, p. 130). For example, it became clear from the data that governance was an issue that nearly all interviewees talked about. It was also apparent that many of the interviewees described how they invest in different types of capital in order to develop capability. At an early stage the researcher shared these emerging themes and tested them out with the interviewees in a participants' conference which was organised to generate discussion and co-construct meaning from the data. Nearly all interviewees attended.

During this conference the researcher's position moved away from the neutral. His presentation to the conference, the structure of it and the way in which he asked questions of the participants showed he was increasingly an actor in the research. The researcher was beginning to work alongside the participants, informing the debate with theoretical ideas, reflecting ideas back to the group and challenging them to contribute to the dialogue about possible conclusions. The neutral position disappeared with the lively debate and the researcher intervening to provoke, stimulate and question the participants. During the conference it was apparent that the researcher's ship had come alongside; he was playing a different role, he engaged in co-construction rather than acting as an external spectator.

Phase 3: Alongsider Research

In the third phase the researcher found himself inside the data, immersed in them and wrestling with meaning. He had come aboard the data ship. The conclusions emerged not only from the rigorous independent and personal data analysis but also from the developing discourse with some key participants and their deeper engagement with the research process. These discussions were often informal but they were very important in shedding further light on ideas and developing the depth of the conclusions. This reflexive process was supported by taking an insider position and emphasising that researcher and participants were all members of the same educational culture constrained by similar sets of rules. The second participants' conference sought to focus on some emerging questions that had caused particular debate, such as whether the Hong Kong context is peculiar or not. By this late stage the expectation of the participants was that the researcher would express his own view; indeed, these views were actively sought. The researcher and participants were now working closely together to understand the data and to co-construct their meaning.

This fluid process through the three phases seems quite simple and linear in this description, but the journey of the researcher towards the practitioners and the heart of the research was complex. Although there are important contextual similarities between the participant schools which support an insider perspective, cultural, linguistic and geographical differences make the environment diverse and a single, static insider viewpoint elusive. Cultural differences emerge from the fact that some of the schools are effectively local schools with an added IB Diploma stream, while others are attached to foreign national systems (e.g. Australia), others are independent, and others are part of the English Schools Foundation. All have very different school cultures. Linguistically, some of the schools are bilingual Chinese schools, some teach through the medium of Cantonese as well as Mandarin, some emphasise European language acquisition, and others only teach Chinese languages. Some of the schools are on Hong Kong island with transient, expatriate families, others are in the New Territories serving the needs of mostly local students. How can one researcher be an insider across such a complex, diverse array? They all have a commitment to the IB Diploma, but does this one curricular similarity outweigh the cultural, linguistic and spatial differences described above?

The distance between researcher and practitioner reduces through the three phases described above, but does this mean the perspective loses its clarity? Or as the viewer moves towards the object does it come into focus? Perhaps the first phase represents the panoramic view with the research object in view within its wider context, and the movement alongside develops an increasing clarity. The art of alongsider research is somehow to retain the perspective of the wider context while zooming in on the complexity of the detail. We argue that there are four additional benefits that emerge from a consideration of the wider literature.

Four Benefits of an Alongsider Approach

1. Exploiting Familiarity and Preunderstanding

Issues of difficult access to data face many researchers, and alongsider research relies on familiarity between participants and researcher. In this case, all participants who were directly approached to contribute to the research accepted the invitation. The approach from a familiar peer facilitated access and this was maintained. The first conference was attended by 17 of the 23 participants.

There was also 'preunderstanding' (Brannick & Coghlan, 2007, p. 68) of the research context. The researcher was well informed about not only the contextual specificity of each institution but also the generic issues faced by school principals in this educational sector. He was able to offer an external, informed perspective on the data and retain some distance from these data until the later stages of the research. An alongsider perspective avoided the problem of 'role duality' (Brannick & Coghlan, 2007, p. 69) as the researcher had no organisational role in the school hierarchy. His role was purely to research. Similarly, the 'political' (Brannick & Coghlan, 2007, p. 71) context of the insider within an organisation was not present in this research methodology, although in some cases a political dimension may have resulted from perceptions of competition between the host school and the researcher's. It was also the case that some interviewees demonstrated higher levels of trust in describing the issues they face than others. This was often related to whether they had worked with the researcher closely in the past and were confident in the relationship.

2. Informing Academic Practice with a Theoretical Perspective

In the discussions during phase 2 the researcher acted as a point of reference both for the emerging data and as a recent student of the theoretical literature. In Hammersley's words (1993, p. 433), he was a 'judicious combination of involvement and estrangement', or able to show both 'empathy and alienation' (Hellawell, 2006, p. 487), in the collaborative research process. Alongsider methodology requires collaboration. It also requires mutual trust and the willingness to disagree and argue. Perhaps school principals are particularly adept at this – they certainly enjoy a good argument!

As collaborators who represent both the practitioner (school principal) and the theoretical (university professor) cultures, we start from the view that educational research has a contextual locus while it presents theoretical possibilities. Our contrasting perspectives give us the opportunity to begin breaking down distinctions and building bridges between academic and lay knowledge. Alongsider research gives the researcher the opportunity to move between the detached theoretical perspective of the outsider and the engaged practitioner perspective of the insider.

We recognise that theory must talk to practice, to engage it. The debates about relevance exemplify this engagement. Some have argued that research must be fundamentally 'relevant' to practice (Kennedy, 1997; Bulterman-Bos, 2008) so that it speaks to practitioners and informs their work in order to improve it, to have an 'impact' (Gardner, 2011). From this point of view the practitioner has a fundamental role to play in demonstrating the relevance of research to their own practice. The practitioner is key and can – indeed, should – also be a successful researcher (Hammersley, 1993). But Labaree (2008) considers the pursuit of relevance 'counter productive' as it narrows our perspectives. Rather, he argues that practitioners should 'adopt the research perspective as an addition to, rather than replacement for, the teacher perspective' (Labaree, 2003). He maintains that the gap between researcher and practitioner is not 'as wide as it seems' and that the differences are a matter of 'emphasis'. He proposes we should work to narrow the gap through the construction of 'hybrid programmes' that marry theory and practice.

We argue that this gap can be creative with different perspectives being brought to play on a particular contextual issue. Research is more likely to be original if it is informed by a dynamic debate rather than comfortable agreement by researchers observing data from the same theoretical position. We need to develop our understanding of the gap to take advantage of the research potential. Therefore practitioners need to go beyond the relevant, the instrumental, the urgent, and develop their skills as academic practitioners in understanding and applying theory. Practitioners need the long view, the distant, neutral perspective to help to interpret the questions they seek to answer and to better appreciate what is actually relevant and what may have an impact.

Given the rapid rise in the number of practitioners engaging in their own research often through participation in university research programmes as academic practitioners and action researchers (see Dick, 2010), these are timely issues for consideration. Persuasive arguments have been developed from contrasting starting points that practitioners should inform themselves by engaging in appropriate research. For example, Hammersley (1993) proposed that research should be 'integrated' with the work of teachers in schools; Hargreaves (1996, 1999) advocated that teaching should be a 'research-based profession' in 'knowledge-creating' schools; Hargreaves and Fullan (2012) argue for building 'professional capital' by teachers taking responsibility for their own solutions; and Dimmock (2012), among others, believes a 'professional learning community' is at the heart of the best schools. In essence, practitioners use external inputs to improve their practice.

Alongsider research reflects this imperative as it starts with the external and sails towards the relevant. It uses the contrasting viewpoints of theory and practice as part of one research process to enable the co-construction of insightful conclusions.

3. Interpreting Interview Data

Mercer (2007) identifies three dilemmas for insider research ('informant bias, interview reciprocity and research ethics'), and it is worth briefly evaluating how this alongsider research resolves these dilemmas. Let's deal with the first two together. Some 'informant bias' emerged as participants who had worked previously with the researcher were more open in their interviews than others who may have been sensitive about sharing problems with an unfamiliar colleague from another school. However, we suspect that this was less of an issue than in pure insider research when 'pragmatism may outweigh candour' (Mercer, 2007, p. 8) as interviewees wrestle with the dilemma of being honest within a professional relationship that extends well beyond the research timescale. It may sometimes be advisable to be diplomatic rather than accurate when being interviewed by powerful insiders! This research process developed in a semi-insulated box and had little impact on future relationships between participants because there were very few power relationships and no hierarchy. Insight was sought without fear of consequence.

To reduce 'interview reciprocity' the researcher didn't offer any of his own perspectives during the interviews (phase 1) even when the interviewee was a close former colleague. He tried to retain a neutral, disinterested position as the data were recorded. This changed during the two conferences, when participants themselves were exposed to what others had said during their interviews and the researcher offered initial interpretations. Therefore there were distinct research phases: intentional neutral data collection; coming alongside with questions; then shared subjective meaning-making.

4. Resolving Ethical Issues

The final dilemma Mercer (2007) describes is 'research ethics'. Interviews are notoriously problematic (see Walford, 2001) as the interviewee may (mis)interpret what is required and give the researcher the story they think he or she wants to hear; furthermore, the researcher may only hear or interpret what they want to hear, and the resulting analysis reflects this complex personal reality. This research attempted to go beyond the narrow ethical assurances about confidentiality and be 'virtuous' (Macfarlane, 2010), using 'academic integrity' (Roland & Wicks, 2009, p. 10) to acknowledge such dilemmas honestly and authentically:

> Being an ethical researcher requires an authentic engagement with our own beliefs and the values of our disciplines. Ethics is a bit like jazz, in that it is about more than simply following the notes on the page. It demands an ability to improvise and to think for ourselves. (Macfarlane, 2010, p. 5)

The second participants' conference towards the end of the research process was an opportunity for a free-flowing discussion, some jazz, between seven participants and the researcher. By this stage in the process the level of trust was high, and those who attended were the most enthusiastic musicians in the ensemble. There was little formal structure and the melody of the emerging findings as presented by the researcher was interpreted in a variety of ways: sometimes it was discordant, sometimes harmonious. Even great jazz is often challenging to understand.

Research Conclusions

So what was this alongsider research methodology able to achieve in Hong Kong? What sort of music was made?

Principals were able to explore the generic challenges all principals face. These included the need to develop a united vision in a diverse context, while reconciling the need for strategic change with the maintenance of existing high standards, and managing issues of concern with governance which often represent the cultural interface between the professional and political worlds.

This methodology also contributed to a deeper understanding of the socio-cultural context of Hong Kong international schools, which is particularly complex and challenging, with homogenising globalisation forces acting against diversifying internationalist values in the peculiar local context of postcolonial aspirational Hong Kong. Leadership responses to these challenges reflect a dialectical search for effective strategies through resolving conflicting contextual forces.

The focus was on *how* principals lead and the generative capability they work to build. The research highlighted that the development of capability in schools is their main strategic intent. This process is achieved through:

- an emphasis on cultural aspects of leadership;
- the widespread use of distributed leadership as a powerful tool;
- investment in three different forms of capital (human capital to develop skills, social capital to build trust, and organisational capital to provide structure) that contribute to a generative culture;
- actions that are 'high leverage' so that outcomes can be maximised for minimum additional effort.

Methodological Potential of an Alongsider Approach

We argue that the alongsider approach has three distinctive qualities that emerge from the discussion above:

- The fluidity along the insider–outsider continuum means the researcher can take advantage of different methodological positions during the research process.

- The movement from detached theory to engaged practice within one piece of research provides a practical solution to the problem of 'managing the gap' between theory and practice.
- The involvement of participants in the co-construction of conclusions maximises the potential for relevance and impact. When participants own the conclusions, they are more likely to use them.

Although the discussion has emerged from a qualitative standpoint, it could be argued that the alongsider approach outlined and justified here also acts as a bridge between the quantitative methods that could be used prominently in phase 1 and the purely qualitative methods that are likely to dominate the third phase. Perhaps it could be used as a methodological justification of mixed methods?

Conclusions

In this study carried out in Hong Kong international schools the researcher was neither an insider working within his own organisation and subject to the direct personal and political forces that buffet and constrain such research, nor was he an outsider looking in a detached, independent way from a different perspective but with only a superficial understanding of the peculiar institutional context. Instead, he was a colleague principal researching the challenges facing principals working within his sector and engaging participants in the interpretation and analysis of the data that emerged. The research viewpoint moved through three phases, from neutral outsider to alongsider researcher who increasingly took on the perspective of an insider. This fluidity of position makes the methodology distinctive. We argue such a methodology has the potential to overcome many of the problems identified in debates about insider–outsider positioning and provides a pathway for future educational research as it embodies the productive use of contrasting perspectives and requires the research practitioner to be able to access contrasting theoretical interpretations.

This alongsider research required a dynamic and active interchange between different skilled and successful practitioners who approached the data from their own personal, professional and experiential viewpoints. There were arguments and disagreements which contributed to the co-construction of emerging conclusions. Alongsider research allows research practitioners to go beyond the confines of the insider and explore an approach which gives a more distant and productively reflexive perspective to the research. This is a perspective that is difficult to achieve from a purely insider position. The collaborative contribution to the research findings by the participants also helps to break down the barriers with theory as practitioners are challenged to use theory to interpret the data they have developed. The dynamic relationships required in such a methodology support professional discourse in the co-construction of mutually owned new meanings which also contribute to the diversity and sustainability of the sector's 'ecology of practice' (Kemmis, 2012).

From the perspective of an academic practitioner, it offers an alternative approach that is neither constrained by the potentially narrow positioning of insider research nor limited by the functionalism of grounded theory or generalist neo-objectivist quantitative methods. It is a methodological positioning that we believe can be useful for others and one that can make a helpful contribution to the wider professional community.

References

Bogdan, R. & Biklen, S. (1998) *Qualitative Research for Education*. Boston, MA: Allyn & Bacon.

Brannick, T. & Coghlan, D. (2007) In Defense of Being 'Native': the case for insider academic research, *Organisational Research Methods*, 10(1), 59-74. http://dx.doi.org/10.1177/1094428106289253

Bulterman-Bos, J. (2008) Will a Clinical Approach Make Educational Research More Relevant for Practice?, *Educational Researcher*, 2008(37), 412. http://dx.doi.org/10.3102/0013189X08325555

Charmaz, K. (2006) *Constructing Grounded Theory*. London: SAGE.

Crossley, M. (2008) Bridging Cultures and Traditions for Educational and International Development: comparative research, dialogue and difference, *International Review of Education*, 54, 319-336. http://dx.doi.org/10.1007/s11159-008-9089-9

Crossley, M. (2010) Context Matters in Educational Research and International Development: learning from the small states experience, *Prospects*, 40, 421-429. http://dx.doi.org/10.1007/s11125-010-9172-4

Crossley, M. (2014) Global League Tables, Big Data and the International Transfer of Educational Research Modalities, *Comparative Education*, 50(1), 15-26. http://dx.doi.org/10.1080/03050068.2013.871438

Crossley, M. & Watson, K. (2009) Comparative and International Education: policy transfer, context sensitivity and professional development, *Oxford Review of Education*, 35(5), 633-649. http://dx.doi.org/10.1080/03054980903216341

Crotty, M. (1998) *The Foundations of Social Research: meaning and perspective in the research process*. London: SAGE.

Dick, B. (2010) Action Research Literature 2008-2010: themes and trends, *Action Research*, 9(2), 122-143. http://dx.doi.org/10.1177/1476750310388055

Dimmock, C. (2012) *Leadership, Capacity Building and School Improvement: concepts, themes and impact*. London: Routledge.

Dimmock, C. & Lam, M. (2012) Grounded Theory Research, in R.J. Briggs, M. Coleman & M. Morrison (Eds) *Research Methods in Educational Leadership and Management*, pp. 188-204. London: SAGE.

Drake, P. (2009) Grasping at Methodological Understanding: a cautionary tale from insider research, *International Journal of Research and Method in Education*, 33(1), 85-99. http://dx.doi.org/10.1080/17437271003597592

Forestier, K. & Crossley, M. (2014) International Education Policy Transfer – borrowing both ways: the Hong Kong and England experience, *Compare*, 1-22, published online 27 June. http://dx.doi.org/10.1080/03057925.2014.928508

Gardner, J. (2011) Educational Research: what (a) to do about impact! *British Educational Research Journal*, 37(4), 543-561. http://dx.doi.org/10.1080/01411926.2011.596321

Gerson, K. & Horowitz, R. (2002) Observation and Interviewing: options and choices in qualitative research, in T. May (Ed.) *Qualitative Research in Action*. London: SAGE.

Glaser, B.G. (1992) *Basics of Grounded Theory Analysis*. Mill Valley, CA: Sociology Press.

Hammersley, M. (1993) On the Teacher as Researcher, *Educational Action Research*, 1(3), 425-445. http://dx.doi.org/10.1080/0965079930010308

Hargreaves, A. & Fullan, M. (2012) *Professional Capital: transforming teaching in every school*. New York: Teachers College Press.

Hargreaves, D. (1996) Teaching as a Research-based Profession: possibilities and prospects. Teacher Training Agency Annual Lecture, London.

Hargreaves, D. (1999) The Knowledge Creating School, *British Journal of Educational Studies*, 47(2), 122-144. http://dx.doi.org/10.1111/1467-8527.00107

Hellawell, D. (2006) Inside-out: analysis of the insider–outsider concept as a heuristic device to develop reflexivity in students doing qualitative research, *Teaching in Higher Education*, 11(4), 483-494. http://dx.doi.org/10.1080/13562510600874292

Hockey, J. (1993) Research Methods – Researching Peers and Familiar Settings, *Research Papers in Education*, 8(2), 129-225. http://dx.doi.org/10.1080/0267152930080205

Kemmis, S. (2012) Researching Educational Praxis: spectator and participant perspectives, *British Educational Research Journal*, 38(6), 885-905. http://dx.doi.org/10.1080/01411926.2011.588316

Kennedy, M. (1997) The Connection between Research and Practice, *Educational Researcher*, 26(7), 4-12. http://dx.doi.org/10.3102/0013189X026007004

Labaree, D. (2003) The Peculiar Problems of Preparing Educational Researchers, *Educational Researcher*, 2003(32), 13. http://dx.doi.org/10.3102/0013189X032004013

Labaree, D. (2008) Comments on Bulterman-Bos: the dysfunctional pursuit of relevance in educational research, *Educational Researcher*, 37, 421. http://dx.doi.org/10.3102/0013189X08325557

Le Gallais, T. (2008) Wherever I Go There I Am: reflections on reflexivity and the research stance, *Reflective Practice*, 9(2), 145-155. http://dx.doi.org/10.1080/14623940802005475

Lichtman, M. (2011) *Understanding and Evaluating Qualitative Educational Research*. London: SAGE.

Macfarlane, B. (2010) The Virtuous Researcher, *Chronicle of Higher Education*, Washington, DC, 4 April.

McNess, E., Arthur, E. & Crossley, M. (2013) 'Ethnographic Dazzle' and the Construction of the 'Other': revisiting dimensions of insider and outsider research for international and comparative education, *Compare*, 45(2), 295-316. http://dx.doi.org/10.1080/03057925.2013.854616

Mercer, J. (2007) The Challenges of Insider Research in Educational Institutions: wielding a double-edged sword and resolving delicate dilemmas, *Oxford Review of Education*, 33(1), 1-17. http://dx.doi.org/10.1080/03054980601094651

Milligan, L. (2014) Insider–Outsider–Inbetweener? Researcher Positioning, Participative Methods, and Cross-cultural Educational Research, *Compare*, published online 26 June. http://dx.doi.org/10.1080/03057925.2014.928510

Phillips, D. & Ochs, K. (2003) Processes of Policy Borrowing in Education: some explanatory and analytical devices, *Comparative Education*, 39(4), 451-461. http://dx.doi.org/10.1080/0305006032000162020

Roland, D. & Wicks, D. (2009) *Qualitative Research in the New Century: Map Points in Insider Research*, pp. 1-15. Kent, OH: School of Library and Information Science, Kent State University.

Sellar, S. & Lingard, B. (2013) The OECD and the Expansion of PISA: new global modes of governance in education, *British Educational Research Journal*, 40(6), 917-936. http://dx.doi.org/10.1002/berj.3120

Silverman, D. (2006) *Interpreting Qualitative Data*. London: SAGE.

Strauss, A.L. & Corbin, J. (1990) *Basics of Qualitative Research: grounded theory procedures and techniques*. Newbury Park, CA: SAGE.

Walford, G. (2001) *Doing Qualitative Educational Research*. London: Continuum.

CHAPTER 13

Sharing Insights: how culture constructs and constricts knowledge

MAROUSSIA RAVEAUD

Introduction

Much uncodified cultural knowledge and behaviour is acquired informally through participation in social activities, and this culturally implicit dimension is usually unarticulated and taken for granted. Sociocultural theory has highlighted the culturally implicit dimension of classroom practice, and comparative education reveals the extent to which classroom practice is firmly situated within a cultural context. However, fewer initiatives have tapped the potential of such research for practitioners. This chapter argues the case for harnessing the insights from comparative studies to promote teachers' reflective thinking. It considers the potential for applying to the field of education novel research procedures developed in social anthropology, based on cross-cultural videos of classroom observations. Indeed, it is argued that cross-cultural video material can be used to elicit practitioners' tacit knowledge and encourage a critical perspective on their values and practice.

As many contributions in this volume point out, the insider–outsider dichotomy is not a clear cut one: each of us can be an insider of various groups and communities, and positions may shift over time. The complexity of social phenomena generates fragmented, fluctuating and hybrid identities (Bhabha, 1994; Calhoun, 1995). In education research this has led to an enriching ability to take into account multiple and shifting perspectives, and to a wariness of simplistic 'them' and 'us' dichotomies based, among others, on national boundaries. However, making sense of classroom practices and of educational thinking requires an understanding of the society and culture within which they are embedded. Jerome Bruner states, 'How one conceives of education, we have finally come to recognize, is a function of how one conceives of culture and its aims, professed and otherwise' (Bruner, 1996, p. x). This does not imply rigidity, permanence or atemporality of a culture that is immutably passed on from generation to generation, but rather that 'the Self too must be treated as a construction that, so to speak, proceeds from the outside in as well as from the inside out, from culture to mind as well as from mind to culture' (Bruner, 1990, p. 108).

While we are aware of having acquired certain beliefs, knowledge and practices that we can consciously examine, much of what we think and do is less readily available for introspection. This chapter explores how an encounter with otherness can trigger an elicitation of taken-for-granted assumptions. My particular focus is on teachers' knowledge and practices, and on fostering awareness of their professional knowledge and practices as sociocultural constructions. To do so, findings from comparative education research were harnessed to generate a cross-cultural experience of outsiderness in order to foster practitioners' reflectivity.

The methodology rests on reflective workshops organised by the researcher, using cross-cultural video to challenge teachers' assumptions and to give them an outsider perspective on their own professional culture. Cross-cultural video is a heuristic tool initially developed within social anthropology, and more recently applied in the field of education by Kathryn Anderson-Levitt (2002), and by Joseph Tobin and his colleagues (Tobin et al, 1989). Here it is applied to teacher development in a pilot study. The chapter first provides a brief outline of the tacit dimension of teacher's professional knowledge. It discusses the potential of comparative education research to foster critical awareness of the cultural embeddedness of classroom practice (Broadfoot et al, 1993; Alexander, 2000, 2006; Broadfoot et al, 2000). I then present the study, which aimed to generate a sense of dissonance in order to explore how culture can both construct and constrict teachers' professional knowledge.

The Tacit Dimension of Teachers' Knowing

The BAICE Thematic Forum on which this publication is based determined to revisit insider/outsider perspectives, which raises the question of what behaviour, values or knowledge such insiderness is based on. While the acquisition of knowledge involves a dimension of individual learning, sociocultural theory shows how that knowledge is situated and distributed, so that the realities that people construct are in fact social realities (Wertsch, 1991; Bruner, 1996). 'To overlook this situated-distributed nature of knowledge is to lose sight not only of the cultural nature of knowledge but of the correspondingly cultural nature of knowledge acquisition' (Bruner, 1990, p. 106). Some of this knowledge is consciously held and can be articulated and formalised. However,

Michael Polanyi highlights that 'we can know more than we can tell' (1967, p. 4). In other words, social actors can act as insiders without knowing why, because their behaviour stems from tacit knowledge. Indeed, 'much uncodified cultural knowledge is acquired informally through participation in social activities; and much is often so "taken for granted" that people are unaware of its influence on their behaviour' (Eraut, 2007, p. 405). Tacit knowledge cannot be codified, but can be transmitted through training or gained through professional experience, and concerns knowledge embedded in a culture (regional, organisational or social) which is difficult to share with others who are not familiar with that culture. This is in part because the transfer of knowledge in a social context rests on tradition, understood as a system of values and norms, a pattern of actions and rules that exist outside the individual and are rooted within a language and social system.

The implications of Polanyi's tacit dimension on education and teacher professionalism were initially explored by Chris Argyris and Donald Schön. They contrast 'espoused theory', which describes the theories one is intellectually and emotionally committed to, and 'theories-in-use', which are implicit in what we do as practitioners (Argyris & Schön 1974; Schön 1983, 1987, 1991). In other words, the 'insiderness' of teacher professionalism is not one that can necessarily be made explicit, for alongside teachers' personal values and pedagogical commitments, their action is also guided by less intentional processes that may not be available in principle to introspection because they rest on tacit knowledge, including taken-for-granted, implicit or unarticulated values, practices and beliefs (Eraut, 1994; Tomlinson, 1999; Atkinson & Claxton, 2000).

Michael Eraut (2000, p. 134) points out benefits of eliciting tacit knowledge: to improve the quality of a person's performance; to help communicate knowledge to another person; to keep one's actions under critical control; and to assist decision-making. Eliciting tacit knowledge comes up against problems of awareness and representation, but Eraut argues it can be triggered by certain events such as 'transgressions' which encourage practitioners to engage with taken-for-granted assumptions and practices. This chapter considers the use of a different educational context as a cross-cultural trigger likely to engender such a sense of dissonance.

Seeing through a Cultural Lens

A tradition of comparative education reaching back to Sir Michael Sadler emphasises the cultural situatedness of practices and social relations inside the classroom from the most routine interactions to organisational models, patterns of thought or student identities (Osborn, 2004; Elliott et al, 2005; Alexander, 2006; Shuayb & O'Donnell, 2008). Culture here is taken in its anthropological sense without normative value judgements, and apprehended at the level of the nation – that is, France and England (as opposed to the United Kingdom as a whole). This level is problematic, as it risks essentialising otherness and suggesting cultures are fixed and homogeneous. Globalisation theorists point to the multiple shifts in policy and practice that bring into question the continuing relevance of the nation-state as a unit of analysis in education (Meyer et al, 1997), and much policy shaping and trend setting takes place at other levels than the nation state. However, converging policies are arguably implemented, mediated and interpreted according to national cultural context (Dale, 2005) and teachers' practices (Crossley et al, 2007). Ethnographic comparative classroom research highlights the degree of coherence that characterises teaching practices and representations in a given cultural context: though primary teachers vary in their pedagogical beliefs, practice and sense of professional identity depending on such factors as age, experience, gender and personality, a core set of representations and assumptions are taken for granted so that 'what teachers do' in one context is largely implicit and not subject to conscious reflection and questioning. The continuing relevance of the national level for conducting comparative research is suggested by the fact that widespread pedagogic practices in one country, such as the use of achievement awards in England, or underachieving French students 'repeating' a year, may surprise or shock the outsider (Sharpe, 1992; Broadfoot et al, 1993; Planel, 2009). Even representations of concepts as fundamental as learning, teaching, achieving, motivation or participating vary from one country to another (Alexander, 2000; Broadfoot et al, 2000; Osborn et al, 2003; Raveaud, 2006; Elliott & Grigorenko, 2007). In appropriate circumstances, being exposed to practices which challenge viewers' assumptions can lead to a feeling of dissonance, which in turn can lead to a re-examination of previously taken-for-granted assumptions (Raveaud, 2005; McAllister et al, 2006). Gaining an insight into an outsider perspective of one's culture can help to deconstruct the socially embedded nature of our beliefs and practices.

Little research exists on teachers who have experienced another education system, but a study into a French–English exchange of trainee primary teachers at the University of the West of England (UWE) in 2002 is illuminating (Newman et al, 2004). Ten French students spent three weeks in placements in Bristol, while their English counterparts experienced primary schools around Rouen. In the interviews after their placements the students from both countries described initial feelings of bewilderment, shock and incomprehension. One French trainee, used to a formal conceptualisation of concepts, remarked, 'I can't really remember having seen a session where a learning concept was formally put across and written down' (p. 291). Conversely, the English trainees were very critical of the lack of differentiation in the French classrooms.

In the most extreme cases, a lack of understanding of the underlying cultural values of the other context led to some students being unable to 'see' what was happening, as when French trainees were unable to recognise differentiation of learning in the English classes. The students who gained most from the experience were those who were able to go beyond the judgement of the other context from their own cultural lens and to progress towards an understanding of the other context. For instance, the use of praise and rewards led some students to conclude that failure, motivation and success were not conceptually similar in England and France (Planel, 2008). The interviews highlighted how exposure to classroom practice in a different culture led to growing critical reflectivity, and to an awareness that practices which had been previously taken for granted were actually context dependent.

The concepts of 'emic' and 'etic' provide a useful conceptual framework to understand the outcomes of this project, as they place the focus on epistemological processes rather than on the more static associations of insider and outsider:

> etics denotes an approach by an outsider to an inside system, in which the outsider brings his own structure – his own emics – and partly superimposes his observations on the inside view, interpreting the inside in reference to his outside starting point. (Harris, 1990, cited by Robinson-Pant, chapter 2 in this volume)

The concepts emic and etic insist on the process of knowledge construction, and invite us to consider the ways in which our tacit knowledge may limit our ability to see beyond our own cultural world. So how can we develop tools to become more aware of our culturally embedded perspectives, and to understand how they might constrict us in our knowledge and practice?

Cross-cultural Video as a Mediating Object

Experience of a different educational context can open up a space for reflectivity, but is hardly a realistic option for most practitioners. However, video can act as a proxy, and is increasingly being used in teacher development. Teachers' learning is arguably at its most receptive when realistic portrayals connect with their professional knowledge, and video has emerged as a powerful engagement tool:

> The use of more multi-modal representations of educational knowledge and practice are needed because they integrate the visual, aural, oral and physical cues that are part of the natural world of communication of teachers. These natural but often tacit aspects of communication are often lost in the 'stream of

> words' print genres that still dominate research dissemination. (Olivero et al, 2004, p. 182)

Video as a means of providing 'authentic' material has long been of interest to anthropologists, and its potential to highlight the cultural situatedness of educational practice has been recognised within the field of education, in particular by Kathryn Anderson-Levitt (2002) in her research on literacy in France and in the USA, and by Tobin et al (1989) in their study of preschool in Japan, China and the USA. In both studies, video from each context was shown in the filming country and cross-culturally, and evidence emerged of differences in what viewers 'saw' and how they constructed meaning. For instance, Anderson-Levitt showed how a pool of shared concepts such as 'participation' translated differently into classroom practice: where the French sought for signs of captivated children showing interest through their immobility, American audiences were more likely to associate interest with movement, taken as a mark of physical engagement.

Critically in such approaches, the video is not supposed to provide an example of 'typical' practice. Neither is it treated as data, nor as a pedagogical tool per se. Rather, it has the methodological function of providing a mediating object which will create a sense of dissonance (Eraut, 2000). It acts as a stimulus for discussion akin to a rich set of non-verbal cues designed to stimulate critical reflection (Tochon, 2007). Scenes that may appear incomprehensible or even shocking at first viewing can lead to a reflective examination of one's own assumptions, thus providing an opportunity to create a distanced vantage point that enables practitioners to elicit taken-for-granted practices and values which are so familiar as to become invisible, and thus to engage in an exercise of values clarification (Erickson, 2007). The constructive dissonance generated by cross-cultural video can give viewers a tool to explore the representations and assumptions they bring to the classroom, and how these might shape their understanding and actions.

However, exposure to cross-cultural video material may not in itself be sufficient to trigger critical reflection and elicit culturally implicit knowledge. The French–English trainee exchange at UWE (see previous section) revealed great differences in students' abilities to distance themselves from their habitual viewing lens and to adopt an outsider perspective. Indeed, the literature shows that what 'gets into' the mind is more a function of the hypothesis in force than a function of the evidence available (Bruner, 1996). Viewers have a propensity to affirm prior interpretations while discounting or even ignoring counterevidence to the point of 'confirmation bias' (Jordan & Henderson, 1995), where what viewers 'see' may not correspond to the visual evidence. In fact, our lens can be so strong as to prevent our seeing. When Frederick Erickson showed footage of a Native American first-grade classroom (with a Canadian Indian teacher and students) to an audience of non-Native

American teachers, the absence of the usual range of voice inflection and lavish praise was overwhelmingly interpreted as a sign of boredom, tiredness or even depression. 'The viewer constructs his or her own narrative understanding of the footage on the basis of prior experience' (Erickson, 2007, p. 153). However, accompanied by appropriate interpretive scaffolding, the medium of interactive video workshops makes it possible to revisit the evidence to uncover such dissonances, and to harness the power of implicit learning by providing a concrete, flexible resource for reflective analysis (Tomlinson, 1999, p. 533).

Pilot Study: creating dissonance

Comparative education studies have developed a wealth of understanding of the cultural embeddedness of classroom practice and, independently, epistemological research has increased our understanding of the culturally implicit dimension of teacher knowledge. However, the two have rarely been combined. This chapter now considers the potential of using comparative research to promote critical awareness and reflectivity in education practitioners, and reports on a pilot study undertaken at the University of Bristol in 2007/08.

France and England were chosen as the cross-national focus for the study because their education systems rest on sharply contrasting pedagogic, philosophical and political traditions (Broadfoot et al, 1993, 2000; Alexander, 2000; Osborn et al, 2003; Raveaud, 2006). The team consisted of a French cameraman and myself. I am bilingual: I grew up and was educated in England and France, so I experienced both education systems as a child, and have returned to them as a researcher, with various ethnographic comparative French and English projects since 1996, focusing on the links between classroom practice and its pedagogical, political and historical underpinnings.

The project focused on five- to seven-year-olds – young children discovering and constructing their roles as pupils. Participant classroom observation took place for six days in a French (greater Paris) and an English (north Bristol) classroom, followed by filming with two cameras for two days in 2007/08. The schools were both located in working-class neighbourhoods, and had clear indicators of relative social disadvantage (parental socio-economic characteristics, proportion of free school meals in England, children repeating a year in France). The classes were not meant to be 'typical' or 'representative' of their cultural contexts, nor did the schools match in all respects: the size of the urban areas (Bristol/Paris) differed; the English class included Year 1 and Year 2 (Y1/Y2) pupils, thus catering for a wider age range than the French Cours Préparatoire (CP) class. The time in the school year was not comparable either, given that the French children were approaching the end of the school year, while their English peers were still settling into their Y1/Y2 classroom. The presence of researchers in the class was also likely to have an influence on the 'reality' that they attempted to study, and these distortions were not culturally neutral. For instance, our presence may have appeared less remarkable to English children, who are used to seeing a range of new faces in their class (substitute teachers, students, governors, visitors), than it did to French children, unused to the presence of anyone other than the class teacher in their room.

Filming lasted two days using two cameras. One was stationary, on a tripod, and captured a wide angle, while the cameraman held a mobile camera for close-ups of individual children or groups and to follow children outside the classroom for such activities as group work, play in shared spaces, assembly and moving about the school as messengers.

The processes of filming and editing themselves constitute acts of representation, with the added factor that the English school had made its agreement conditional on the right to request editing changes in the video. Following a preview by the governing body of the rough-cut version of a 15-minute film, the head teacher requested the removal of an incident showing bad behaviour and the teacher dealing with it. In the French case, only the teacher viewed the edited film, and considered it as a research and training tool which she did not seek to influence. These differences were seen not as detrimental to the project, but as instances of the embeddedness of classroom practice within a wider educational culture where the image of a school carries high stakes in an English context of parental choice, league tables and competition.

In order to maintain perspective in filming, key themes had been identified. These were themes that had been identified in my experience and in a review of comparative research literature as reflecting the influence of cultural context, and that were most likely to create a sense of dissonance in viewers from a different country. They included aspects of teaching and learning such as classroom organisation; strategies for dealing with a heterogeneous attainment range (e.g. differentiation by ability, peer support, time management); the degree and nature of pupil autonomy; and the promotion of values and attitudes and the development of identities through such things as reward mechanisms and behaviour policies, conflict resolution, attitudes to student diversity, whole-school situations (e.g. assemblies in England), and parental contact and involvement.

The video material arising from the project took the shape of a 15-minute narrative film for each class, and short (2-3-minute) thematic clips chosen for their potential to parallel and contrast with material from the other context. Pilot workshops then took place within research seminars and teacher development sessions. The protocol included a first continuous viewing of subtitled video material, following which a few minutes were reserved for individual note-taking in order to minimise the risk of a dominant voice influencing the group. A first round of group discussion elicited spontaneous reactions and provided an opportunity for participants to request clarification and to ask for more background information if deemed necessary. After a phase of discussion with minimal input on the part of the researcher, there was a second viewing of the video to identify critical incidents by asking participants to stop the video to discuss situations they found perplexing or even provocative. When relevant, I introduced input such as the filmed teachers' stated aims, or contextual clarifications of the practices under discussion, and moderated a group discussion. The final phase invited practitioners to critically reflect on their own practice and representations.

Outcomes: through the (cultural) looking glass

This section retraces some outcomes of the practitioner workshops, and highlights thought processes evidenced in participants: growing awareness of a particular viewing lens; reassessment of practices thought to be 'universal'; eliciting taken-for-granted values and beliefs; and in some cases a newfound sense of agency, redefining perceptions of insiderness.

Not Seeing the Other: being constricted by the insider viewpoint

Initial reactions to cross-cultural video footage often included polarising dichotomies, and confirmed instances of viewer bias as documented in the literature. The following French video clip was shown in both countries.

French extract (Cours Préparatoire, six-year-olds)

> A new sound is the focus of the day's lesson. The children are seated around tables in groups with their individual slates. They listen to the teacher saying the sound and repeat it in unison. They then proceed to a familiar exercise in which the teacher speaks out a word, and pupils draw a succession of squares on their slates to represent each syllable, and put a cross in the syllable-square that contains the new sound. After each word the teacher claps her hands and upon this signal the children raise their slates towards her; she scans the class to monitor how each child has done. The process is repeated six times.

During a seminar with the Centre for Research on Language and Education (CREOLE, University of Bristol), a teacher from Kenya – where classes of 80 are not exceptional since primary education became free and compulsory in 2003 – described this as a participative approach based on student–teacher exchange and pupil contributions. A Taiwanese student reacted by pointing out that though the children sat in groups there was no sign of interaction between them or of collaboration in the extract, and that the activity was under the control of the teacher in terms of content, pace and assessment. Understandably, viewers interpreted what they saw through their own culturally situated lens, as insiders of their own education systems. In fact, in this case several participants could draw on multiple insider perspectives as the seminar included various international students but was situated within the English educational frame of reference. The Taiwanese response may thus constitute an instance of chosen insiderness, with the English frame of reference considered more appropriate than the Taiwanese one in this context.

Participants on each side of the English Channel tended to 'see' different aspects of identical clips, and group discussions reflected debates that were salient in the viewing country rather than in the filmed context. In Bristol, the discussion of the situation described above focused on differentiation and on self-esteem, which one English participant saw as being potentially threatened. Upon hearing that the French lesson was not followed by an exercise differentiated by attainment, a lively debate ensued on the effects this lack of individualisation might have in terms of the French pupils' learning, motivation and self-confidence. At a teacher development workshop for French primary teachers, secondary teachers and head teachers (Université d'Automne, Reims), participants also commented on the teacher's pedagogy and style and discussed differentiation sometimes in similar terms to those used in the English seminar; however, the teacher-led style and pupils' self-esteem were barely mentioned. The concern with differentiation was voiced essentially by younger teachers. This suggested that teacher career stages and evolutions in policy and training were also likely to have an impact on responses. When the French discussion moved to peer interaction, the focus was less on self-confidence and engagement than on socialisation and citizenship, which underpin the ethos of the French education system.

Crossing Boundaries: reassessing the insider perspective

A group of French primary teachers viewed English material in which children were seen working autonomously in groups of 5-8 around a table while the teacher was seated at one of the tables, and later heard children reading individually at her desk. They offered the mistaken assumption that the school must be in a socially privileged area:

> With our pupils you can't do that. If they haven't learnt at
> home to be autonomous ... If I were in the city centre [i.e. in a

> middle-class area] I could work like that, but not here.
> (CP teacher, working-class area)

Yet this particular school was situated in an area belonging to the lowest income quintile according to national statistics. This came as a shock: 'But then ... Congratulations to the teacher! But it can't be like that in all classes, can it?' I explained that working in autonomous groups and differentiation by attainment is a key characteristic of English primary teaching (Galton et al, 1999; Osborn et al, 2000). This input freed the participants from their initial tendency to categorise and polarise, and enabled them to look at their own system with a fresh perspective and critical distance. A heated discussion followed where the French teachers considered the constraints they face in taking into account differences between pupils, and debated the influence, practical or symbolic, exerted by national curricula, the possibility of students being held back to 'repeat' a year, and the spatial and temporal organisation of the French classroom:

> We think we can't differentiate [by attainment], that we are hemmed in by the curriculum, by student numbers, but actually it's also a matter of choice and of priorities. They [in England] also have a curriculum, and they have bigger classes than we do, and yet they do it. (Maternelle teacher, working-class area)

A first crucial step had been taken: the group had shifted from an uncritical insider perspective, dismissing the other context as too alien to be relevant, to a position where they were able to challenge the taken-for-granted nature of some of their pedagogical practices and beliefs. Aspects of their thinking which had previously been uninterrogated became available for critical thought and reassessment.

A second step in the reflective process was an eliciting of implicitly held assumptions and beliefs. One French teacher contrasted how her training had taught her to assess a range of teaching options, but given her no understanding of the values she was unconsciously promoting:

> I had never stood back to think of the values we transmit to the children. As far as pedagogy is concerned, yes. Daily. I think we all do it: 'Have I chosen the right method to explain this notion?'; 'Have I given an appropriate answer to this child's question?', etcetera. But concerning the values we transmit, never. I didn't even think about them. I must have thought they were more or less universal. (French teacher approaching the end of her career)

Some participants were able to take the process further, adding critical reflectivity and a sense of agency to previously intuitive practices. This was the case of two participants in particular who requested further reading material, and contacted me subsequently. They were both French teachers, one about to retire, the other newly qualified. Both described the workshop as opening up possibilities by making previously taken-for-granted assumptions or 'necessities' appear contingent and therefore subject to their active choice and agency. The experienced teacher reported experimenting with methods she had (re)discovered through the cross-cultural video workshop, not necessarily trying to implement practices she had seen in the English class, but rather devising her own procedures in accordance with deeply held convictions that had sometimes become sidelined in her practice. She described herself as freed from the auto-pilot which had led her to unquestioningly reproduce practices she had probably experienced as a pupil. Her young colleague explained how she felt more at ease with certain practices which she now felt she could articulate and justify:

> Last year I set up a rota for children's duties in the classroom. That was just the way it was, I hadn't stopped to wonder why, I suppose I liked the idea without really knowing why. Now, if a child is dragging her feet, I tell her 'There you go, you're in France, you're a member of a group, you're a citizen, that's just how it is.' Now I know why I'm doing it, I'm quite committed to it. (French teacher, newly qualified)

The experience gained from her first year of teaching and the sense of perspective she brought to her practice after the comparative detour arguably gave her a new layer of insiderness. Bakhtin describes this process of reaching a perspective where insider and outsider meet as a 'dialogic encounter' in which 'a meaning only reveals its depths once it has encountered and come into contact with another, foreign meaning' (1986, p. 7, cited in McNess et al, 2013, p. 306).

Implications for Practice

Comparative research has not been widely tapped in teacher training or development (Alexander, 2006, Planel, 2008). This may be linked to a wider policy trend promoting forms of teacher professionalism based on skills rather than critical thinking. The preferred forms of comparative studies associated with this technicist view of teaching are international league tables and the search for evidence of transferable 'best practice' techniques which are considered outside their contextual cultural significance. The relationship between cultural context and practice then tends to be reduced to a set of 'culturally rooted teaching scripts' (Stigler & Hiebert, 1999) considered as a default form of action that constrains teaching practice and constitutes a barrier to change. By contrast, for the workshops in our project to foster reflective analysis – potentially leading to a renewed sense of agency – it was necessary to lead participants away from the temptation to lend the video content a normative function or to judge/censor/praise the observed practice, thus essentialising cultural differences. This required the availability to participants of clarifying input, mediation and scaffolding. I was thus involved in all the workshops, and encouraged participants to engage critically with any sense of dissonance so as to foster a reflection on their own practices.

For me as a researcher, the project created insider/outsider boundaries at various levels. In terms of cultural background I could be perceived as an insider of both research cultures: I am bilingual and have an institutional position in both countries, as a senior lecturer at a French university and as a visiting fellow of the University of Bristol. My educational and research background as a bilingual-cum-academic gave me dual cultural belonging, which participants resorted to when calling on me to clarify practices from the other context. A dual perspective, as both an insider and an outsider, was central to this project: I needed to be able to understand the rationale for particular educational practices and their meaning within a broader social and educational framework, but also to see how these practices might challenge assumptions within the other context. In the course of the workshops I consciously switched from an insider to an outsider perspective, and aimed to help participants gain awareness of such layered and multiple meanings. Such a dual perspective can be recreated within multi-national teams, and projects such as the ENCOMPASS study on learner identity in English, French and Danish secondary schools explicitly harnessed multiple insider/outsider views – for instance, by having the description of a French *collège* written from a Danish viewpoint (Broadfoot et al, 2000).

While I was a research insider, I was an outsider of the primary teacher's professional world, of which I had only theoretical knowledge (my own teaching and training had taken part mainly at higher education (HE) level, with only a year as a trainee secondary teacher of English in France). Here the insiders were the participants, and their insights into the videos offered me understandings I would not have gained without them. As a researcher I gained much from 'cannibalising' their responses (Jordan & Henderson, 1995) and feeding their recorded responses and discussions back into the research loop on tacit teacher knowledge. In such a process the interaction between researcher and researched is integrated in an iterative process (Holy, 1984), where teachers are posited as co-constructors of meaning and their responses become new research data, generating new insider/outsider boundaries and sharing of perspectives.

Concluding Remarks

This chapter has considered how cross-cultural classroom evidence, whether experienced directly or indirectly, as with video, can make a contribution to teacher professional development by enabling the eliciting of tacit knowledge and making culturally situated taken-for-granted assumptions available for introspection. This can generate an increased sense of agency as the outsider perspective uncovers layers of meaning of familiar practices, potentially making practitioners experience a renewed sense of purpose, or conversely making it possible for them to envision alternatives where they might previously have felt trapped by a sense of inevitability. The dilemmas and insights they express can in turn be fed back into the research process, thus attaining more collaborative research procedures with more porous boundaries between researcher and researched.

Cross-cultural classroom research also raises the issue of insiders and outsiders at the societal level. For instance, Anderson-Levitt (2002) makes a powerful critical analysis of education policy when she reveals that the skills regarded by teachers as 'learning to read' in the USA and in France rest on criteria of success that are so different as to lead to the classification of the same performance (e.g. correct sounding out of a word without understanding its meaning) as 'successful' reading in one context but as 'failing' in the other. Beyond the impact on a child's present experience and prospects for the future, this also has implications at the pedagogical level within the classroom, and in shaping support and remedial policies which do not address the same difficulties and objectives, or target the same groups either side of the Atlantic. Defining the legitimate insider whose point of view will be recognised as authoritative (Bourdieu & Passeron, 1977) carries high stakes in terms of power, and the establishment or reinforcement of social hierarchies.

Such power issues are also relevant at the micro level of the classroom. Indeed, each classroom has its codes governing expectations of pupil and adult behaviour, language and interactions. Each child needs to be enculturated into their role as a schoolchild and to unpick many tacit, implicit or unarticulated codes (Bernstein, 1990; Pollard with Filer, 1996). These insider codes are rarely neutral in terms of social, ethnic or gender identities, thus potentially distancing certain groups from the school culture. Thus North American research in the 1980s showed how African American and Hispanic children were considered disrespectful because their cultural codes for eye contact reversed the white norm of looking away while talking, and making eye contact while listening (Harper et al, 1978; Hanna, 1984). It is hugely difficult to bring to light such deeply rooted unconscious habits, and to make teachers aware of the implicit codes they perpetuate within their classrooms. Yet these may be so fundamental as to jeopardise the establishment of a learning situation for certain children/groups. Cross-cultural dissonance can foster an enhanced awareness of such tacit expectations, thus bridging a cultural gap which can generate exclusion.

If insiderness constructs itself in contrast to outsiderness, a heightened critical awareness of what it is that makes us an insider can promote understanding and tolerance of difference, and foster more inclusive practices. This is of significance as the tacit knowledge embedded in classroom practice is not only about professional teaching knowledge, but also conveys a representation of society with its ideals, its defining boundaries, and its hierarchies of power. In fact the insiders and outsiders we have encountered here are rarely unambiguously one or the other. The idea of a 'Third Space' (Bhabha, 1994) has increasingly been put forward (see McNess et al, 2013) to open up a constricting dichotomy. Here we have emphasised a process (*becoming* an in/outsider) rather than a static unchanging quality (*being* an in/outsider), and the constructive interplay between one and the other (i.e. between insider and outsider) which has been a useful tool for professional learning.

References

Alexander, R. (2000) *Culture and Pedagogy*. Oxford: Blackwell.

Alexander, R. (2006) Dichotomous Pedagogies and the Promise of Cross-cultural Comparison, in H. Lauder, P. Brown, J.A. Dillabough & A.H. Halsey (Eds) *Education, Globalization and Social Change*, pp. 722-733. Oxford: Oxford University Press.

Anderson-Levitt, K. (2002) *Teaching Cultures: knowledge for teaching first grade in France and the United States*. Cresskill, NJ: Hampton Press.

Argyris, C. & Schön, D. (1974) *Theory in Use: increasing professional effectiveness*. San Francisco: Jossey-Bass.

Atkinson, T. & Claxton, G. (Eds) (2000) *The Intuitive Practitioner. on the value of not always knowing what one is doing*. Oxford: Oxford University Press.

Bernstein, B. (1990) *Class, Codes and Control. Vol. 4: The Structuring of Pedagogic Discourse*. London: Routledge. http://dx.doi.org/10.4324/9780203011263

Bhabha, H. (1994) *The Location of Culture*. London: Routledge.

Bourdieu, P. & J.-C. Passeron (1977) *Reproduction in Education, Society and Culture*. London: SAGE.

Broadfoot, P., Osborn, M., Gilly, M. & Brucher, A. (1993) *Perceptions of Teaching: primary school teachers in England and France*. London: Cassell.

Broadfoot, P., Osborn, M., Planel, C. & Sharpe, K. (2000) *Promoting Quality in Learning. Does England have the Answer?* London: Cassell.

Bruner, J. (1990) *Acts of Meaning*. Cambridge, MA: Harvard University Press.

Bruner, J. (1996) *The Culture of Education*. Cambridge, MA: Harvard University Press.

Calhoun, C. (1995) *Critical Social Theory: culture, history and the challenge of difference*. Oxford: Blackwell.

Crossley, M., Broadfoot, P. & Schweisfurth, M. (Eds) (2007) *Changing Educational Contexts, Issues and Identities: 40 years of comparative education*. London: Routledge.

Dale, R. (2005) Globalisation, Knowledge Economy and Comparative Education, *Comparative Education*, 41(2), 117-150. http://dx.doi.org/10.1080/03050060500150906

Elliott, J. & Grigorenko, E. (2007) *Western Psychological and Educational Theory in Diverse Contexts*. London: Routledge.

Elliott, J., Hufton, N., Ilyushin, L. & Willis, W. (2005) *Motivation, Engagement and Educational Performance: international perspectives on the contexts of learning*. Basingstoke: Palgrave Macmillan. http://dx.doi.org/10.1057/9780230509795

Eraut, M. (1994) *Developing Professional Knowledge and Competence*. London: Falmer Press.

Eraut, M. (2000) Non-formal Learning and Tacit Knowledge in Professional Work, *British Journal of Educational Psychology*, 70, 113-136. http://dx.doi.org/10.1348/000709900158001

Eraut, M. (2007) Learning from Other People at Work, *Oxford Review of Education*, 33(4), 403-422. http://dx.doi.org/10.1080/03054980701425706

Erickson, F. (2007) Ways of Seeing Video: toward a phenomenology of viewing minimally edited footage, R. Goldman, R. Pea, B. Barron & S.J. Derry (Eds) *Video Research in the Learning Sciences*, pp. 145-155. New Jersey: Lawrence Erlbaum.

Galton, M., Hargreaves, L., Comber, C. & Wall, D. (1999) *Inside the Primary Classroom: 20 Years On*. London: Routledge. http://dx.doi.org/10.4324/9780203269329

Hanna, Judith L. (1984) Black/White Nonverbal Differences, Dance, and Dissonance: implications for desegregation, in Aaron Wolfgang (Ed.) *Nonverbal Behavior Perspectives, Applications, Intercultural Insights*, pp. 373-410. Lewiston: Hogrefe Publications.

Harper, R.G., Wiens, N.A. & Matarazzo, J.D. (1978) *Non-verbal Communication: the state of the art*. New York: John Wiley.

Holy, L. (1984) Theory, Methodology and the Research Process, in R. Ellen (Ed.) *Ethnographic Research: a guide to general conduct*, pp. 13-34. London: Academic Press.

Jordan, B. & Henderson, A. (1995) Interaction Analysis: foundations and practice, *Journal of the Learning Sciences*, 4, 39-103. http://dx.doi.org/10.1207/s15327809jls0401_2

McAllister, L., Whiteford, G., Hill, B., Thomas, N. & Fitzgerald, M. (2006) Reflection in Intercultural Learning: examining the international experience through a critical incident approach, *Reflective Practice* 7(3), 367-381. http://dx.doi.org/10.1080/14623940600837624

McNess, E., Arthur, L. & Crossley, M. (2013) 'Ethnographic Dazzle' and the Construction of the 'Other': revisiting dimensions of insider and outsider research for international and comparative education, *Compare*, 45(2), 295-316. http://dx.doi.org/10.1080/03057925.2013.854616

Meyer, J.W., Boli, J., Thomas, G.M. & Ramirez, F.O. (1997) World Society and the Nation-State, *American Journal of Sociology*, 103(1), 144-181. http://dx.doi.org/10.1086/231174

Newman, E., Taylor, A., Whitehead, J. & Planel, C. (2004) 'You just can't do it like that – it's just wrong!' Impressions of French and English Trainee Primary Teachers on Exchange Placement in Primary Schools Abroad: the value of experiencing difference, *European Journal of Teacher Education*, 27(3), 285-298.

Olivero, F., John, P. & Sutherland, R. (2004) Seeing is Believing: using videopapers to transform teachers' professional knowledge and practice, *Cambridge Journal of Education*, 34(2), 179-191. http://dx.doi.org/10.1080/03057640410001700552

Osborn, M. (2004) New Methodologies for Comparative Research? Establishing 'Constants' and 'Contexts' in Educational Experience, *Oxford Review of Education*, 30(2), 265-285. http://dx.doi.org/10.1080/0305498042000215566

Osborn, M., Broadfoot, P., McNess, E., Ravn, B., Planel, C. & Triggs, P. (2003) *A World of Difference? Comparing Learners across Europe*. Milton Keynes: Open University Press.

Osborn, M., McNess, E., Broadfoot, P., Pollard, A. & Triggs, P. (2000) *What Teachers Do*. London: Continuum.

Planel, C. (2008) The Rise and Fall of Comparative Education in Teacher Training: should it rise again as comparative pedagogy? *Compare*, 38(4), 385-399. http://dx.doi.org/10.1080/03057920701467867

Planel, C. (2009) Les pratiques en classe, partie emergée de l'iceberg des valeurs culturelles. Pédagogies à l'oeuvre dans les ecoles anglaises et françaises, *Revue Internationale d'Education*, 50, 75-85.

Polanyi, M. (1967) *The Tacit Dimension*. New York: Anchor Books.

Pollard, A., with Filer, A. (1996) *The Social World of the Primary School*. London: Cassell.

Raveaud, M. (2005) Hares, Tortoises and the Social Construction of the Pupil: differentiated learning in French and English primary schools, *British Educational Research Journal*, 31(4), 459-479. http://dx.doi.org/10.1080/01411920500148697

Raveaud, M. (2006) *De l'enfant au citoyen*. Paris: Presses Universitaires de France.

Schön, D. (1983) *The Reflective Practitioner. How Professionals Think in Action*. London: Temple Smith.

Schön, D. (1987) *Educating the Reflective Practitioner*. San Francisco: Jossey-Bass.

Schön, D. (1991) *The Reflective Turn: case studies in and on educational practice*. New York: Teachers Press, Columbia University.

Sharpe, K. (1992) Catechistic Teaching Style in French Primary Education: an analysis of a grammar lesson with seven-year-olds, *Comparative Education*, 28(3), 249-268. http://dx.doi.org/10.1080/0305006920280303

Shuayb, M. & O'Donnell, S. (2008) Aims and Values in Primary Education: England and other countries. Primary Review Research Survey 1/2. Cambridge: University of Cambridge Faculty of Education.

Stigler, J.W. & Hiebert, J. (1999) *The Teaching Gap*. New York: Free Press.

Tobin, J., Wu, D. & Davidson, D.H. (1989) *Preschool in Three Cultures*. New Haven, CT: Yale University Press.

Tochon, F. (2007) From Video Cases to Video Pedagogy: a framework for video feedback and reflection in pedagogical research praxis, in R. Goldman, R. Pea, B. Barron & S.J. Derry (Eds) *Video Research in the Learning Sciences*, pp. 53-65. Mahwah, NJ: Lawrence Erlbaum Associates.

Tomlinson, P. (1999) Conscious Reflection and Implicit Learning in Teacher Preparation. Part II: Implications for a Balanced Approach, *Oxford Review of Education*, 25(4), 533-544. http://dx.doi.org/10.1080/030549899103973

Wertsch, J. (1991) *Voices of the Mind*. Cambridge, MA: Harvard University Press.

Notes on Contributors

Joanna Al-Youssef is a tutor in English for Academic Purposes at the University of Nottingham. Joanna has an EdD (Doctor of Education) from the University of Bath and an MA in English Language Teaching from the University of Nottingham. Her teaching experience includes undergraduate, postgraduate and doctoral supervision levels. Her research interests are in the areas of the internationalisation of higher education, international policy, international students, and language and culture.

Lore Arthur (PhD) is a research consultant at the Open University, supervising doctoral students. Previously she was senior lecturer at the OU's Faculty of Education for many years. She has researched and published widely in areas of comparative education, lifelong learning, higher education and language learning. She was chair and vice chair of the British Association for International and Comparative Education (BAICE) from 2006 until 2010 and chair of the editorial board of *Compare* (2008–2010). She is co-director of the BAICE 'Insider–Outsider Research' Thematic Forum.

Sughra Choudry Khan is an EdD graduate of the University of Bristol. She has formerly worked in the UK as a teacher and teacher educator and more recently in international educational development in Pakistan.

Mindy Colin is an American educational researcher and consultant living in Mauritius. Prior to her PhD studies at the University of Bristol on education reforms in small island developing states, Mindy worked in the academic technology group at Loyola Marymount University in Los Angeles. She currently teaches at a Mauritian tertiary institution, consults with Mauritian private schools and tertiary organisations, and conducts research for NGOs and other agencies involved in local schooling initiatives. Her research interests are in educational technology in small states contexts.

Michael Crossley is Professor of Comparative and International Education, director of the Centre for Comparative and International Research in Education at the Graduate School of Education, and director of the Education in Small States Research Group (www.smallstates.net), at the University of Bristol, UK. Professor Crossley is a former editor of the journal *Comparative Education* and former chair of the British Association for International and Comparative Education (BAICE). He is currently Adjunct Professor of Education at the University of the South Pacific, and is an elected fellow, FAcSS, of the British Academy of Social Sciences. He is co-director of the BAICE 'Insider–Outsider Research' Thematic Forum.

Hania Salter-Dvorak, MA, Ed.D, is a lecturer in TESOL Education at Exeter University Graduate School of Education. Her experience in language education (teaching Italian, French and Arabic, and acting as subject leader for English for academic purposes in two UK universities) led to her interest in the development of academic literacy of second language graduate students, particularly in relation to identity formation in academic social spaces and socialisation into disciplinary genres. By examining the dynamic between culture, language, identity and power in learning processes, she is interested to identify ways in which universities can accommodate such students through appropriate course design and community building.

Cecilia Garrido is a senior lecturer in modern languages at the Open University, where she has performed a variety of roles, including being Head of Spanish and Associate Dean (Learning and Teaching) in the Faculty of Education and Language Studies. She has extensive teaching experience in the UK and abroad. Her research interests and publications are mostly in the area of intercultural competence and its implications for language teaching and learning, teacher education and cultural integration.

Qing Gu is Professor of Education at the University of Nottingham, School of Education. She is vice chair of the British Association of Comparative and International Education (BAICE) and a member of the editorial boards of *Compare*, the *International Journal of Educational Development*, the *International Journal of Research and Method in Education*, and the *Journal of Educational Administration*. She is the author of *Teacher Development: knowledge and context* (Continuum, 2007); editor of *The Work and Lives of Teachers in China* (Routledge, 2014); and co-author of *Teachers Matter* (Open University Press, 2007), *The New Lives of Teachers* (Routledge, 2010), *Successful School Leadership: linking with learning and achievement* (Open University Press, 2011) and *Resilient Teachers, Resilient Schools* (Routledge, 2014).

Nilou M Hawthorne is an independent education researcher in sociolinguistics and education and works supporting non-formal and community education capacity-building in the rural parish of Hanover in western Jamaica. She has experience in higher education marketing, widening participation project development and academic librarianship in the UK, and community project development in Jamaica. Her research interests include the impact of discourses on higher education and the international education policy environment.

Peter Kelly is Reader in Comparative Education at Plymouth University. His main interests are European education policy and comparative pedagogy. Since 2007 he has been working with colleagues at Aarhus University, Denmark and Freiburg Pedagogic University, Germany on a comparative pedagogy project titled Comparing and Analysing Teaching in Northern Europe (CATE). A second project is now in its third year, comparing the reading assessment of eleven-year-old children in primary schools in England with that of their peers in *folkskoles* in Denmark.

Juliet McCaffery, MEd, PhD, is a research associate at Sussex University, UK. Juliet specialises in literacy, gender and equalities. She has worked in school and adult literacy in the USA, Brighton and London. She was the first gender and development officer at the British Council. She is now an independent consultant. She became interested in English Gypsies and Irish Travellers as an elected councillor and researched their attitudes towards education. Her research interests and publications concern literacy and marginalised communities.

Elizabeth McNess, MEd, PhD, is a senior lecturer at the University of Bristol, Graduate School of Education and former director of the Document Summary Service, a policy briefing service for head teachers, teachers, educational administrators and those involved in policy research. She has a background in comparative research and has worked on several large ESRC-funded projects, publishing widely in the areas of education policy, teachers' values and pupil experience of learning at home and in school in England, Wales, Denmark, France and Belgium. Elizabeth was previously secretary to the British Association for International and Comparative Education (BAICE) and an elected member of the executive committee. She is co-director of the BAICE 'Insider–Outsider Research' Thematic Forum.

Lizzi O. Milligan is a lecturer in international education at the University of Bath. Her research interests focus on issues of social justice, equity and educational quality in low-income countries, particularly in eastern Africa. She is currently involved in a number of DfID-funded projects related to Rwandan primary education. She completed an ESRC-funded PhD at the University of Bristol. Until recently, she was the secretary of the British Association for International and Comparative Education (BAICE).

Claire Planel, BSc, MA, PhD, has an academic background in anthropology and linguistics. She has been a research fellow in comparative education at the Graduate School of Education, University of Bristol, where her particular focus was in comparative pedagogy in England and France. That same interest in culture, language and learning has underpinned her work in primary schools, teaching English as an Additional Language. She supports primary schools, teachers and ethnic minority children in Gloucestershire, UK.

Maroussia Raveaud was educated in the UK and in France, and graduated in English with teaching qualifications and a PhD in education. She held an ESRC postdoctoral fellowship at the University of Bristol in 2002–2003 and is currently a lecturer at the Université du Maine, France, and research associate at the University of Bristol, Graduate School of Education. Her research focuses on socialisation, citizenship, comparative education, teacher development, primary schools and qualitative methods. She is a member of the editorial board of the *Revue Internationale d'Education de Sèvres.*

Anna Robinson-Pant is Professor of Education at the University of East Anglia. She was previously based for around ten years in South Asia (particularly Nepal) as a teacher trainer, educational planner and researcher. Her ethnographic research on women's literacy and development in Nepal received the UNESCO International Award for Literacy Research. In UK higher education she has conducted research with international students and is particularly interested in internationalisation policy and practice.

Nicola Savvides is a lecturer in higher education at King's College London. Her research interests lie within the fields of intercultural, international and comparative education and qualitative research methodology. She has published widely on the intergovernmental European Schools and on the European dimension in education and has undertaken research on Erasmus students' needs and experiences and students' sense of citizenship and identity. She holds an ESRC-funded doctorate and two master's degrees in education from the University of Oxford.

Ed Wickins has been the principal of King George V School, an English Schools Foundation School in Hong Kong, since 2004. Prior to this, most of his teaching career had been in the UK, where he was the head teacher of two different comprehensive schools in Gloucestershire, UK. He also spent two years as a geography teacher in Malaysia. His interest in education research was stimulated by the University of Bristol EdD programme, and he completed his doctorate in 2014. He is particularly interested in the context of school leadership and he has worked with the Asia Pacific Centre for Leadership and Change in Hong Kong, the International Baccalaureate Organisation and various principal networks within Hong Kong to try to understand this better. His blog edwickins.me shares his perspectives.